Free at Last

Free at Last

The Message of Galatians

Derrick McCarson

RESOURCE *Publications* • Eugene, Oregon

FREE AT LAST
The Message of Galatians

Copyright © 2015 Derrick McCarson. All rights reserved. Except for brief quotations in critical publications or reviews, no part of this book may be reproduced in any manner without prior written permission from the publisher. Write: Permissions. Wipf and Stock Publishers, 199 W. 8th Ave., Suite 3, Eugene, OR 97401.

Resource Publications
An Imprint of Wipf and Stock Publishers
199 W. 8th Ave., Suite 3
Eugene, OR 97401

www.wipfandstock.com

ISBN 13: 978-1-4982-1903-7

Manufactured in the U.S.A. 03/02/2015

This book is dedicated to the people of Liberty Baptist Church in Candler, NC. Thank you for giving me a chance to learn, grow and serve as your pastor.

Contents

Acknowledgments | ix

1 The Let Freedom Ring! (1:1–3) | 1
2 Only One Gospel (1:1–9) | 10
3 Countering the Critics (1:10–24) | 20
4 The Freedom Fighter (2:1–10) | 30
5 Peter vs. Paul/Law vs. Liberty (2:11–21) | 38
6 Breaking the Law (3:1–14) | 48
7 Law and Grace: A Dynamic Duo (3:15–25) | 60
8 Who Do You Belong To? (3:26–29) | 70
9 Trading Sonship for Slavery (4:1–11) | 76
10 Velvet Steel (4:12–20) | 88
11 A Tale of Two Sons (4:21–31) | 99
12 Standing Firm in Liberty (5:1–6) | 108
13 Facing-off Against False Teachers (5:7–12) | 116
14 Risky Business (5:13–15) | 124
15 The War Within (5:16–21, 24–26) | 132
16 The Fruit of the Spirit (5:22–23) | 143
17 No Man Left Behind (6:1–6) | 161
18 Spiritual Laws of the Harvest (6:7–10) | 170
19 Boasting Only in the Cross (6:11–18) | 180

Bibliography | 191

Acknowledgments

I would like to express gratitude to my helpmate, Caitlin McCarson, for the countless hours of diligently proofreading, editing and correcting my mistakes both on the written page and in life. Without you this work would not be possible.

CHAPTER 1

Let Freedom Ring!

Since 1886 immigrants to America arriving through New York Harbor have been greeted by a 300 foot lady who stands proudly. She holds a torch in her hand giving light to those in the dark. Atop her head is a crown with seven points which represent the seven continents of the globe. Attached to this lady's feet is a chain that has been broken signifying her abolition from tyranny and oppression. An inscription upon the pedestal has the immortal words of Emma Lazarus' sonnet:

> Give me your tired, your poor,
> Your huddled masses yearning to breathe free,
> The wretched refuse of your teeming shore.
> Send these, the homeless, tempest-tost to me,
> I lift my lamp beside the golden door!

We know this special ambassador of freedom as Lady Liberty and she invites those beleaguered refugees from around world to come to America—the land of the free and home of the brave. Christ is holding out the same promise of freedom to those who are looking to escape spiritual bondage. Jesus, in the original emancipation proclamation, said in John 8:36, "If the Son sets you free, then you are free indeed."

The epistle of Galatians has been called the Magna Charta of spiritual liberty, the battle cry of the Reformation, the Christian's Declaration of Independence, and the rough-draft for Romans. Many church historians maintain that Galatians was the catalyst which sparked the Protestant Reformation. Martin Luther, the great reformer, said, "The epistle to the Galatians is my epistle. To it I am, as it were, in wedlock. Galatians is my

Katherine (the name of his wife)."[1] Meanwhile, renowned Biblical scholar, Merrill C. Tenney, wrote of Galatians:

> Christianity might have just been one more Jewish sect and the thought of the Western world might have been entirely pagan had it never been written. Galatians embodies the germinal teaching on Christian freedom which separated Christianity from Judaism and which launched it upon a career of missionary conquest. It was the cornerstone of the Protestant Reformation, because its teaching of salvation by grace alone became the dominant preaching of the Reformers.[2]

Think of Galatians as an invitation to freedom. In fact, the word "liberty" is used eleven times in this book. In this letter God invites us to throw off the shackles of man-made religion and embrace His grace completely. Say "goodbye" to legalism and performance-based religion—there is no place for that where we are going.

The Apostle to the Galatians (1:3, 6:11)

The author of this fiery letter is the Apostle Paul. In typical fashion he identifies himself in the greeting (1:1–2). Many scholars believe that this was one of the earliest letters written in the New Testament, penned sometime around 48 AD. In my estimation, Paul is the perfect candidate to write Galatians because of his background as a former Pharisee. If there were ever a man who knew anything about rule-keeping and adhering to religious traditions, it was Paul. Remember that before Paul was gloriously zapped by Jesus in Acts 9 on the road to Damascus, he was a card-carrying, law-loving, Christian-killing Pharisee.

Paul was born as Saul in the city of Tarsus, which is in the modern-day country of Turkey. He was a well-educated Roman citizen. Acts 22:3 says that he received his theological training at the feet of Gamaliel, who was the most prominent Hebrew scholar of the first century. You can get a feel for the kind of zealot that Paul used to be before Christ rocked his world when he wrote in Philippians 3:4–6:

> If anyone else thinks he has reason for confidence in the flesh, I have more: circumcised on the eighth day, of the people of Israel,

---

1. MacArthur, *Galatians*, ix.
2. Tenney, *Galatians*, 15.

of the tribe of Benjamin, a Hebrew of Hebrews; as to the law, a Pharisee; as to zeal, a persecutor of the church; as to righteousness under the law, blameless.

This man had the equivalent of a PhD in the minutia of theological hair-splitting, so there was nobody better qualified to deal with the problems plaguing the Galatian church than Paul. More than any other apostle he understood the bondage of the law and the freedom of grace. Bible commentator John Phillips wrote:

> Paul's signature on a letter was worth millions, not in the coin of the realm, but in spiritual terms. The name Paul on an epistle is like the name Mozart on a musical score, the name Rembrandt on a painting, the name Rockefeller on a check, or the word sterling on silver. It indicates worth. Paul! He was the church's greatest thinker, the church's greatest missionary, the church's greatest apologist, the church's greatest theologian, the church's greatest enthusiast, and the church's greatest apostle."[3]

It's ironic to think how God used Paul so mightily—even though he was a Jew, the Lord would use him to reach gentiles; even though he once persecuted the early church, he would become the greatest promoter of the early church; even though he was once the greatest Pharisee, he would become the greatest freedom fighter for Christian liberty.

God performed a similar miracle with Martin Luther. Before Luther became the great champion of justification by faith. Luther was a German monk who was completely sold-out to the burdensome traditions of the Catholic Church. Luther wrote of himself:

> When I was a monk I depended on such willing and exertion, but the longer [I worked at it] the further away I got . . . I was very pious in the monastery, yet I was sad because I thought God was not gracious to me . . . When I had prayed and said my mass I was very presumptuous. I didn't see the scoundrel behind it all because I didn't put my trust in God but in my own righteousness . . . the most pious monk is the worst scoundrel . . . I was a good monk and kept my rule so strictly that I could say if ever a monk could get into heaven through monastic discipline, I was that monk . . . And yet my conscience would not give me that certainty, but I always doubted and said, "You didn't do that right. You weren't contrite enough. You left that out of your confession. Although I

---

3. Phillips, *Exploring Galatians*, 19.

lived a blameless life as a monk, I felt that I was a sinner with an uneasy conscience before God. I could also not believe that I had pleased him with my works. Far from loving that righteous God who punished sinners, I actually hated him . . ."[4]

There is a well-known story from Luther's monastic life when he took a trip to Rome as a spiritual pilgrim. Luther made his way to a building called the Lateran. Outside there was a series of ancient stairs that had been transported from Jerusalem to Rome. Supposedly, Jesus had walked on those stairs outside Pilate's hall. The Catholic Church taught that if you got on your hands and knees and crawled up the twenty-eight stone stairs, and said a prayer on each one of the stairs, by the time you got to the top stair you could reduce your time in purgatory. Thousands of pilgrims would come and climb those stairs on their hands and knees. Martin Luther—now deeply troubled—got on his hands and knees and crawled up those stairs, kissing each one as he crawled and saying "Our Father" along the way. When he got to the top, he looked back at the stairway and asked himself a question, "What if it is not so?"

God used that experience in Luther's life to help him see the utter futility and bankruptcy of the Catholic religion. The turning point came in 1515 when Luther was allowed to teach the Bible. It was then that he began reading the Scriptures as never before. The single verse that changed his life was, "the just shall live by faith," written by Paul some 1,500 years earlier, found in Gal 3:11 and Rom 1:17.

The Audience of Galatians (1:3)

This letter was written to several churches across the region of Asia Minor. Paul knew these people very well because on his first and second missionary journeys he and Barnabas planted these churches on their evangelistic crusades. Acts 13–14 chronicle the journeys of Paul across the cities of Galatia. Every step of this mission trip was met with resistance and persecution.

When Paul and Barnabas went into the city of Iconium they preached the Gospel in the synagogues and many Gentiles believed. However, there was a contingent of unbelieving Jews who poisoned Paul's efforts. Paul and Barnabas were undeterred and they dug in their heels at Iconium. The harder they preached, the more intense the opposition became. Finally,

---

4. Mullett, *Martin Luther*, 42.

when the Jews in the city had enough of Paul they hatched a plot to stone him. However, Paul learned of this assassination attempt and he escaped the city unscathed (Acts 14:1–5).

On another occasion in the city of Lystra, Paul nearly lost his life after preaching the Gospel and performing miracles among the pagans. When the Jews from Iconium and Antioch found out that Paul was just down the road a few miles, doing the same thing he did in their cities, they traveled to Lystra and stirred up opposition against him. Dr. Luke tells us what happened in Acts 14:19, "Then Jews from Antioch and Iconium came there; and having persuaded the multitudes, they stoned Paul and dragged him out of the city, supposing him to be dead."

With the help of some believers Paul recovered from his wounds, and later he and Barnabas traveled the sixty miles to Derbe, preached the Gospel, and made many more disciples. After they appointed elders for the churches they headed back to Antioch and Jerusalem. When Paul wrote to his young friend Timothy years later, he recounted this trip to Galatia over again:

> My persecutions and sufferings that happened to me at Antioch, at Iconium, and at Lystra—which persecutions I endured; yet from them all the Lord rescued me. Indeed, all who desire to live a godly life in Christ Jesus will be persecuted (2 Tim. 3:11–12).

The churches that Paul wrote to in this letter were churches that he planted with his own blood, sweat, and tears. Most of the people who were saved out of his ministry in this area were totally pagan and had no knowledge of Christ. Paul founded the church where previously there was nothing but the temples of the Greek gods. Every soul won to Christ was precious to him and he was not about to let his hard work be destroyed by false teachers.

The Attack on the Galatians (1:6, 2:4, 3:1, 4:9)

Paul's letter is in response to a problem that secretly snuck into these churches after he left and went back to Jerusalem. The churches in Galatia had been infiltrated by a group of false teachers which became known as the "Judiazers." Just as the Gentile believers in Galatia were getting established in the faith, a group of legalistic teachers came from Jerusalem and began to teach them that their faith was incomplete. They poisoned the simplicity of the gospel by saying in addition to grace, the Galatians needed to observe and keep the Old Testament law. These false teachers were preaching a hijacked, hybrid religion of grace + works = salvation. Notice how this attack from the outside emerges in various places throughout the letter.

> "I marvel that you are turning away so soon from Him who called you in the grace of Christ, to a different gospel" (1:6).

> "And this occurred because of false brethren secretly brought in (who came in by stealth to spy out our liberty which we have in Christ Jesus, that they might bring us into bondage)" (2:4).

> "O foolish Galatians! Who has bewitched you that you should not obey the truth, before whose eyes Jesus Christ was clearly portrayed among you as crucified?" (3:1).

> "But now after you have known God, or rather are known by God, how is it that you turn again to the weak and beggarly elements, to which you desire again to be in bondage?" (4:9).

This is Paul's most passionate letter. You can tell he is seething with anger over what was going on inside these churches. His stylus was pushing deep into the papyrus as he wrote with urgency.

Chief among their heresies, the Judiazers told the Galatian men before they became Christians that they needed to be circumcised like the Jewish men (5:2). The law-lovers also taught the Galatians that although they were first saved by grace, what kept them righteous before God was keeping the Mosaic laws, regulations, and ceremonies (2:15–16). To add insult to injury, Paul's critics bashed him by saying that he was not a real apostle and that his message was a counterfeit (1:12). The Galatians traded their freedom in Christ for legalistic bondage.

There is a legendary story about a Persian spy who was captured by the Spartan army. Of course, the spy was imprisoned, interrogated, and sentenced to death, but before the execution the Spartan general went through an unusual ritual. He gave the spy twenty-four hours to make a choice between beheading or what lay behind a black door. The spy deliberated and finally chose the chopping block. Moments after his life was extinguished, the Spartan leader turned to his aide and said, "They always prefer to the known to the unknown." The aide did not know what fate was behind the black door so he asked his commander. "Freedom," replied the general. "And I've only known a few brave enough to take it."

Perhaps the Galatians had a fear of the unknown. After all, grace was a totally new and radical concept. So they chose slavery over freedom. This is what Paul couldn't understand. Why would the Galatians trade the freedom of grace only to go back into the bondage of the law?

The Argument of Galatians (2:20, 3:13, 5:1)

One reason why the Galatians went backward instead of forward was because they didn't have a full understanding of grace or what Christ accomplished when He went to the cross.

Paul was writing to set the record straight so that there could be a grace awakening in every believer's heart. As we shall see, the fearless apostle is going to demonstrate that the different Gospel the Judiazers were preaching was not really the Gospel at all. In order to make his point, Paul approaches the issue from several angles. The structure of the epistle follows a three-fold purpose.

Chapters 1–2 are an explanation of Paul's *personal vindication*. Here Paul takes on those who have damaged his reputation and called into question his credentials. He is going to prove to the Galatians why his message is valid and why his ministry is true. This section climaxes with his grand statement in 2:20, "I have been crucified with Christ; it is no longer I who live, but Christ lives in me; and the life which I now live in the flesh I live by faith in the Son of God, who loved me and gave Himself for me."

Chapters 3–4 are the heart of the letter and they build a *doctrinal foundation*. Here Paul launches into an all-out defense of the Gospel and why the law is insufficient and superfluous for a Christian who has been saved by grace. The crux of his theological defense comes in 3:11, "Now it is evident that no one is justified before God by the law, for 'the righteous shall live by faith.'"

The last section, chapters 5–6, is where Paul makes some *practical application*. Having laid out the Gospel from a theological basis, this is where Paul explains how a Christian lives in the arena of grace. The rallying cry of this section can be found in 5:1, "Stand fast therefore in the liberty by which Christ has made us free, and do not be entangled again with a yoke of bondage."

I like how Bible commentator Philip Ryken summarizes the purpose of Galatians:

> Galatians is a letter for recovering Pharisees ... Most Pharisees have a problem, however. It is hard for them leave their legalism behind. Although initially they received God's grace for free, they keep trying to put a surcharge on it. They believe that God loves them, but secretly they suspect that His love is conditional, that it depends on how they are doing in the Christian life. They end up with a performance based Christianity that denies the grace of God. To put this in theological terms, they want to base their justification on their sanctification. This means that most former Pharisees—indeed most Christians—are still in recovery. There is still something of the old legalist in us. Although we have been saved by grace, we do not always know how to live by grace. Galatians was written for people like us.[5]

Galatians

	Personal Vindication Chapters 1-2	Doctrinal Foundation Chapters 3-4	Practical Application Chapters 5-6
	"I have been crucified with Christ; it is no longer I who live, but Christ lives in me; and the life which I now live in the flesh I live by faith in the Son of God, who loved me and gave Himself for me (2:20)."	"Now it is evident that no one is justified before God by the law, for 'The righteous shall live by faith (3:11)."	"Stand fast therefore in the liberty by which Christ has made us free, and do not be entangled again with a yoke of bondage (5:1)."
Focus	The enemies of liberty	The explanation of liberty	The exercise of liberty
Conflict	authority vs. opinion	freedom vs. bondage	spirit vs. flesh
Purpose	Defending the Gospel	Understanding the Gospel	Living out the Gospel
Style	Passionate, direct, blunt	intellectual, persuasive	pastoral, didactic
Lesson	Exclusivity of the Gospel	Justification by Faith	Walk by the Spirit

Called to Freedom! Don't Miss Out!

In his book *Ghost Soldiers*, Hampton Sides tells the story of a dramatic mission during World War II. On January 28th, 1945, 121 hand-selected Army

---

5 Ryken, *Galatians*, 3–4.

Rangers slipped behind enemy lines in the Philippines in an attempt to rescue 513 American and British POWs who had spent three years in a hellish prison camp near the city of Cabanatuan.

Sides described the first effects of liberation as chaos and fear. The prisoners were too mentally brittle to understand what was taking place. Some even scurried away from their liberators. One particular prisoner, Bert Bank, refused to budge, even when a Ranger walked right up to him and tugged his arm. "C'mon, we're here to save you," he said. "Run for the gate."

Bank still would not move. The Ranger looked into his eyes and saw they were vacant, registering nothing. "What's wrong with you?" he asked. "Don't you want to be free?" A smile formed on Bank's lips as the meaning of the words became clear, and he reached up to the outstretched hand of the Ranger.

The Rangers searched all the barracks for additional prisoners, then shouted, "The Americans are leaving. Is there anybody here?" Hearing no answer, they left. But there was one more POW left behind—Edwin Rose—who had been on latrine duty and somehow missed all the shooting and explosions. When he wandered back to his barracks, he failed to notice the room was empty. He laid down on his straw mat and fell asleep. Edwin had missed the liberation, but there was a reason why. Edwin was deaf.

It wasn't until early the next morning that Edwin realized the other prisoners were gone and that he was left behind. Nevertheless, he took the time to shave and put on his best clothes that he had been saving for the day he would be rescued. He walked out of the prison camp, thinking that he would soon be found and led to freedom. Sure enough, Rose was found by passing Filipino guerrillas and led to safety.[6]

Edwin Rose nearly missed out on his freedom. Yet in many ways, I would argue that there are scores of Christians who are in the same predicament. Don't make the same mistake. Have you become deaf to the announcement of liberation? Galatians was written so that everyone would know that freedom has arrived. Our Great Emancipator—Jesus Christ—has announced liberty to the captives (Luke 4:18). Don't let this opportunity pass you by. Accept His invitation to freedom today!

---

6. Sides, *Ghost Soldiers*, 295–296.

CHAPTER 2

Only One Gospel (1:1–9)

During WWII the Axis and Allies not only fought with bullets and bombs, but covertly with deception and misinformation. One such silent operation that came to light after the fog of war cleared was code-named "Operation Bernhard." Listen to how one historian records the discovery of this Nazi scam:

> Early in the morning of May 13, 1945 a fisherman who had just left his house on the shore of Truan Lake in western Austria came pounding back up the stairs. "Wake up! Wake up! Everybody! Come out here! You won't believe this." His half-awake family stumbled into their yard and gazed out at the water in astonishment. The little lake was totally covered by a gently bobbing blanket of thousands of British banknotes! Soon hundreds of fully dressed villagers were thrashing about in the lake, frantically stuffing sodden banknotes into pails and baskets. The air was filled with delighted shrieks, gasps, and exclamations. Some rushed home to dry their money in ovens or on stove tops. Others laid out the bills on the beach and in a nearby field to dry in the sun . . . Several people hurried to the nearby town of Endsee to the village bank. A cashier tested the sample bill with ultraviolet light and passed it around among her colleagues for their opinions. Everyone agreed: the bills were genuine.[1]

Soon after the discovery of the millions of British banknotes, Allied forces arrived at the little Austrian village and explained the situation. The recovered currency was actually part of the biggest counterfeiting operation in world history. The Nazi's had stolen printing plates from the British treasury and secretly produced over 650 million pounds of fake British money. The Nazis even used prisoners from the Sachsenhausen concentration

---

1. Schroeder, *Scams*, 73–75.

camp to help process the currency. The motive behind Operation Bernhard was to introduce enough fake money into the British economy to cause it to collapse.

Fortunately, the fake bills never made it into circulation. As the Allies advanced deeper into German territory the stores of cash were crated up and thrown into the Truan River. When the crates of cash were cracked open, the bills floated downstream and ended up in Truan Lake where the villagers inevitably discovered the fake fortune. Disaster was averted, but imagine the tremendous disappointment that those poor villagers must have felt when they were told that they had handfuls of soggy, worthless paper.

Counterfeits are empty lies mixed with just enough truth to make them seem believable. What is so disconcerting is that counterfeits are everywhere—there's bogus money, look-alike jewelry, bootlegged media, faux furs, imitation leather, artificial flavoring, and even false faiths. For every one of God's truths, Satan has cleverly invented a fraud to deceive, delude, and distort. That's what the apostle Paul was dealing with when he wrote to the Galatian believers. The true Gospel had been hijacked by spiritual hucksters and a mutant form of faith and works was being taught to the Galatian Christians. The result was counterfeit Christianity.

The issues that Paul was dealing with were not theological rabbit trails. Paul was fighting for the very essence of the Christian message—the Gospel. Perhaps that's why his opening words to the Galatians were so forceful and pungent. The souls of men and women were at stake as well as the fundamental doctrine of salvation. With no time to waste Paul does away with the pleasantries and wades into the middle of controversy.

The Credibility of the Apostle Paul (1:1–2)

One of the first lines of attack by the Judiazers was an attempt to discredit the character of Paul. The critics believed that if they could deny or explain away Paul's apostleship, they would be able to destroy his message. The accusation went something like this: since Paul was not a personal disciple of Jesus, like the original twelve, then he could not claim to have the same inspiration as Peter, James, or John. Paul's enemies also said that his gospel had been communicated to him by a human source and therefore had no authority.

This is why Paul opens up by establishing the fact that he was indeed a true messenger of God. "Paul, an apostle—not from men nor through man, but through Jesus Christ and God the Father, who raised him from the dead." Paul comes out of the gate by saying, "Look people, I'm legit!" His authority was not bestowed upon him by a committee or self-appointed. It was God-given. His ordination came at the nail-pierced hands of Jesus. He indignantly denied the lies that his enemies were telling about him.

The word "apostle" comes from the Greek word *apostolos* and it simply means "one who is sent." An apostle was an ambassador, messenger, or emissary sent by a king or dignitary to deliver a message. In the New Testament, there were some prerequisites for being an apostle. First, they had to be earthly companions of Jesus during His ministry (John 15:22, Acts 1:22). Paul was the only exception. He refers to himself as "being born out of due time" (1 Cor. 15:8). Second, they had to be an eyewitness of the risen Lord Jesus, which Paul was (1 Cor. 15:5–8). Third, they had to be called by God and receive direct revelation from Jesus Christ (Mark 1:16–20, John 15:16). Paul saw the resurrected Jesus and received his calling when Christ appeared to him on the road to Damascus (Acts 9:1–19). Lastly, the apostles were confirmed by supernatural works (Acts 2:43, 5:12; 2 Cor. 12:12). Paul performed several miracles including healing a lame man at Lystra (Acts 14:8–10), casting out demons (Acts 16:16–18), and raising a man from the dead (Acts. 20:9–11). By the way, it's significant to note that because nobody today can meet these qualifications, there is no such thing today as a "modern apostleship." John Phillips wrote about the significance of Paul's greeting:

> Paul! As soon as they saw the name on the letter, the Galatians would see him in their mind's eye. They would recall at once the extraordinary Jew who spoke like a Roman and reasoned like a Greek. Paul! He was the man who could preach like an archangel, who was as bold as a lion, as tender as a nurse, as honest as the sunshine, wiser than Solomon, more patient than Job, and armed with spiritual authority and power. No foe could daunt him; no fear could haunt him. He had taken their little corner of the Roman world by storm![2]

Not too long ago I saw an advertisement for a product that left me shaking my head in disbelief—Spray-on Mud! Not kidding. This was fake mud in an aerosol can. Spray-on Mud is designed for use on the outside

---

2. Philips, *Exploring Galatians*, 19.

Only One Gospel (1:1–9)

of your truck or SUV. A liberal application makes it appear as if you use your expensive gas-guzzler for more than taking the kids to soccer practice. Spray it on along the tire wells and mud flaps and friends might think you've just returned from a wilderness adventure. Apparently, $15 a can seems a reasonable price for the appearance of authenticity.

There are many expressions of imitation Christianity that we can try to pass off as the real thing. Success can be misconstrued as spiritual blessings. Inspirational bumper stickers and religious symbols dangling on gold chains can be interpreted as signs of spirituality. Excellent music can cover for authentic worship of the heart. Feel-good motivational messages can pass for inspired preaching. Christian clichés can be handed out as biblical wisdom. An attractive personality can be mistaken for a Spirit-filled life.

But we all know that authenticity is much deeper than appearances. Paul knew that his calling was real and deep down, so did the Galatians. They just needed a friendly reminder in the midst of all the fake mud that was being tossed around. Yet there is a reminder for us in the example of Paul. As a follower of Christ, you can expect folks to criticize, especially when you endeavor to undertake something in the ministry. You will never make everyone happy and the quickest way to failure is to try to please everyone. But I have found that the best way to nullify slander and criticism is to live in such a way that nobody will believe the critics.

The Content of the Gospel (1:3–4)

Paul moves on to make the content of the Gospel message clear and concise. "Grace to you and peace from God our Father and the Lord Jesus Christ, who gave Himself for our sins to deliver us from the present evil age, according to the will of our God and Father, to whom be the glory forever and ever. Amen."

Since the beginning of Christianity, there have been heretics in every generation who have tried to redefine and change the Gospel to suit their needs. Generally, this usually happens in one of two ways—legalism or liberalism, addition or subtraction. Legalists always want to add things to the Gospel, while liberals want to subtract things from the Gospel.

For example, a legalist would say, "You need to be baptized in order to go to heaven." A legalist argues, "The King James Version is the only inspired translation of the Bible and all others are inferior." Another legalistic lie goes like this, "Unless you confess your sins to a priest, God will not hear your prayers." With legalism, it's always Jesus plus works equals salvation.

On the other end of the spectrum, there is liberalism which always takes away from the Gospel. A liberal might say, "Sure, I'm a Christian. But I don't believe that Jesus actually rose physically from the dead." Another claim from a liberal might say, "God is too big to fit into one religion and, therefore, we need to be open to the possibility that Jesus is not the only way to heaven." With liberalism, it's always the Gospel minus truth which equals heresy.

Undoubtedly, if Paul were alive today, he would tear into heretical statements like that in a split second. Paul was a buzz-saw when it came to the truth and he clearly lays out the Gospel message so there is no confusion. The Gospel was about Christ's deity, death, and resurrection. Nothing more, nothing less. Instead of falling off into a heretical ditch, Paul keeps his teaching in the middle of the road by pointing out three core truths:

First, the death of Christ was voluntary. Notice that he says Christ "gave Himself" for our sins. No one made Jesus go to the cross. He did it on His own free will out of His love for sinners. Jesus said, "No one takes my life from me, but I lay it down of my own accord. I have authority to lay it down, and I have authority to take it up again. This charge I have received from my Father" (John 10:18).

Second, the death of Christ was vicarious. Paul says that Christ died for "our sins." He went to the cross taking our place as the sin-bearer of humanity. He died the death we deserved. He paid the penalty we could not. Jesus said in Mark 10:45, "The Son of Man came not to be served but to serve, and to give His life as a ransom for many."

Third, the death of Christ was victorious. Jesus' death and resurrection "delivered us from this present evil age." In other words, Christ conducted a successful rescue operation and set us free from sin, Satan, death, and the evil world system. Jesus said, "I am the resurrection and the life. Whoever believes in me, though he die, yet shall he live again" (John 11:25).

The result of Christ's death and resurrection is grace towards repentant sinners, which is why Paul begins with, "Grace to you." Grace is a word that is often thrown around by preachers, yet few take time to define it. Even though we may know what it is initially, if asked on the spot, "What is grace?" we may not have the ability to give an answer. I once heard Billy Graham tell a story about himself that illustrates how the Gospel of grace operates.

Only One Gospel (1:1–9)

Dr. Graham was driving through a small, southern town when he was stopped by a policeman and charged with speeding. Graham admitted his guilt, and was told by the officer that he would have to appear in court. The judge asked, "Guilty, or not guilty?" When Graham pleaded guilty, the judge replied, "That'll be ten dollars—a dollar for every mile you went over the limit. You have violated the law and the penalty must be paid." Billy said that's when he started reaching for his wallet and suddenly the judge recognized the famous evangelist and said, "The fine must be paid—but I am going to pay it for you." The judge took a ten dollar bill from his own wallet, attached it to the ticket, and then took Graham out and bought him a steak dinner! "That," said Billy Graham, "is how grace works."

If justice is getting what you deserve and mercy is not getting what you deserve, then grace is getting what you can't earn and don't deserve. The simple message of the Gospel is faith alone, in Christ alone, who saves us by His grace alone. When man tries to add something to the Gospel it's like saying, "Thank you, Jesus, for your death on the cross, but it's not enough!" In God's economy, its grace plus nothing or else you have man-made religion. With grace, you can't add anything to it, nor can you subtract anything from it. It's God's unmerited favor—or God's Riches At Christ's Expense!

The Counterfeit Gospel (1:6–7)

Paul is astonished, bewildered, and angered that the Galatians have so quickly turned away from the simplicity of the Gospel of grace. It's worthy of noting that at this point in all of Paul's other letters there is usually a prayer of thanksgiving for the believers to whom he is writing. However, in this case Paul is boiling hot and he's not exactly in the praying mood. "I am astonished that you are so quickly deserting him who called you in the grace of Christ and are turning to a different gospel—not that there is another one, but there are some who trouble you and want to distort the gospel of Christ" (1:6). As soon as Paul heard about the corruption of the Gospel in Galatia, he started composing his heated response. We can imagine how he did it, grabbing a parchment, slamming an inkwell on his desk, calling for his secretary. As he paced back in forth in his chamber he dictated his letter in short, angry outbursts.[3]

---

3. Ryken, *Galatians*, 16.

Notice that Paul refers to "a different Gospel." The particular word used in the Greek is *heteros*. We use that word in our English language as a prefix to describe opposite pairings—like a heterogeneous mixture or a heterosexual couple. Paul is livid that these people have gone to a *heteros* Gospel, an aberration that is the opposite of what they first believed. They had exchanged the real thing for a counterfeit. In essence, Paul accuses his readers of being turncoats to the Gospel. The verb that he uses to describe their desertion is a colorful one that refers to a military revolt. Paul is saying they are traitors—they have changed sides.[4]

This reminds me of the Brett Favre controversy that disgruntled many life-long Packers fans. For sixteen years Brett Favre was the hero of the Green Bay Packers. Favre was considered one of the greatest quarterbacks of all-time when he was at the helm of the Packers from 1992 to 2008. He even led them to a Super Bowl victory in 1997. He was to forever be a legend with "Cheese-heads" until the unthinkable happened. He came out of retirement for a second time and joined the divisional rivals, the Minnesota Vikings. Packers fans were so incensed over Favre's defection to the "dark side" that when the Vikings came to Lambeau Field, they took old Brett Favre jerseys and replaced his name with the title "Judas." Ouch! The way those jilted Packers fans felt betrayed gives us an inkling of how Paul felt. John MacArthur writes:

> The Galatians had been privileged to be taught by the greatest teacher the church had ever known apart from the Lord Himself; yet they readily rejected the truths of grace they had learned from him . . . a single drop of poison in a large container can make all the water lethal. And a single false idea that in any way undercuts God's grace poisons the whole system of belief. Paul would not tolerate a single drop of legalism being intermixed with God's pure grace."[5]

Any system that places value on religious merit, human effort or man's ability to work for God's love and favor is not the grace of Christianity. This is where Jesus stands in opposition to all other religious leaders. Every world religion says "do," but Christianity says "done." There is no compromise. It's either grace or works. Paul was adamant about this and unwilling to budge.

---

4. Jeremiah, *Claiming Faith, Finding Freedom*, vol. 1, 14.
5. MacArthur, *Galatians*, 13–14.

Only One Gospel (1:1–9)

The Curse of the Counterfeit Gospel (1:8–9)

Did you realize that throughout the Bible the strongest language of judgment is not reserved for the murderer, or the adulterer, or the thief, but for those who propagate religious error? In fact, Paul uses one of the strongest words in the Greek language to pronounce a curse on those that distort and pervert the Gospel—*anathema!* He even repeats himself in verse 1:9 to make sure his readers get the message loud and clear. "But even if we or an angel from heaven should preach to you a gospel contrary to the one we preached to you, let him be accursed [*anathema*]. As we have said before, so now I say again: If anyone is preaching to you a gospel contrary to the one you received, let him be accursed [*anathema*]."

It's fascinating that Paul mentions the angels. Of course, a heaven-sent angel could never contradict God's word, so Paul is speaking in exaggeration to make his point abundantly clear that even if Michael the archangel were to arrive at their church trumpeting another gospel, he is to be damned! Maybe Paul was exercising some sanctified foresight here because two of the world's largest false religions are based on angels communicating "new truth" to prophets. In both Islam and Mormonism the source of the religious doctrine is reported to have come from angels.

Supposedly, in 610 AD while praying in a cave near Mecca, an illiterate merchant by the name of Muhammad received his first revelations from Allah through the angel Gabriel. In fact, if you read the Quran it mentions that Muhammad felt the angel choking him, telling him to recite all he was told (Sura 96:1–3). The result of this angelic revelation was eventually written down into the Quran.[6]

Fast forward 1,200 years to the 1820s in upstate New York. A young man by the name of Joseph Smith says that the angel Maroni appeared to him with two golden tablets that contained God's unspoiled truth. Maroni said that Smith needed only to translate the message on the tablets and become the true prophet who would restore the worship of God. The result was the Book of Mormon and the Latter Day Saints Church.

The common thread of angelic revelation shows that these two religions are taken from the same demonic lie. Moreover, both of those religions are works-based. Every Muslim must keep the five Pillars of Islam and every Mormon must achieve perfection for their salvation. Also, both of those religions revere Jesus, but He most definitely is not regarded as

---

6. Federer, *What Every American Needs to Know about the Qur'an*, 38–40.

God's only unique Son. In Islam, Jesus is merely a respected prophet—a man and nothing more. Sura 43:59 states, "Jesus was no more than a mortal whom Allah favored and made an example to the Israelites. They are unbelievers who say God is Messiah, Mary's son." In Mormonism, Jesus is known as the spirit-brother of Lucifer and the first of many spirit-children born to the Heavenly Father.

Both of those religions have their sources in an angel, Maroni and Gabriel. However, Paul reminds us here and in 2 Cor. 11:14 to beware of look-a-likes because "Satan can present himself as an angel of light." I believe that rather than angelic revelation, these false prophets were victims of demonic deception. It's almost as if Paul, under the inspiration of the Holy Spirit, can see these errors coming later and so these warnings in 1:8–9 are penned as a preemptive strike against such theological quackery.

In case you think Paul's words are too harsh for our tolerant and politically correct culture, let me remind you that the Gospel is not up for debate. Truth is not determined by feelings or a majority vote. God does not offer many paths to heaven but one way through the blood of Christ (Acts 4:12). Christians need not apologize that the Gospel is narrow or that grace cannot be earned or deserved. We are not more godly if we side-step doctrinal issues, nor do we truly love people if we sugarcoat the Gospel to make it more palatable. The reason why Paul is so adamant about protecting the Gospel is because the distortion of it results in everlasting destruction. Mess with the Gospel and you mess with the eternal souls of men and women.

In his book, *The Shepherd*, the famous writer Frederick Forsythe tells a story about a pilot on Christmas Eve of 1957. A young Royal Air Force pilot is stationed at a base in Germany. As Christmas approaches, he yearns to visit home, but his hopes are dashed when his commanding officer tells him that he has to stand duty on Christmas day. He resigns himself to the prospect of a lonely holiday when suddenly late on Christmas Eve, the word comes: he is released from duty and can fly home to England.

At ten o'clock on Christmas Eve, the young aviator climbs into the cockpit of his single-seat Vampire fighter jet and takes off under a moonless sky for the 400-mile flight home to Kent, England. But just ten minutes out over the North Sea, there's a short in the jet's electrical system. His instrument panel goes dark, and both the compass and the standby compass fail. Fighting a rising sense of panic, the pilot realizes he only has 80 minutes worth of fuel for the flight home.

Only One Gospel (1:1–9)

Recalling what he has been taught to do in such an emergency, he descends in altitude, slows his airspeed, and flies in an emergency triangular pattern in order to be picked up on radar. He wonders: Will anyone see me? Will help come in time? He begins to pray: "O Heavenly Father, lead me home..."

Suddenly, from out of nowhere there appears beneath him a dark object—a plane that dips its wing as a signal for him to follow. This plane leads the young aviator to a landing field with a lighted runway. As he gets into his landing pattern, the plane disappears into the night. In aviation parlance, such a plane is known as a "shepherd." As he touches down, the young pilot breathes a prayer of thanks for that unknown shepherd who found and led him home.

In the same way, Jesus is the only reliable guide to our heavenly home—our Good Shepherd (John 10:11). He knows the way home. "I am the way, the truth, and the life, no man comes to Father except through me" (John 14:6). It may seem narrow and insensitive to say, "Jesus is the only way to the Father," but our job isn't to serve as His speech writers or spinmeisters, seeking to reinvent His message and improve His poll numbers. Our job is not to try to improve on what He said, but to believe it, share it, and preach it. There is only one Gospel.

CHAPTER 3

Countering the Critics (1:10–24)

THERE IS A STORY about a salesman who was getting a haircut and he mentioned to his barber that he was about to take a trip to Rome. The barber chimed in, "Rome is a terribly overrated city. I've been there." There was an awkward silence in the room. "What airline are you taking?" asked the barber. The salesman told him the name of the airline and the barber responded, "What a terrible airline! Their seats are cramped, their food is bad, and their planes are always late." "What hotel are you staying at?" the barber wanted to know. The salesman named the hotel and the barber exclaimed, "Why would you stay there? That hotel is in the wrong part of town and has horrible service. You'd be better off staying home!" Getting a little exasperated, the salesman sat forward in the barber chair and said, "But I'm expecting to close a big deal while I'm there and I'm hoping to meet the pope." The barber came back, "You'll be disappointed trying to do business in Italy and don't count on seeing the pope. He only grants audiences to VIPs."

Three weeks later the salesman returned to the barber shop. The barber asked, "How was your trip?" "Wonderful! I made a big sale and I got to meet the pope!" said the salesman. "You got to meet the pope?" Finally, the barber was impressed, "Tell me what happened!" The salesman explained, "Well, when I approached him, I bent down and kissed his ring." The barber was getting drawn into the story, "No kidding. What did he say?" The salesman replied, "He looked down at my head and said, 'My son, where did you get that lousy haircut?'"

As one wag put it, "Too bad the only people who know how to run this country are busy driving cabs and cutting hair." The ancient Greek philosopher Aristotle said, "Criticism is something you can avoid easily—by saying nothing, doing nothing, and being nothing." John Maxwell also

Countering the Critics (1:10–24)

has a colorful saying, "When you get kicked in the rear, you know you're out in front."

One of the occupational hazards of being a leader is receiving criticism. In the face of that kind of heat, there's a strong temptation to "go under," "throw in the towel," or "bail out." Many have faded out of leadership because of the fiery darts of an armchair quarterback. No matter what you do, if you are in a position of leadership, dealing with criticism is inevitable.

The apostle Paul was no stranger to criticism and the venomous attacks of enemies. As a church planter and a champion of the Gospel he was always on the frontlines of battle and he came away with many wounds. Perhaps, no greater assault came upon Paul's ministry than from the Judiazers who tried to subvert his work in the Galatian churches.

Not only did these false teachers pervert the gospel of grace, but they discredited Paul's character and credentials. In order to cause as much controversy as possible, the Judaizers spread the false accusations around that Paul was not a legitimate apostle because he was not one of the original twelve disciples. Furthermore, they claimed that Paul's message of grace was not authentic and that he stole it or invented it to make himself look good in the eyes of the Gentiles. The strategy worked and many believers in the Galatian churches began doubting Paul's apostolic legitimacy. Paul's message of grace was under fire.

The remaining verses in chapter one are Paul's defense in response to his critics. In this passage Paul gives his readers an autobiographical sketch of his life before meeting Christ and after his conversion as proof that the radical change in his life was a work of God's saving grace.

Paul's Convictions (1:10–12)

The apostle begins by answering the accusations that he was purposely watering down God's standards in order to make it easier to get converts. According to the Judaizers, the message of grace was just too simple and Paul was merely telling the people what they wanted to hear.

First, Paul makes the point that *his motive was not to please men*. "For am I now seeking the approval of man, or of God? Or am I trying to please man? If I were still trying to please man, I would not be a servant of Christ." The words of Paul do not sound like the soft intonations of a man looking to win a popularity contest. Granted, there was a point in his life when he tried to measure up to the standards of his superiors in Judaism, but he gave up that futile exercise when Christ freed him from the bondage of the law and opened his eyes. The persecution that Paul endured for the sake of Christ proved that he was not in it to make a name for himself or to go another rung higher on the social ladder.

A preacher of the Gospel is called to take an unpopular stand against many sins, doctrinal errors, and corruption in high places. He is called to persuade men of the Gospel by any means he can, but he is never authorized to be a silk-tongued orator who sugarcoats evil and compromises the truth. I admire men like Paul who dug in their heels when opposition came.

When Peter Cartwright, the pioneering Methodist preacher of the 1830s, was doing his itinerant ministry across America, it came to his attention that the president of the United States, which at that time was Andrew Jackson, had intentions of attending the church where he was to preach. Cartwright was undaunted, but the president's advisors came to Cartwright before the service and very gently asked him not to say anything which would offend the president.

When Cartwright ascended to the pulpit, he opened his sermon with the following remarks. "I understand that Andrew Jackson is here this morning. And I have been requested to be very guarded in my remarks. Let me say this: Andrew Jackson will go to hell if he doesn't repent of his sin." After the service the president met the evangelist at the door and is reported to have said to the preacher, "Sir, if I had a regiment of men like you in my army, I could whip the world."[1]

Second, Paul notes that *his message was not from men* (1:11–12). The apostle reinforces the idea that the Gospel he received was not an imitation, fabrication, nor an assimilation of other ideas. "For I would have you know, brothers, that the gospel that was preached by me is not man's gospel. For I did not receive it from any man, nor was I taught it, but I received it through a revelation of Jesus Christ."

Paul did not invent grace, nor did he learn it from a book, but rather it was a direct revelation from God. In fact, the Greek word that is translated in the text as "revelation" is the word *apokalupsis* which means "an unveiling of something previously secret." In other words, God let Paul in on something that mankind was previously blind to see. John MacArthur has written:

> Had Paul proclaimed a gospel that was according to man, it would have been permeated by works righteousness, as is every humanly

---

1. Michael, *Spurgeon on Leadership*, 105–106.

Countering the Critics (1:10-24)

devised system of religion. Man's sinful pride is offended by the idea that only God's mercy and grace can save him from sin, and he therefore insists on having part in his own salvation. The very fact that Paul preached a message of salvation in which works play absolutely no part was itself evidence that his message was from God and not man.[2]

Let's face it, the Gospel is offensive. No one likes to have their personal sinfulness exposed and be called a wicked rebel who deserves God's wrath. Furthermore, no prideful person wants to hear that there is nothing they can do to merit or earn God's approval. If the Gospel was man-made, then it would be more palatable—certainly there would be no mention of sin, no need for the Cross, and not a hint of future judgment. If the Gospel were man-made, then it would look like a twelve-step program to personal success. A man-centered Gospel would replace bloody Mt. Calvary with a set of scales where men could earn their way to heaven by being fifty-one percent good. Perhaps one theologian, Rienhold Niebuhr, best summarized a humanistic gospel like this: "A God without wrath brought men without sin into a kingdom without judgment through the ministrations of a Christ without a cross."[3]

Paul's Conversion (1:13-16)

Now on a roll, Paul launches into his personal testimony to make the point that he is the most unlikely person to ever adopt a Gospel according to grace. He begins by explaining what he was like when he was a card-carrying Pharisee.

In verses 1:13-14, we notice *his conduct as a Pharisee*. "For you have heard of my former life in Judaism, how I persecuted the church of God violently and tried to destroy it. And I was advancing in Judaism beyond many of my own age among my people, so extremely zealous was I for the traditions of my fathers." Before Paul was confronted by the risen Jesus he was totally sold-out to squashing the early church. As a hardcore Jew, Paul thought that Jesus was a blasphemer and he believed that killing Christians was a noble service to God. According to his own statements, Paul took twisted pleasure in his job. In Acts 22:4-5, Paul shared his testimony with a hostile crowd:

---

2. MacArthur, *Galatians*, 23.
3. Niebuhr, *The Kingdom of God in America*, 193.

> I persecuted this Way to the death, binding and delivering to prison both men and women, as the high priest and the whole council of elders can bear me witness. From them I received letters to the brothers, and I journeyed toward Damascus to take those also who were there and bring them in bonds to Jerusalem to be punished.

Later on, when Paul is giving his defense to Agrippa in Acts 26:10–11, he added:

> And I did so in Jerusalem. I not only locked up many of the saints in prison after receiving authority from the chief priests, but when they were put to death I cast my vote against them. And I punished them often in all the synagogues and tried to make them blaspheme, and in raging fury against them I persecuted them even to foreign cities.

If that wasn't enough, according to Phil. 3:4–6, Paul wrote:

> If anyone else thinks he has reason for confidence in the flesh, I have more: circumcised on the eighth day, of the people of Israel, of the tribe of Benjamin, a Hebrew of Hebrews; as to the law, a Pharisee; as to zeal, a persecutor of the church; as to righteousness under the law, blameless.

If Paul had a space in your high school yearbook, he would be "most likely not to convert to Christianity." He was one of Gamaliel's star pupils and a shoe-in to be the president of the NAACP—that's the National Association for the Advancement of Committed Pharisees. Paul was at the top of his game in Jerusalem and he had no reason to leave the tradition that he had practiced so perfectly. It's not like Paul just woke up one morning and thought, "I wonder what it would be like to preach the Gospel of grace?" So what happened to radically change the direction of Paul's life?

Verses 1:15–16 relate to us *his call to preach*. "But when he who had set me apart before I was born, and who called me by his grace, was pleased to reveal his Son to me, in order that I might preach him among the Gentiles, I did not immediately consult with anyone . . ." When Paul was on the road to Damascus going to kill more Christians, he got laser-beamed by Jesus Christ. The conversion of Paul was so important that it is recorded in the New Testament at least four times (Acts 9:1–18, Acts 22:4–5, Acts 26:1–18, and 1 Tim. 1:12–14).

What Paul is getting across here is that his divine election and call to preach were not even on his radar. Those were God's supernatural and sovereign plans for him from the foundation of the world, not his own choosing. God totally interrupted his meteoric rise up the ladders of Judaism and wrecked Paul's life with His amazing grace. It's safe to say that the ole' boy never recovered.

David Jeremiah has a great illustration of how amazing grace works. Suppose that you look out the window of your home and you see someone stealing your car. You phone the police and give a description of the person along with the make, model, and description of your vehicle. Later that day, the phone rings. It's the police department. "Can you come down to the police station?" the officer inquires. "We have your car and we have the culprit."

So you go down and he is there—a woebegone-looking teenager. You inspect your car and it is undamaged. The officer asks, "Do you want to press charges?" If you say, "Yes, the young man stole my car and deserves to go to prison," that would be justice. If you say, "No, he's young and maybe he's learned his lesson, so let him go," that would be forgiveness. But suppose that you were to turn to the culprit and say, "Young man, I not only forgive you, but I also want to help you. Don't ever steal a car again. Here are the keys to the car. You can have it." That would be grace, unmerited favor, giving him something he didn't deserve and couldn't repay.[4]

God's grace is His active favor bestowing the greatest gift upon those who deserve the greatest punishment. That is the way God saved Saul of Tarsus and that is the way that He saves each and every sinner. Often times we read about the dramatic conversion of someone like Paul and we say, "My testimony isn't like that," and we might feel a little unsure of our election. For me personally, I was saved when I was seven years old. I never got into drugs or alcohol and I never became a prodigal son. God did not appear to me in a blinding light or speak to me with a booming voice. I don't say those things with a boasting heart. I know my sins aren't as public as others might be. Then one day I finally realized that it was God's grace all along that kept me from a life of bad choices, pain, and heartache. But I was just as much a sinner as anyone else. I needed God's grace just as much as Saul of Tarsus, John Newton, or the thief on the cross. Though the depth of our pit may have differing degrees, it takes the same amount of grace to save a death-row murderer as it does a child of seven.

---

4. Jeremiah, *Claiming Faith, Finding Freedom*, vol. 1, 24.

Free at Last

Paul's Commute (1:17–24)

The apostle now gives a detailed account of his travels and adventures since his conversion. The first stop on his journey was Arabia, "Nor did I go up to Jerusalem to those who were apostles before me, but I went away into Arabia" (1:17). After his conversion, Paul went into the desert of Arabia to be schooled by the Lord. There is much speculation about what exactly went on during this period, but we really don't know for sure. I happen to believe that just as Jesus spent three years with His disciples teaching and training them, so too did He do that for Paul. John Stott reinforces this interpretation:

> A veil of thick darkness hangs over St. Paul's visit to Arabia. We know neither where he went nor why he went there . . . We believe that in this period of withdrawal, as he meditated on the Old Testament Scriptures, on the facts of the life and death of Jesus that he already knew and on his experience of conversion, the gospel of the grace of God was revealed to him in its fullness. It has even been suggested that those three years in Arabia were a deliberate compensation for the three years of instructions which Jesus gave the other apostles, but which Paul missed. Now he had Jesus to himself, as it were, for three years of solitude in the wilderness.[5]

The point is that Paul was not taught by the other apostles as his critics might claim. It also underscores the importance of preparation and discipleship. We minimize the importance of preparation, but everyone who was used of God to do a great work spent a time in isolation with the Lord.

The next leg of the journey took Paul back to Damascus, "and returned again to Damascus" (1:17). Remember this is where Paul was initially going until Jesus made him take a detour. If we fill in the gaps with Dr. Luke's account in Acts, a harrowing adventure took place while Paul was in Damascus. Paul first went to Damascus to be the hunter, but this time he was the hunted. The Jews in the city wanted Paul dead so he had to get creative and improvise an escape plan. In Acts 9:19–25 we read of Paul being let down over the city wall in a basket.

From there, Paul tells us that he made his way back to Jerusalem, "Then after three years I went up to Jerusalem to visit Cephas and remained with him fifteen days. But I saw none of the other apostles except James the Lord's brother. (In what I am writing to you, before God, I do not lie!)."

---

5. Stott, *The Message of Galatians*, 34.

Countering the Critics (1:10-24)

When Paul first arrived in Jerusalem, the Church didn't exactly roll out the red carpet for him. There is an interesting detail in Acts 9:26, "And when he [Paul] had come to Jerusalem, he attempted to join the disciples. And they were all afraid of him, for they did not believe that he was a disciple." With good reason the other disciples were a bit standoffish. At one time Paul was the Church's greatest persecutor. This would be like Osama Bin Laden or some other al-Qaeda big shot converting to Christianity, coming to your church, and sitting down on the front row. Naturally, you might be a bit reserved if the man responsible for a worldwide terror organization came and told you that Jesus appeared to him personally. In fact, were it not for Barnabas vouching for him Paul may have been an outsider for much longer (Acts 9:27).

Once their guard was lowered, Paul tells us that he spent some time in Jerusalem getting acquainted with Peter and James. His short visit of fifteen days was not to learn the gospel message but to meet these two men who had spent time with Jesus. Could you imagine being a fly on the wall during their meetings? I can assure you they didn't talk about weather or sports. Imagine some of the stories Peter could have told him. He could have explained to Paul what it was like to momentarily walk upon the water or what it was like to see the fishes and loaves multiplied. He could have shown Paul the gnarled olive trees in Gethsemane where Jesus prayed and no doubt their time included a tour of the empty tomb.

After a fifteen day trip in Jerusalem, Paul headed north again, "Then I went into the regions of Syria and Cilicia" (1:21). During this part of his travels some scholars believe that Paul took a trip back to his hometown of Tarsus, which is mentioned briefly in Acts 9:30. Imagine how much courage this must have taken as Paul went back to his family and told them about the powerful change that had taken place in his life. Historians think that Paul spent about seven years in Tarsus until Barnabas called him to help in the ministry at Antioch (Acts 11:25). That means that about ten years passed for Paul from conversion to full-time ministry.

Finally, Paul wraps up this biographical account, "And I was still unknown in person to the churches of Judea that are in Christ. They only were hearing it said, 'He who used to persecute us is now preaching the faith he once tried to destroy.' And they glorified God because of me." For obvious reasons it was difficult for the churches to believe that the conversion of Paul was totally genuine. I'm sure that many thought Paul's story was just a ploy to get into the churches so he could persecute them even more.

However, when the churches saw that Paul was the real deal, they glorified God because of the complete 1800 U-turn from Saul to Paul.

The story of Paul's conversion made me begin thinking of other calloused men like him who were eventually overtaken by the Hound of Heaven. History is replete with examples of skeptics who were turned into believers after examining the evidence concerning the resurrection.

Sir Lionel Luckhoo was known in the legal world as the greatest defense attorney that ever lived (1914–1997). In fact, *The Guinness Book of World Records* has him listed with the most wins ever by a defense attorney with 245 consecutive murder acquittals. He was knighted twice by the Queen of England. Luckhoo was an avowed atheist. Someone asked him if he had ever investigated the evidence for the resurrection and challenged him to apply his legal prowess to the New Testament. He accepted the challenge and at the end of his investigation he went from being an atheist to being a Christian. He said, "I say unequivocally that the evidence for the resurrection of Jesus Christ is so overwhelming that it compels acceptance by proof which leaves absolutely no room for doubt."[6]

In the 1930s, a rationalistic English journalist named Frank Morrison set out to debunk the crazy idea of Jesus' resurrection once and for all. He examined the historical evidence with all his legal logic and evidential expertise. Morrison sifted through every possibility that might account for the disappearance of Jesus' body, yet the only logical solution was the biblical explanation. In the end, he wrote a book called *Who Moved the Stone?* The only thing his investigation debunked was his skepticism. His book has become a classic apologetic text for the historical authenticity of the resurrection of Christ. In the opening chapter entitled, "The Book that Refused to Be Written," Morrison said, "The book that was originally planned was left high and dry, like those Thames barges when the great river goes out to meet the incoming sea. The writer discovered one day that not only could he no longer write the book as he had once conceived it, but that he would not if he could."[7]

Finally, let's consider Josh McDowell. As a pre-law student, Josh McDowell was also an out-spoken skeptic of Christianity. In his own words, Josh believed that "every Christian had two minds: one was lost while the other was out looking for it." McDowell was eventually challenged by a group of Christian friends to investigate the Christian truth claims.

6. Clifford, *The Case for the Empty Tomb*, 112.
7. Morrison, *Who Moved the Stone?*, 8.

Countering the Critics (1:10–24)

Thinking this a farce, he accepted the challenge and decided that he would write the definitive book which would make a laughingstock of Christianity. McDowell only made it a year or so into his research before he realized that the weight of the evidence in favor of the Bible was too great for his skepticism to hold up. Josh wrote:

> One day while I was sitting in a library in London, England, I sensed a voice inside me saying, "Josh, you don't have a leg to stand on." I immediately suppressed it. But just about every day after that I heard the same inner voice. The more I researched, the more I heard His voice. I returned to the United States and to the university, but I couldn't sleep at night. I would go to bed at ten o'clock and lie awake until four in the morning, trying to refute the overwhelming evidence I was accumulating that Jesus Christ was God's Son. I began to realize that I was being intellectually dishonest."[8]

McDowell eventually gave his life to Christ and wrote a number of important texts in defense of Christianity, among them are *Evidence That Demands a Verdict* and *More Than a Carpenter*.

The Gospel is the most powerful force ever unleashed on the Earth. When Christ moves into a sinner's life, radical change occurs. It changed Paul from persecutor to preacher, from Pharisee to pastor, from adversary to apostle. As it turns out, the best way to deal with critics is to point them in the direction of Christ and let Him deal with them.

---

8. McDowell, *Evidence for Christianity*, xxiii.

CHAPTER 4

The Freedom Fighter (2:1–10)

PATRICK HENRY. NELSON MANDELA. Mahatma Gandhi. Spartacus. Martin Luther King, Jr. These names have become synonymous with the fight for freedom and equality. Some of them resorted to military action, while others took the road of peaceful resistance. All of them refused to be in bondage to a political or social structure that kept them locked up like an animal in a cage.

When historians talk about great freedom fighters, one name that usually emerges at the top of the list is William Wallace (1272–1305). His story of courage and valor has been told and re-told, most recently in the 1995 blockbuster movie *Braveheart*. For those of you who aren't familiar with the history, the Scottish people had lived for many years under the oppressive iron fist of the British crown. King Edward I (also known as "Longshanks") was cruel to the Scots and forced them into serfdom. Not only were the Scots forced to pay high taxes and suffer other injustices, they also had to deal with an occupying army that mistreated them.

William Wallace was born under this tyranny and he inspired a group of beleaguered Scots to fight against great odds for their freedom from the British. Through guerrilla tactics Wallace led his band of soldiers to some improbable victories against the King's armies. It looked like there was nothing that could stop his battle cry from advancing to the King's front door. However, Wallace was eventually betrayed by fellow Scotsman John de Menteith, tried as an insurrectionist, and executed by being "drawn and quartered." His decapitated head was dipped in tar and placed on one of the spires of London Bridge. There is much about the legend of Wallace that is exaggerated, but one thing all historians agree on is that Wallace wanted a free Scotland and he was willing to pay the ultimate price for that freedom with his own life.

The Freedom Fighter (2:1-10)

The movie *Braveheart* climaxes with an emotional scene on the day Wallace's death sentence is to be carried out. Wallace is before an angry mob—his body tied to a torture rack. An executioner displays an array of knives, axes, and sharp objects. Wallace faces death undaunted. The executioner finally asks Wallace if he has any last words. His one word reply shouted at the top of his lungs was, "FREEDOM!"

The bagpipes crescendo. A lump forms in the throat. Goosebumps rise up and down the spine and every man in the theater wishes he had courage like that. Wallace became a martyr for the Scottish war of independence and the film ends with the following voice over, "In the year of our Lord, 1314, patriots of Scotland, starving and outnumbered, charged the fields of Bannockburn. They fought like warrior poets. They fought like Scotsmen. And won their freedom."

The story of Wallace illustrates the truth that some men would rather die than live as a slave. Nearly 1,300 years before Wallace another freedom fighter took up the cause of liberty. However, the weapons of Paul's war were not swords and spears but pen and ink. Armed with the truth of God, Paul was standing against the traditions of the Judaizers which sought to drag the believers of Galatia back into religious bondage. In this autobiographical passage, Paul describes his most significant trip to Jerusalem after his conversion. His goal is to demonstrate that the gospel he preached to the Gentiles was the same gospel being preached by the other apostles.

Paul's Appearance in Jerusalem (2:1-2)

The apostle begins by giving us a brief timeline of his early ministry. Recall that after Paul was converted he spent three years in the desert of Arabia (1:17). After his time alone with the Lord he visited Peter and James in Jerusalem for about fifteen days (1:18). Paul spent 14 years on missionary journeys through the region of Galatia and then he made a second trip to Jerusalem. Acts 15 should be studied in tandem with this passage because it gives the reason why Paul made a second trip to Jerusalem. Acts 15:1-2 reads:

> But some men came down from Judea and were teaching the brothers, "Unless you are circumcised according to the custom of Moses, you cannot be saved." And after Paul and Barnabas had no small dissension and debate with them, Paul and Barnabas and

some of the others were appointed to go up to Jerusalem to the apostles and the elders about this question.

This is what is known as the "Jerusalem Council" and it is the first unofficial conference of the Church. The meeting was vitally important because it dealt with the issue of salvation. Specifically, what does a person have to do in order to be saved? Is faith in Christ enough? Should the Gentiles be made to become Jews by circumcision? And what about the Old Testament law? Where did that fit into the offering of grace? The council put their conclusions and recommendations into a letter to be taken back to the church at Antioch.

Two of the decisions made at this meeting related directly to Paul. First, they made it known that those who had gone to Antioch from Jerusalem advocating circumcision for Gentiles had done so without the permission of the leaders in Jerusalem (Acts 15:24). Second, the letter vindicated the ministry of Paul and Barnabas who risked their lives to declare the gospel of grace to Gentiles in Cyprus and Asia Minor (Acts 15:25-26).

As Paul was reliving the Jerusalem Council over again in his mind, he first notes *his companions in the Gospel*, "Then after fourteen years I went up again to Jerusalem with Barnabas, taking Titus along with me" (2:1). On this trip, Paul took two of his closest friends with him—Barnabas and Titus.

Barnabas was Paul's constant companion on the mission field and these guys had been through thick and thin together. You'll recall that his original name was Joseph; however, the apostles changed his name to Barnabas, which means "son of encouragement," (Acts 4:36) after he sold a piece of land and gave the money to the church. True to his name, every time you see him in Acts he is building someone up. Acts 11:24 says that "he was a good man, full of the Holy Spirit and of faith." If you were going into war, this was the kind of guy you wanted to have in the trenches with you. Paul and Barnabas were the dynamic duo—the first foreign missionaries in the church age.

Paul's other friend along for the ride was Titus. He was an uncircumcised Gentile that Paul had won to the Lord. In fact, Paul thought of Titus like his spiritual son (Titus 1:4). Titus was a product of the very ministry the Judiazers were attacking, so if anyone was going to claim that you needed to be circumcised in order to be saved, Titus would dispute that heresy.

Next, Paul notes *his concern for the Gospel*. "I went up because of a revelation and set before them (though privately before those who seemed influential) the gospel that I proclaim among the Gentiles, in order to make

The Freedom Fighter (2:1–10)

sure I was not running or had not run in vain" (2:2). The phrase, "Those who seemed influential," refers to the pillars of the Jerusalem church. Paul's trio met up with the original apostles in Jerusalem—Peter, James, and John. There he shared with them privately the content of the Gospel message he had been preaching publically to the Gentiles. As it turns out, both Paul and the other apostles were preaching the same gospel of grace. Paul's preaching was vindicated, proving that he had not labored in vain.

As I thought about Paul and his companions going up to Jerusalem to deal with the controversies in the ministry, I tried to imagine how Paul must have been encouraged by the fact that Titus and Barnabas had his back no matter what. Paul didn't have to fight the battle alone because he had the support of his closest brothers.

I doubt you have ever heard the name Donald Vairin, but he was a U.S. veteran of World War II and his story of how he survived the invasion of Guam is pretty amazing:

> Suddenly our boat came to a grinding halt. We had hit a coral reef and the commanding officer ordered everyone off the ship. I jumped into the ocean and sank like a rock, my carbine rifle, medical pack, canteen, and boots dragged me down. I somehow forced myself to the surface, gasping for air, only to sink again. I tried to pull off my boots, but the effort was exhausting and I realized I wasn't going to make it. Just then I saw a man thrashing in the water not too far away. In desperation I reached out and clung to him. That proved to be enough to enough to hold me up so that I could get to the reef where I was picked up by a rescue boat. I felt so guilty about grabbing the drowning man to save myself that I never told anyone what had happened. About six months later, on shore leave in San Francisco, I stopped in a restaurant. As I entered an unknown sailor in uniform waved me over to his table and announced to his friends, "This is my buddy. He saved my life." "What are you talking about?" I asked. "Don't you remember?" said the sailor, "We were in the water together at Guam. You grabbed onto me. I was going down and you held me up.[1]

Often times we don't realize it, but just by being there in the midst of crisis we can hold each other up. Paul, Barnabas, and Titus—this band of brothers—held each other up as they faced one of many fierce battles of the ministry. We can do the same for each other. "A friend loves at all times,

---

1. Vairin, "His Mysterious Ways."

and a brother is born for adversity," so says Proverbs 17:17. A true friend is someone who walks into your life while everyone else is walking out.

Paul's Adversaries in Jerusalem (2:3–5)

When Paul got to Jerusalem there were wolves in sheep's clothing waiting to sabotage his every move. The Greek word that Paul uses to refer to the "false brethren" is *psuedadelphos* or quite literally, "pseudo-Christians" or "counterfeit Christians." These guys were religious con-artists who somehow wormed their way into the Jerusalem Council and saw the gospel of grace as a threat to the traditions of Judaism. In fact, they even tried to get Titus tied up in their long list of rules and regulations. Paul writes in 2:3–5:

> But even Titus, who was with me, was not forced to be circumcised, though he was a Greek. Yet because of false brothers secretly brought in—who slipped in to spy out our freedom that we have in Christ Jesus, so that they might bring us into slavery—to them we did not yield in submission even for a moment, so that the truth of the gospel might be preserved for you.

The central issue was over circumcision and whether it was necessary to keep the Mosaic Law in order to be a Christian. The Judiazers could not fathom how Christ's life and death on the cross fulfilled the Old Testament, so they held onto their traditions. Commenting on the pressure the Judiazers placed upon Titus, John Phillips has written:

> They would cite the long, hallowed sanctity of the Law with its inflexible insistence on obedience to all of its commands. They would press upon him even Abraham's need for circumcision and God's displeasure with Moses for neglecting to circumcise his sons. They would urge him to start keeping the Sabbath, to participate in the ritual law, to offer sacrifices, and to adhere to the strict observance of the Mosaic dietary laws. And, with the tireless zeal and persistence of cultists in all ages, they would pursue him day and night, urging, badgering, and persuading.[2]

Do you get the sense that these guys were as pushy as a used car salesman at the end of the month? Much to Titus' relief, the Jerusalem Council voted unanimously in the negative. Titus was living proof that circumcision was not necessary for salvation. I don't know about you, but any religion

2. Phillips, *Exploring Galatians*, 63–64.

that requires me to undergo surgery in order to join can take a long walk off of a short pier. But such is the case with legalism—it makes you do crazy things in order to gain God's approval. It's a totally insane way to live because you never know when you've done enough to meet those lofty standards. Just when you think you've met one rule, you find out there are rules behind those rules and it never ends.

Paul's Acceptance in Jerusalem (2:6–10)

Paul's second trip to Jerusalem was a resounding victory for his ministry. Not only was his ministry authenticated by the other apostles, but the Judiazers' attack against Paul ran out of steam. Paul notes that *his authority was confirmed*. "And from those who seemed to be influential (what they were makes no difference to me; God shows no partiality)—those, I say, who seemed influential added nothing to me" (2:6). Notice again that Paul refers to the apostles in Jerusalem in seemingly derogatory terms, "those who seemed to be influential."

Paul was not disrespecting Peter, James, or John, but he was saying that the men whom the Judiazers put on a pedestal were in no way superior to Him. Paul explains that the original disciples in Jerusalem "added nothing to him," meaning that the Gospel that Peter, James, and John preached was identical to the one Paul preached.

Finally, we are told that *his ministry was commissioned*:

> On the contrary, when they saw that I had been entrusted with the gospel to the uncircumcised, just as Peter had been entrusted with the gospel to the circumcised (for he who worked through Peter for his apostolic ministry to the circumcised worked also through me for mine to the Gentiles), and when James and Cephas and John, who seemed to be pillars, perceived the grace that was given to me, they gave the right hand of fellowship to Barnabas and me, that we should go to the Gentiles and they to the circumcised. Only, they asked us to remember the poor, the very thing I was eager to do" (2:7–10).

Though they had different fields of service, the apostles in Jerusalem confirmed they were on the same team as Paul, Barnabas, and Titus. Paul's apostolic ministry was to the Gentiles, while Peter's was first and foremost to the Jews. Through these two powerful preachers God had an evangelistic mission of "divide and conquer." This scene of unity dealt a death blow to the false teachers who tried to put Paul at odds with the church in Jerusalem. For his perseverance and undying love of Christian liberty, Paul was rewarded with victory over his enemies.

Paul's struggle reminded me of another freedom fighter who was another link in the long chain of great Church reformers. The Bible stayed in the hands of the Catholic clergy until an Englishmen by the name of John Wycliffe came along in the middle of the fourteenth century (1330–1384). He has often been called "The Morning Star of the Reformation" because he was one of the first proponents for the translation of the Bible into the common tongue.

Wycliffe became a popular preacher in London, and he was quick to point out the unbiblical traditions of the Catholic Church and their abuse of power. As Wycliffe deepened his study of Scripture, he wrote more about his conflicts with official church teaching. He challenged indulgences, "It is plain to me that our prelates in granting indulgences do commonly blaspheme the wisdom of God." He repudiated the confessional, "Private confession was not ordered by Christ and was not used by the apostles." He reiterated the biblical teaching on faith: "Trust wholly in Christ; rely altogether on His sufferings; beware of seeking to be justified in any other way than by His righteousness." He was also one of the first to criticize the Pope—calling him "the Antichrist." He said that the bishops were like "dumb hounds that failed to bark in time of need."

In response, Pope Gregory XI issued five bulls (church edicts) against Wycliffe, in which Wycliffe was accused on eighteen counts and was called "the master of errors." Eventually, Wycliffe was put under house arrest. However, Wycliffe didn't waste his imprisonment. Believing that every Christian should have access to Scripture (only Latin translations were available at the time), he began translating the Bible into English with the help of his good friend John Purvey.

In those days before the printing press it would take a scribe working full time for nine months to copy one Bible, so it was very expensive for a common peasant to get a Wycliffe Bible. It has been said that farmers in those days would trade a wagon-load of hay just for the privilege of renting the Bible for one day of reading. Families would scrimp and save for months just for the opportunity to buy a few pages of Scripture.

Of course, the Catholic Church bitterly opposed Wycliffe's Bible. Their official statement read, "By this translation, the Scriptures have become vulgar, and they are more available to lay, and even to women who can read,

The Freedom Fighter (2:1–10)

than they were to learned scholars, who have a high intelligence. So the pearl of the gospel is scattered and trodden underfoot by swine." Wycliffe replied, "Englishmen learn Christ's law best in English. Moses heard God's law in his own tongue; so did Christ's apostles."

Sadly, Wycliffe died before the translation was complete; however, his friend Purvey is considered responsible for the version of the Wycliffe Bible we have today. Though Wycliffe's followers (who came to be called "Lollards") were driven underground, they remained a persistent irritant to English Catholic authorities until the English Reformation made their views the norm.

John Wycliffe left quite an impression on the Church. Forty-three years after his death, officials dug up his body, burned his remains, and threw the ashes into the River Swift. Yet they still couldn't get rid of him. Wycliffe's teachings, though suppressed, continued to spread. As a later chronicler observed, "Thus the brook hath conveyed his ashes into Avon; Avon into Severn; Severn into the narrow seas; and they into the main ocean. And thus the ashes of Wycliffe are the emblem of his doctrine which now is dispersed the world over."[3]

Freedom fighters like Paul and Wycliffe endured the tongue-lashings and stumbling blocks placed in their path because they knew the truth of God was more important than their own comfort. Because of Paul's grit and perseverance his letters are forever recorded in the New Testament. The church marches on while his critics remain nameless nay-sayers for all time. Likewise, with Wycliffe, Luther, Tyndale, Calvin, and the other men of God who stood in the gap and refused to be enslaved by man-made religion.

I like what David Jeremiah said, "As we read of Paul's courage for the sake of the Gospel we are reminded of the many men and women of God who throughout the ages gave their lives to preserve the message of the Gospel. Perhaps, tonight, all of us who call ourselves Christians ought to get down on our knees before we go to bed and say, 'God thank you for Paul, who did not give an inch to the people who wanted to destroy the Gospel of Jesus Christ.'"[4]

---

3. Galli and Olsen, *131 Christians Everyone Should Know*, 211–213.
4. Jeremiah, *Claiming Faith, Finding Freedom*, vol. 1, 43.

CHAPTER 5

Peter vs. Paul/Law vs. Liberty (2:11–21)

SHOKOI YOKOI SPENT TWENTY-EIGHT years needlessly living a life of desperation and survival. Yokoi's long ordeal began in July of 1944 when U.S. forces stormed Guam as part of their offensive against the Japanese in the Pacific. The fighting was fierce and casualties were high on both sides, but once the Japanese command was disrupted, soldiers such as Yokoi and others in his platoon were left to fend for themselves.

From the outset of the American invasion, the abandoned Japanese soldiers took enormous care not to be detected, erasing their footprints as they moved through the undergrowth. But fearing detection from US patrols and later from local hunters, they gradually withdrew deeper into the jungle. Yokoi made a cave his home, digging an underground shelter supported by strong bamboo canes. For over a quarter of a century he only came out at night. He survived on frogs, rats, bugs, and mangoes. Yokoi made a trap from wild reeds for catching river eels. He later learned the war was over and that the Japanese had surrendered by reading one of the thousands of leaflets that were dropped into the jungle by American planes. Still, Yokoi feared being taken prisoner, so he remained in his cave.

Finally, when he was discovered by local hunters on January 24, 1972, the 57-year-old former soldier still clung to the notion that his life was in danger. He was wearing a pair of burlap pants and a shirt which he said he had made from the bark of a tree. Startled by the sight of other humans after so many years on his own, Yokoi tried to grab one of the hunter's rifles, but weakened by years of poor diet, he couldn't put up much of a fight. As they led him away through the tall foxtail grass, Yokoi cried for them to kill him.

When Yokoi returned to Japan he became a national hero for his dramatic tale of survival and his unflinching adherence to the Imperial Army's

Peter vs. Paul/Law vs. Liberty (2:11–21)

code of "never surrender." Understandably, his family members said that Yokoi never really adjusted back to normal life.[1]

What happened to Yokoi happens to many Christians today. We can live under a set of rules that no longer apply to the land we inhabit. For Yokoi it was the rules of war even though V-J Day had come and gone. For Christians it's the rules of man-made religion that we cling to, even though the victory of Calvary has already been secured. It's a tragic thing when a man wastes his life in a jungle cowering in fear, but it's equally as pitiful when a Christian can't seem to shake off the fetters of legalism and live in liberty.

In fact, this was a problem for many of the first century Jews who converted to Christ. Even the great "rock," the apostle Peter, still dragged around the ball and chain of the Mosaic Law. Like Yokoi slinking in his cave, the Apostle Peter struggled with giving up his old ways of keeping the law. Just as Yokoi went kicking and screaming when liberators came to drag him out of his cave, so too Peter put a fight when Paul tried to unlock his chains with the key of grace.

Paul records for us one of the first-century Church's most famous conflicts. The opponents were the two pillars of the church: Peter—the apostle to Jews—and Paul—the apostle to the Gentiles. These men are so prominent in the New Testament that their lives literally outline the entire book of Acts. The first twelve chapters of Acts record Peter's ministry, while Acts 13–28 is the record of Paul's missionary adventures.

Recall that Peter and Paul had met once already. When Paul visited Jerusalem in Gal. 2:1–10, Peter, James, and John extended the right-hand of fellowship. However, controversy arose when Peter came to Antioch where Paul and Barnabas were ministering (Acts 13:1). Conflict in the church is nearly inevitable. The early church was no different, except in this case they were not fighting over some of the petty things we do today (like the color of the carpet or the style of the music). No, this was a battle between law and grace, tradition and truth, legalism and freedom in Christ.

A Confrontation Over Legalism (2:11–14)

The passage begins with Paul giving Peter a public rebuke. The struggle was not over the preaching of the Gospel. Paul and Peter already established

---

1. Lanchin, "Shoichi Yokoi, the Japanese Soldier Who Held out in Guam."

that they preached the same message of grace (2:6). The source of the controversy was over the *practice* of the Gospel.

Frist, we must take note of *Peter's compromise*. "But when Cephas came to Antioch, I opposed him to his face, because he stood condemned. For before certain men came from James, he was eating with the Gentiles; but when they came he drew back and separated himself, fearing the circumcision party. And the rest of the Jews acted hypocritically along with him, so that even Barnabas was led astray by their hypocrisy" (2:11–13).

When Peter first arrived in Antioch he must have been quite a celebrity among the growing church. This was the man who had spent three years with Jesus and seen His amazing miracles. Peter was there on Pentecost when the Holy Spirit descended with power. Thousands had been saved by his preaching. We can imagine the tiny church in Antioch bulging with people trying to hear Peter preach.

I'm sure the best part of Peter's visit to Antioch was the potluck dinners and the invites he must have received to go eat with the Gentile believers. No doubt Peter was enjoying his freedom in Christ because the dietary restrictions that were formerly placed on him by the Mosaic Law were nullified by God's grace.

In Acts 10:9–16, Peter received a powerful vision from God instructing him that there was no longer any such thing as clean and unclean meat. While on a rooftop in Joppa, Peter saw a great sheet descend from heaven and with it all kinds of animals. Peter resisted the Lord three times, but he finally received the message that Jews were no longer to look down upon the Gentiles as unclean.

Later, Peter was used by God to convert Cornelius, the first Gentile believer, to Christ. Peter even preached a message in Cornelius' home saying, "In truth I perceive that God shows no partiality" (Acts 10:34). God broke down Peter's prejudice by showing him that both groups were on equal footing and that he and the Jewish Christians were free to fellowship with the Gentiles. J. Vernon McGee has a vivid way of describing the scene in Antioch for us:

> When Peter came to visit Antioch and it was time for the love feast, Simon Peter went over to the kosher table, while Paul went over to the Gentile table. Peter noticed that there was pork roast on the Gentile table and after dinner Peter joined Paul and they went on a little walk. Peter said, "I noticed that you ate at the Gentile table." "Yes" Paul said. "And I noticed," said Peter, "that you ate pork tonight. Is it good? I've never tasted it." Paul said, "It's delicious."

Peter vs. Paul/Law vs. Liberty (2:11–21)

> Then Peter said, "Do you think it would be alright if I ate over there?" Paul said, "Well, it's my understanding that we are having some nice pork chops in the morning for breakfast. Why don't you come and try it." So in the morning when he came to breakfast Peter went over to the Gentile table, sat down gingerly, and rather reluctantly took a pork chop. After he tasted it, he said to Paul, "It is delicious, isn't it?" Paul said, "Yes, after all, under grace you can either eat it or not eat it, it makes no difference. Meat won't commend you to God." So Simon Peter said, "I will be here for dinner tonight, I hear they are having ham for dinner tonight."[2]

So it was pork chops and good times in Antioch until verse 2:12 informs us that James and a delegation from Jerusalem arrived and found out what Peter was doing. Apparently, "James the Just" was also having a difficult time giving up the regulations of the law and when he got word that Peter was fraternizing with the Gentiles and eating their food, he went straight into "killjoy mode."

Paul adds in 2:13 that many other Jewish Christians in Antioch and even Barnabas gave in to the peer pressure of James and his cronies. Because Peter was such an important figure in the Church, his actions influenced the others to withdraw from fellowshipping with the Gentile believers. Paul called them "hypocrites" for abandoning the freedom they had in Christ and reverting back to the law so they could win back the approval of the Jewish-Christians. The fact is that Peter knew better, and he sent a mixed message to the believers in Antioch. This reminds me of a story Charles Swindoll tells in one of his books:

> I heard about a fellow who attended a legalistic college where students were to live according to very strict rules. They weren't supposed to do any work on Sundays. None! Guess what? He spied on his wife and caught her hanging out a few articles of clothing she washed on a Sunday afternoon. Are you ready? The guy turned his wife into the authorities of the school! I'll bet she was fun to live with the next day or so.[3]

Legalism has no pity on people and it turns its practitioners into squinty-eyed heresy hunters. Legalism makes my belief your burden, my opinion your boundary, and my fallible interpretation of Scripture your obligation.

---

2. McGee, *Galatians*, 33–34.
3. Swindoll, *The Grace Awakening*, 87.

The story unfolds with *Paul's correction*. Paul noticed that Peter's behavior sent a conflicting message to the other believers in Antioch, namely that if the Gentiles wanted to receive God's grace then they would have to behave as Jews. Because Peter's compromise affected the whole church, Paul had no choice but to make a public rebuke. So he got up in Peter's grill. Eugene Peterson's paraphrase of 2:14 brings some colorful insight into Paul's words:

> If you, a Jew, live like a non-Jew when you're not being observed by the watchdogs from Jerusalem, what right do you have to require non-Jews to conform to Jewish customs just to make a favorable impression on your old Jerusalem cronies?[4]

Paul's words must have stung Peter, but Paul was reinforcing the fact that Peter simply could not have it both ways. He couldn't preach the principles of grace and then practice the law. It was inconsistent to hold others to those man-made traditions when he didn't keep them regularly. Paul was not afraid to practice in-your-face grace!

I will never forget one of my first preaching experiences. It was on a hot summer evening at my home church. Because it was so sticky and humid, I decided that I would be more comfortable wearing a short-sleeve polo shirt rather than the customary long-sleeve, button-up shirt and tie. After the message was over a man came up to me and said, "Can I talk to you privately?" So we walked over to the corner of the sanctuary where the man proceeded to tell me that "real preachers" knew better than to expose their arms and that if I ever wanted to preach again in that church, I had better make sure to wear a long-sleeve shirt from now on. The funny thing was that he had no problem himself wearing a short-sleeve shirt to church that evening. Inside I was raging mad and I thought to myself, "Who died and made you Barney Fife of the fashion police? Would you like to show me a chapter and verse for your conviction?"

Legalists are like neighborhood bullies, except they carry Bibles and they use them as a means of suppressing other people to their standards. They think they are doing God's business by belittling other Christians with their made-up checklists. If you don't have the guts to stand up to legalists and tell them to "get lost," they will walk all over you and others.

---

4. Peterson, *The Message*, Gal. 2:14.

Peter vs. Paul/Law vs. Liberty (2:11–21)

A Condemnation of Legalism (2:15–21)

In the second half of this passage, Paul launches into a theological argument explaining why Peter's actions were wrong, while at the same time presenting the heart of the Gospel message. Notice how Paul brilliantly exposes the deficiencies of legalism compared to grace.

Paul begins by explaining in 2:15–17 that *legalism cannot achieve salvation*. Three times Paul repeats the rallying cry that "a man is not justified by the works of the law." Yet, at its core, legalism is a system of achievement that tries to measure man's ability to make himself righteous before God. However, Paul's simple point here is that man's works don't work. Once again, *The Message* paraphrase throws a great deal of light on Paul's words:

> We Jews know that we have no advantage of birth over "non-Jewish sinners." We know very well that we are not set right with God by rule-keeping but only through personal faith in Jesus Christ. How do we know? We tried it—and we had the best system of rules the world has ever seen! Convinced that no human being can please God by self-improvement, we believed in Jesus as the Messiah so that we might be set right before God by trusting in the Messiah, not by trying to be good.[5]

The law is like an x-ray scan. It can show you that you are broken, but it can't heal you. The law acts like a mirror which reveals that our face is dirty, but it can't turn on the faucet and wash away the dirt. In Romans 3:20, Paul would explain, "For by works of the law no human being will be justified in his sight, since through the law comes knowledge of sin." Charles Spurgeon illustrated man's hopeless predicament in clinging to works when he explained:

> Some fancy that they have done a great many good works. In cherishing that delusion, they are like a Hindu of whom I once heard. He believed that he must not eat any animal substance and that if he did, he would perish. A missionary said to him, "That idea is ridiculous. Why, you cannot drink a glass of water without swallowing thousands of living creatures." He did not believe it, so the missionary took a drop of water and put it under a microscope. When the man saw the innumerable living creatures in the drop of water, he broke the microscope. That was his way of settling the question. So when we meet with persons who say, "Our works are pure and clean and excellent," we bring the great microscope

---

5. Peterson, *The Message*, Gal. 2:15–17.

of the law of the Lord, and we bid them look through that. When they do look through it and discover that even one sinful thought destroys their hope of salvation by self-righteousness, and when they see a whole host of sins in one of their prayers or acts or thoughts, then they are angry with the preacher. They try to break the microscope![6]

The only way to be saved is through what Paul calls "justification." Justification is God's judicial declaration that a sinner who believes in Christ is counted righteous instead of guilty based on Jesus' perfect life and sacrificial death on their behalf. Christ's righteousness is credited to the sinner, while the sinner's guilt was placed on Christ when He died on the cross. To be justified means that we are declared righteous, innocent, and free before the justice bar of God.

The story is told from years ago about a wealthy Englishman who purchased a Rolls Royce and drove it on a vacation to the south of France. However, his car broke down and he called back to the factory. The company sent down a mechanic to the south of France to diagnose the problem. When the mechanic figured out what needed to be fixed, he called in the part and it was shipped immediately to his location. A day later he fixed the car and sent the Englishman on his way. The man expected to get a sizeable bill, but after a few weeks, no bill came. He finally called the Rolls Royce factory, thanking them for the excellent service and he asked them for the bill. The attendant at the factory said, "Sir, we have no record of anything ever having gone wrong with your car."

That's not a perfect illustration, but it gets across the idea of what it means to be justified. God picks up the bill and wipes our record clean. There is no record of our sin in His spiritual ledger. Please understand, to be justified does not simply mean "just-as-if-I'd-never-sinned." I hear that from time-to-time and it makes me grit my teeth. Why? Because I think it weakens the full impact of justification. Justification really means that even though I still sin periodically and have found myself unable to stop sinning on a permanent basis, God declared me righteous when I believed the gospel. If that's the case, then how much more amazing is God's grace which continually covers us and declares us legally innocent!

Paul expands his argument in 2:17–18 by pointing out that *legalism contradicts the Gospel*. "But if, in our endeavor to be justified in Christ, we too were found to be sinners, is Christ then a servant of sin? Certainly not!

---

6. Spurgeon, *Spurgeon at His Best* (Grand Rapids, MI: Baker, 1988), 316.

Peter vs. Paul/Law vs. Liberty (2:11–21)

For if I rebuild what I tore down, I prove myself to be a transgressor." Paul's opponents argued that since justification by faith eliminated the need to keep the law, it encouraged sinful living. In other words, a person could believe in Christ then live any way he pleased and use God's grace as a license to sin. This is like sinning on Saturday night knowing that you could stroll into church on Sunday morning and ask for forgiveness. Paul denied this charge by laying out the inevitable and ugly consequence—Christ would be a promoter of sin! In Romans 6:1–2 we find a parallel passage, "What shall we say then? Are we to continue in sin that grace may abound? By no means! How can we who died to sin still live in it?" Moreover, 1 John 3:8 adds, "Whoever makes a practice of sinning is of the devil."

When Peter succumbed to the legalistic pressures of the Jerusalem crowd, he approved of their message that the law still held sway on their spiritual condition. Implicitly, Peter's actions said that grace was not enough and that he had made a mistake; therefore, he "rebuilt what he had previously torn down." Paul's point is that Peter is caught in a catch-22. If Peter was right in going back to the Mosaic Law, then he was wrong by eating with the Gentiles and, therefore, a transgressor of the law which told him in the first place never to eat with Gentiles. However, if Peter preaches grace and then still practices the law, then he inevitably denies the freedom he has in Christ. So we arrive at the conclusion Paul wants us to accept—its either grace or law. We cannot live by both and still have the benefit of the Cross.

One time I was in a conversation with a group of proud Christians who leaned heavily toward legalism. Our talk found its way to the topic of food. I started raving about a favorite Mexican restaurant. I told them about how the chips and salsa are so addicting, and how the fajitas are still sizzling when they bring them out to you. Looking for common ground, I was turned away. One woman frowned at me, knowing that the restaurant also had a bar, she said, "I would never go into a restaurant that served alcohol." I thought for a second and retorted, "Well, then I'm glad you don't buy groceries." She inquired, "What do you mean?" I said, "Where do you buy groceries?" She told me the name of the store. Knowing that the store sold beer and wine (like every grocery does), I said, "Too bad because they have all those cases of beer right across from the eggs, milk, and butter." She was speechless.

This is the problem with legalism—on the one hand it says that I'm free, while on the other hand it says that God is still keeping track of how well I am following the rules. Legalism always leads to contradiction because it tries to earn a salvation that cannot be earned. The law says "Do! Try! Behave!" Meanwhile, the Gospel says, "Done! Trust! Believe!" All that the law could do was bring us to the threshold of the Gospel of grace, but it cannot get us in the door.

Another problem is that *legalism cancels out the effect of the Cross*. The legalist misses the entire point of Jesus dying on the Cross, which is why Paul writes with soaring words, "For through the law I died to the law, so that I might live to God. I have been crucified with Christ. It is no longer I who live, but Christ who lives in me. And the life I now live in the flesh I live by faith in the Son of God, who loved me and gave Himself for me" (2:19–2:20).

Methodist missionary, James Calvert (1813–1892), committed his life to reaching the indigenous peoples of the Fiji Islands. It is widely reported that upon his voyage, the ship's captain warned him to turn back, saying, "You will lose your life and the lives of those with you if you go among such savages." Calvert purportedly replied, "We died before we came here." Calvert understood the implications of Galatians 2:20, "I have been crucified with Christ." The first and most essential act of discipleship is firing the planning committee in your heart and dying to self.

Paul goes further to say that when we believe in Christ we are not only *identified* with Him, but we are *indwelt* by Him. Our old-self dies and Christ's life becomes our own. The Christian life is an exchanged life—Jesus' life for your life. The Bible says that when we come to Jesus for salvation we enter into a permanent, spiritual union. The life of Christ becomes our own. The righteousness of Christ is credited to our spiritual ledger. Everything Christ has ever done becomes something we have done. God attaches us to the events of Christ's life so that they become part of our lives. His story—the story of the cross and the empty tomb—becomes our story. So the true Christian life is not so much a believer living for Christ as it is Christ living in and through the believer.

The problem with legalism is that it tries to regulate the person from the outside-in without changing the person at all, whereas Christ sanctifies the person from the inside-out. In other words, the law does not have any sanctifying power. It can't do what the indwelling Christ can do. To illustrate how the grace of God can change our hearts in ways that religion cannot, J. D. Greer writes:

Peter vs. Paul/Law vs. Liberty (2:11–21)

Think of our relationship with Christ like a balloon. There are two ways to keep a balloon afloat. If you fill a balloon with your breath, the only way to keep it in the air is to continually smack it upward. That's how religion keeps you motivated: it repeatedly "hits" you. "Stop doing this!" "Get busy with that!" This is my life as a pastor. People come on Sunday so I can "smack" them about something. "Be more generous!" And they do that for a week. "Go do missions!" And they sign up for a trip. Every week I smack them back into spiritual orbit. No wonder people don't like being around me. But there's another way to keep a balloon afloat. Fill it with helium. Then it floats on its own, no smacking required. Seeing the size and beauty of God is like the helium that keeps us soaring spiritually.[7]

Finally, Paul wraps up by reminding us that *legalism cheapens grace*. In 2:21, he writes, "I do not nullify the grace of God, for if righteousness were through the law, then Christ died for no purpose." If man's righteousness could have been attained by keeping the law, then Jesus' sacrificial death on the Cross was a monumental failure and a needless waste. If we can keep the law perfectly in thought, word, and deed to merit salvation, then we don't need the Cross. Legalism is an insult to Christ because in effect it says that Christ's death was not enough and that God's grace is insufficient

Imagine the following scenario: A man standing before a judge has been given the choice of paying $100 or serving 90 days in jail. The man doesn't have any money, but he does have a wife and five hungry children at home who are depending on him and him alone. He tells such a heartrending story that the courtroom spectators are moved with pity and take up a collection to help pay the man's fine. Although it is unlike him, even the judge chips in. Altogether they raise $99.95. Even though they are only five cents short, the judge declares that the entire $100 must be paid, and orders the bailiff to take the man to jail. He dejectedly walks out of the courtroom, thrusting his hands deep into his pockets where he finds—a nickel! Elated, he rushes back into the courtroom and slaps it on the bar before the judge, declaring, "I'm free, I'm free!" In his mind, what saved him? The $99.95 or the five cents? In the same way, if we did anything to merit our salvation, we would be forever boasting about it in heaven. The fact is that there was nothing we could do, so Jesus paid it all.

---

7. Greer, *Gospel*, 97–98.

CHAPTER 6

Breaking the Law (3:1–14)

We can all agree that laws are generally a good thing for society, especially the rules that prevent looting, killing sprees, and anarchy. Laws are necessary as long as they serve a practical purpose, for without them bedlam rules. This is also true in sports as well. Rules protect the game and maximize the enjoyment of the sport. Imagine playing in a baseball league where the strike zone was never the same or in a basketball tournament where the out-of-bounds lines were not clearly defined. Laws are meant to protect life and rules are designed to make a level playing field.

However, we can go overboard in the legislative process. There are some laws which are totally unnecessary and quite ridiculous. In many states there are laws still in effect that either ban something no sane person would ever do, or show their age with respect to culture. If you plan on doing some traveling be warned because these laws are still on the books:

- In Missouri, it is illegal to drive down the highway with an un-caged bear in your car.
- In Orlando, Florida, when parking your elephant be sure to deposit the same amount of change in the parking meter as you would for a regular motor vehicle or else you could be jailed.
- In Salem, West Virginia, it's against the law to eat candy less than an hour and a half before church service.
- In Alabama, it is illegal for a husband to beat his wife more than once a month.
- In Memphis, Tennessee, women can't drive a car unless there is a man with a red flag in front of the car warning the other people on the road.

Breaking the Law (3:1–14)

- In Texas, a law requires criminals to give their victims notice, oral or written, 24 hours in advance of the crime they're planning to commit and the nature of that crime.[1]

While these laws are nearly impossible to enforce, they are still legally valid because no one has bothered to repeal them. Most of these laws are so old and outdated, that lawmakers themselves aren't even aware that many of them exist.

Therein lies one of the problems with legalism—the making of one law, inevitably leads to the making of another law, and pretty soon you have more laws and lists to follow than you can remember. The Pharisees of Jesus' day had accumulated so many outrageous laws that it was impossible for any one man to know them all, much less keep them. The Jews had laws concerning what constituted work on the Sabbath, laws defining what foods were permissible for one to eat, laws delineating what things were permissible to touch, laws dealing with what kinds of clothes were deemed appropriate to wear, ad infinitum. In fact, first-century rabbis expanded the Ten Commandments to include 365 prohibitions and 248 positive commands for a grand total of 613 laws.

Believe it or not, that same propensity for rule-making is still alive today. Christian author, Philip Yancey, attended a super-conservative church in the south during the 1960s. He often writes about the boot camp environment that dominated his early years:

> I grew up in a church that drew sharp lines between "the age of Law" and "the age of Grace." While ignoring most moral prohibitions from the Old Testament, we had our own pecking order rivaling the Orthodox Jews. At the top were drinking and smoking (this being the South, however, with its tobacco-dependent economy, some allowances were made for smoking). Movies ranked just below these vices, with many church members refusing even to attend *The Sound of Music*. Rock music, then in its infancy, was likewise regarded as an abomination, quite possibly demonic in origin. Other proscriptions—wearing makeup and jewelry, reading the Sunday paper, playing or watching sports on Sunday, mixed swimming (curiously termed "mixed bathing"), skirt length for girls, hair length for boys—were heeded or not heeded depending a person's level of spirituality. I grew up with the strong impression that a person became spiritual by attending

1. McGlynn, "17 Ridiculous Laws Still on the Books in the U.S."

to these grey-area rules. For the life of me, I could not figure out much difference between the dispensations of Law and Grace.[2]

Yancey wasn't the only one having a difficult time seeing the difference between liberty and law. The Christians living in Galatia were also torn between two worlds. The apostle Paul couldn't understand why the believers in Galatia, who had been granted complete freedom from the Old Testament laws when they accepted Christ, wanted to suddenly revert back to keeping them. Even though the Galatian believers had been given a declaration of independence by Christ, they opted to live like slaves. This strange reversal left Paul bewildered. Perhaps the people in Galatia needed a refresher course from the Old Testament to help them understand that no one, not even father Abraham, was saved by keeping a laundry list of regulations. Paul argues against the lifestyle of legalism by going back into the Old Testament to show how even the father of the faithful, Abraham, was justified by belief not behavior.

An Interrogation of Their Spiritual Life (3:1–5)

Paul begins asking a series of five rhetorical questions designed to show the utter foolishness of trying to revert back to the law when the Galatians were saved by grace. He is drawing on their personal experience with Christ to remind them that it was all by grace and not of works that they were saved.

First, Paul *reminded them that they believed in the Son of God*. In 3:1 it's apparent that Paul was hot under the collar. Normally, when Paul wrote a letter he referred to his audience as "dearly beloved," but here he calls them "fools" because of the way they had so quickly abandoned grace. "O foolish Galatians! Who has bewitched you? It was before your eyes that Jesus Christ was publicly portrayed as crucified." The J.B. Phillips paraphrase of verse 3:1 is humorously rendered, "O you dear idiots of Galatia, who saw Jesus Christ the crucified so plainly, who has been casting a spell over you?" Paul is essentially telling the Galatians they had lost their minds! He actually uses the word "bewitched" or *baskaino* in the Greek, which literally means to "hypnotize" or "mesmerize," to describe what happened to them. In secular writings from the same period, the same word described sorcerers who cast spells and incantations on their enemies. Paul preached the Gospel of Christ so vividly that people could almost imagine the scene

---

2. Yancey, *What's so Amazing about Grace?*, 30.

Breaking the Law (3:1–14)

at Calvary in their mind's eye. But somehow the Judiazers had cast a spell over them and led them away from Calvary and back to Mt. Sinai, away from grace and back to the law.

Second, Paul *reminded them that they received the Spirit of God.* "Let me ask you only this: Did you receive the Spirit by works of the law or by hearing with faith? Are you so foolish? Having begun by the Spirit, are you now being perfected by the flesh?" (3:2–3). Paul wants to know from them, "Galatians, when you were saved and received the Holy Spirit. Did that happen because you kept all kinds of rules and traditions or was that a result of your faith in Christ?" In other words, Paul is saying, "Surely you aren't so dull to believe that the Holy Spirit was good enough to get you going, but not enough to keep you going." In a parallel passage found in Romans 8:14–15 we find a similar line of reasoning, "For all who are led by the Spirit of God are sons of God. For you did not receive the spirit of slavery to fall back into fear, but you have received the Spirit of adoption as sons, by whom we cry, 'Abba! Father!'"

When I presented this passage to my church congregation, I used the following illustration to help underscore what Paul is getting at here:

> Suppose we all get in a brand new bus and head down to the beach for a vacation. We fill the bus with gas and just take off with the radio blaring and windows down enjoying the cruise control. However, as we get outside of Asheville we notice that people are just pushing their cars along the interstate. It's odd, but we just wave as we pass them. Eventually we have to stop for gas and while filling up, a car-pusher asks, "Where are you going?" We say, "Well, we're going down to the beach." The car-pusher asks, "Well, why are you driving? We're all pushing." "Yes, we can see that, but why are you pushing?" They reply, "Oh, well, if you push your car it cuts down on air pollution, you save money on gas, not to mention you don't have to worry about getting speeding tickets, and it's just good exercise. That's why we're pushers and not drivers." Convinced this is a good idea we let the bus run out of gas. Then everyone gets out and we begin to push this plush, air-conditioned bus down to the beach. Anyone want to be first out of the bus?

That is what Paul is writing about in Galatians 3:2–3. In essence, he says, "You're telling me that you who began with a full tank of the Spirit are pushing your way through life? You're telling me that's an advantageous message?" Cars are made to drive, not push. In the same way, the Christian life is meant to be lived in tandem with the Holy Spirit. Tragically, the

Galatians had let Christ save them but not change them. They had yet to discover what it meant to live by the Spirit and not in the energy of the flesh.

Herbert Jackson, a missionary to the Philippines, told a humorous story when he was just getting started on the mission field. He was given a car that wouldn't start without a push, so he quickly devised different ways of getting that car started without him having to push it. He would park the car on a hill or leave it running. One time he even went to a school near his home and got the children out of class to push the car to get it started. He did this kind of thing for two years. Then when a new missionary came, Dr. Jackson was showing him the car, proudly explaining all the creative methods he used to get around the starting problem.

While he was talking, the new man looked under the hood, saw that the problem was a loose cable, tightened it, turned on the ignition, and the car engine roared to life! Can you imagine Dr. Jackson's embarrassment? He had spent two years without ever finding out what the problem was and how easy it was to fix. The power was there all the time. Only a loose connection kept Jackson from putting that power to work. This is the way it is with life in the Spirit. How many Christians are pushing or pulling their way to heaven when the untapped power they need is there all along?

Paul also *reminded them that they saw the signs of God*. "Did you suffer so many things in vain—if indeed it was in vain? Does he who supplies the Spirit to you and works miracles among you do so by works of the law, or by hearing with faith?" (3:4–5). When the Galatians initially broke away from the law, they suffered great persecution. To return back to the law would mean that their suffering was meaningless. Moreover, when Paul was doing his missionary work in Galatia, the people experienced miracles. Recall that Paul healed a lame man in the city of Lystra (Acts 14:8–10). Paul is reminding them that when God worked supernaturally in their midst, it wasn't because they were good at keeping the Ten Commandments. It was because of faith.

What was going on in the church at Galatia reminds me of a news article that I read about an ex-convict who was caught trying to break back into prison. Johnny Cash famously sang about the doldrums of Folsom Prison, but one man apparently had never heard the album. In 2011, authorities said they caught 48-year-old Marvin Lane Ussery when he was spotted late one night scaling the 7-foot tall, barbed wire-topped fence that encircles a large wooded area behind the California State Prison in Sacramento. When authorities asked Ussery why he was trying to break back into the prison, the man said, "I don't know how to live on the outside. My home is inside, and I want to stay here for the rest of my life."[3]

Perhaps it was the cable TV and the promise of three square meals a day that enticed him to go back into bondage. We look at that and say, "Who would do such a thing?" Yet there are believers who, spiritually speaking, choose to put themselves back in fetters when they nullify grace for man-made laws. I know this may sound strange, but adhering to external religious restraints can be easier than serving God in the liberty of the Spirit. Grace always raises the bar. It never lowers it. For instance, the Pharisees thought they were doing a pretty good job keeping the seventh commandment, "You shall not commit adultery" (Ex. 20:14). By the wooden interpretation of the law all a man had to do was keep himself out of bed with another man's wife and he could check that one off the list. However, when Jesus came along he raised the standard by pointing out that adultery actually begins in the heart. "But I tell you that anyone who looks at a woman lustfully has already committed adultery with her in his heart." (Matt. 5:28). Living under grace comes with its own set of challenges. Grace desires to change our heart, while the law only cares about reforming behaviors.

Perhaps this explains, in part, why some first-century believers in Galatia wanted to live under the Mosaic Law, even though in Christ they were no longer bound by it. Apparently, they discovered that "freedom" can be frightening and even more demanding. Christians today are still susceptible. We can look for security by living under a legalistic system that calls for no more than good external behavior. In many instances, the do's and don'ts are merely cultural, not biblical. Although outward conduct may be honorable, they are actually escaping into a subtle kind of bondage.

An Illustration of Salvation by Faith (3:6–9)

Now that their folly has been exposed, like a good teacher Paul drives the point home by giving the Galatians a refresher course in the basics. The apostle explains how that everyone who has ever been saved by God has been saved by faith and not works, thus making legalism useless. Paul brilliantly chooses Abraham as an Old Testament example of this. Remember that the Judaizers were teaching that in order to experience salvation, one had to combine grace plus the works of the law. To refute this error, Paul

---

3. Janes, "Former Inmate Arrested after Jumping Fence onto Folsom Prison Property."

took their number one hero, Abraham—the father of the Jewish nation—to make his case for justification by faith. If he could show that Abraham was saved by faith and not the law, then the Judaizers wouldn't have a leg to stand on.

Paul began his argument by quoting from Genesis 15:6 and the context of this verse refers to the moment when God made a covenant with Abraham promising him a son. The text says in Genesis, "And he brought him outside and said, 'Look toward heaven, and number the stars, if you are able to number them.' Then he said to him, 'So shall your offspring be.' And he believed the LORD, and he counted it to him as righteousness" (Gen. 15:5–6).

The only problem was that at the particular time God made this promise to Abraham, he was a geriatric and his wife wasn't exactly a spring chicken either. Sarah had been barren for many years and had all but given up the hope of being a mother. However, God made Abraham a promise that his descendants would give rise to a nation of people. Abe's response was to simply take God at His word. In that moment, despite his old age and Sarah's infertility, the Bible says that God credited to Abraham's spiritual bank account His righteousness.

Twenty-five years after the initial promise, when Abraham finally did get a son, Isaac, God tested his faith when he told Abraham to go to Mount Moriah and sacrifice Isaac on an altar. Genesis 22:1–2 says, "After these things God tested Abraham and said to him, 'Abraham!' And he said, 'Here I am.' He said, 'Take your son, your only son Isaac, whom you love, and go to the land of Moriah, and offer him there as a burnt offering on one of the mountains of which I shall tell you.'"

Think about the contradictory information that Abraham was getting from God. On one hand, Abraham was being told that his son Isaac would be the progenitor of nations, while on the other hand, God told him to kill Isaac. Question—if Isaac was supposed to be the son of promise, how could he fulfill this if he was dead?

It seems like God was on the horns of an unresolvable dilemma. However, Galatians 3:8 tells us that "Abraham had the Gospel preached to him." What is the Gospel? The Gospel is the message of the deity, death, and resurrection of Jesus Christ. Abraham knew that even if he followed through with killing Isaac, God was going to keep His initial promise.

Hebrews 11:17–19 tells us what was going through Abraham's head when he was getting ready to plunge the knife into Isaac. "By faith

Breaking the Law (3:1–14)

Abraham, when he was tested, offered up Isaac, and he who had received the promises was in the act of offering up his only son, of whom it was said, 'Through Isaac shall your offspring be named.' He considered that God was able even to raise him from the dead, from which, figuratively speaking, he did receive him back."

On Mt. Moriah Abraham and Isaac were literally acting out the Gospel. Just as Abraham was willing to sacrifice Isaac, 2,000 years later on top of Mt. Calvary God would offer up his only Son on a cross—except that time there would be no substitute. Jesus was the Lamb of God, prefigured by the ram caught in the thicket atop Moriah. Abraham believed that even if he went through with the slaying of Isaac, God had the power to raise him from the dead. In the same way, three days after the horror of Golgotha, God the Father resurrected the Son, Jesus Christ, from the dead.

Abraham's obedience proved that he was living by incredible faith. By placing Isaac on the altar, only to have his hand stayed at the last minute, Abraham came to understand that one day God would substitute Himself on an altar of nails and wood. God would become the lamb slain. Thus, the episode with Isaac was merely a shadow of what was to come in Christ.

This leads us back to Paul's argument. In the end, what saved Abraham? It wasn't keeping the law because it didn't even exist until God revealed it to Moses some 400 years later. Abraham was justified by trusting God. Thus, the Lord saved Abraham on credit, so to speak. God knew that Abraham's sin (and all sins of the Old Testament believers) would eventually be paid for at the cross of Christ.

Notice that Paul quotes again from Genesis, this time 12:3, "In you [Abraham] all the nations shall be blessed." This quote pertains to the original covenant that God made with Abraham when he told him to leave Ur and head for Canaan. It's important to remember that when Abraham was called out by God, he was an uncircumcised pagan worshipping the false deities of Mesopotamia. Paul is reminding the Judaizers that Abraham, their hero, was a gentile at one time. Wow! Talk about a zinger for all those Jews who prided themselves on being descendants of Abraham. They weren't really any different from the Gentiles.

The reason why every nation, Jew or Gentile, would be blessed on account of Abraham was because from his loins would burst forth the Jewish nation, and from the Jewish nation would be born Jesus Christ, the Savior of the world. In that way, any Gentile who trusts in Christ for salvation is like Abraham who also believed God and was saved.

Paul's point is that every person in the Old Testament was saved just like every person in the New Testament—by faith alone in Christ alone. The only difference is that those in the Old Testament were looking forward in anticipation to the Cross, while believers after Christ are looking back in remembrance of the Cross.

An Invitation to Be Set Free (3:10–14)

Paul was brilliant in using Abraham as a picture of salvation by faith. By doing so, he undercut the belief system of the Judaizers and showed that it was possible to be a Jew and not be a son of Abraham, while at the same time it was possible to be a Gentile and be a son of Abraham. How could this be? Faith in Christ. Those with no faith in Christ are not true children of Abraham, as Jesus said to the Pharisees, "Your father Abraham rejoiced to see My day, and he saw it and was glad." (John 8:56). Abraham believed and trusted in a coming Redeemer and so all that follow in his footsteps by trusting in Christ are part of the same spiritual family.

Paul had turned the tables on the Judaizers and now he will do it again. In the following section he is going to use the law to prove that salvation by works is impossible. Like a well-trained attorney, Paul will use their rule book against them. Imagine using Darwin's *Origin of Species* to disprove evolution to a skeptic or David using Goliath's own sword to cut off the giant's head—this is what Paul does. He demonstrates man's need for grace by quoting the law back to the legalists.

Paul points out *the curse of the law*. "For all who rely on works of the law are under a curse; for it is written, 'Cursed be everyone who does not abide by all things written in the Book of the Law, and do them.' Now it is evident that no one is justified before God by the law, for 'The righteous shall live by faith.' But the law is not of faith, rather 'The one who does them shall live by them.'"

In just a few short breaths Paul throws out three Old Testament proof texts. In 3:10, he quotes from Deuteronomy 27:26 and from Leviticus 18:5 to show the Galatians that if they decided to revert back to the law, then they had better be prepared to keep every aspect of it. Did you know that the Old Testament literally teaches that you can be saved by the law? In fact, Paul quotes the verses to prove it. However, that is only possible if a man can keep every aspect of the law in thought, word, and deed.

Breaking the Law (3:1–14)

If you want to get a feeling for how oppressive this would be, start reading the book of Leviticus for fun. It's about as enjoyable as copying words out of a medical dictionary. When I first started preaching, I had the distinct privilege of teaching out of Leviticus. At the time, our church was going through a series called "Route 66" where each message was focused on the overall theme of each book in the Bible. The pastoral staff was teaching this on a rotating basis and when it was my turn, Leviticus was my assignment. To be honest, I had never even seriously looked at the book of Leviticus in my young life. Skimming through its dense repetitions reminded me of trying to make sense of IRS tax forms. As you go from one regulation to another, you start feeling the drudgery and the weight of the law. It's just rule, after rule, after rule. It's written in such a dry and monotonous way that you can feel the chains dragging the floor. It's exhausting just trying to make it through the book. No wonder that's why most Bible's creak when they open up to that section. Max Lucado hit the nail on the head when he wrote:

> A legalist believes the supreme force behind salvation is you. If you look right, speak right, and belong to the right segment of the right group, you will be saved. Legalism is just enough religion to keep you, but not enough to nourish you. So you starve. Your teachers don't know where to go for food, so you starve together. Your diet is rules and standards. No vitamins. No zest. Just bland, predictable religion.[4]

Moreover, keeping the law sounds good in theory, but in practice it's utterly impossible because the first time we slip, it's all over. James said, "For whoever keeps the whole law but fails in one point has become accountable for all of it" (James 2:10). In other words, the law was treated by God as a unit. Break one part and the whole thing shatters. A ship that is moored to a dock by a chain is only as secure as the weakest link in that chain. If a severe storm comes and causes even one link to break, the entire ship breaks away. So it is for those who try to come to God by their own perfection and break even one law along the way. They will be lost and forever wrecked.[5]

Paul knew that legalism was pointless. He had tried it himself. That's why he so loved to quote Habakkuk 2:4, "the just shall live by faith," which is found in verse 3:11. This verse is also referenced in Romans 1:17 and Hebrews 10:38. Supposedly, this was the verse which started the Reformation.

---

4. Lucado, *He Still Moves Stones*, 119.
5. Jeremiah, *Claiming Faith, Finding Freedom*, vol. 1, 87.

Someone has passed along the legend (whether it's fact or fiction, I don't know) that Martin Luther, when he came to see the truth that a person is justified only by faith and not works, was staggered under the blow of it. He supposedly stepped out of his cell and made his way through the cloistered halls of the monastery and saw a rope. He was about to fall and he grabbed the rope to support himself. When he did, his weight pulled it, and it happened to be the rope that led to belfry. And so it rang the bells in the middle of the night as if to announce to the world, "The just shall live by faith! The just shall live by faith!"

Ravi Zacharias pointed out in a sermon that the Mosaic Law gave 365 prohibitions and 248 positive commands. David reduced them to 11 in Psalm 15. Isaiah made them 6 (Isaiah 33:14, 15). Micah 6:8 binds them into 3 commands. Finally, Habakkuk reduces them all to one great statement: "The just shall live by faith."

Finally, Paul concludes this passage by pointing us to *the cure from the law*. "Christ redeemed us from the curse of the law by becoming a curse for us—for it is written, 'Cursed is everyone who is hanged on a tree'—so that in Christ Jesus the blessing of Abraham might come to the Gentiles, so that we might receive the promised Spirit through faith."

There was only One who perfectly fulfilled the letter and spirit of the law—Jesus Christ (Matt. 5:17). However, Jesus was treated as if He had broken every law possible. When He died on the Cross, He took the curse of the law upon himself—death. According to the Old Testament law, the accepted form of capital punishment for criminals was death by stoning. Deuteronomy 21:23 (where Paul is quoting from in 3:13) instructed that after a criminal was executed, his body would be tied to a wooden post, or a "tree," where his body would hang until sunset as a visible representation of God's rejection.

The "tree" of Calvary advertised that Jesus was under the curse of the law. The Cross publically showed His rejection by the world and the Father. Atop his brow sat a crown of thorns (Matt. 27:29). That was no accident either. The Roman soldiers who hammered it into Jesus' skull for sadistic sport did not realize that they were actually fulfilling an ancient prophecy. According to Genesis 3:17–19, thorns and thistles were the symbol of God's curse on the Earth for Adam's sin. Yet Jesus the Sinless One wore the crown as if it were His own. The glorious truth is that when we place faith in Christ, like Abraham trusted in God, we receive the blessing of adoption

Breaking the Law (3:1–14)

into the family of God through the Holy Spirit. Jesus bore our curse so that we might receive His righteousness.

Chuck Colson once told a story that I think vividly illustrates what it means when Paul says, "Christ became a curse for us." Near the city of Sao Jose dos Campos, Brazil, there is a remarkable facility. Several years ago the Brazilian government turned a prison over to two Christians. The institution was renamed Humaita, and the plan was to run it on Christian principles. With the exception of two full-time staff, all the work is done by inmates. Families outside the prison adopt an inmate to work with during and after his term. Chuck Colson visited the prison and made this report:

> When I visited Humaita, I found the inmates smiling—particularly the murderer who held the keys, opened the gates, and let me in. Wherever I walked I saw men at peace. I saw clean living areas, people working industriously. The walls were decorated with Biblical sayings from Psalms and Proverbs. My guide escorted me to the notorious prison cell once used for torture. Today, he told me, that block houses only a single inmate. As we reached the end of a long concrete corridor and he put the key in the lock, he paused and asked, "Are you sure you want to go in?" "Of course," I replied impatiently, "I've been in isolation cells all over the world." Slowly he swung open the massive door, and I saw the prisoner in that punishment cell: a crucifix, beautifully carved by the Humaita inmates—the prisoner, Jesus, hanging on a cross. "He's doing time for the rest of us," my guide said softly.[6]

---

6. Colson, "Making the World Safe for Religion."

CHAPTER 7

Law and Grace: A Dynamic Duo (Gal. 3:15–25)

SOMETIMES THE WORLD OF sports intersects with the Bible. When this rare convergence happens, there is an unusual connection between sweat and the Scriptures. Such was the case when the Chicago Cubs took to the baseball field during the 1989 and 1990 seasons. Philip Ryken writes:

> For two glorious summers, the Chicago Cubs taught baseball fans the fundamentals of Reformation theology. First, the Cubbies made a trade for Vance Law and started him at third base. Then a few months later, marvelous to say, they brought first baseman Mark Grace up from the minor leagues. There they were, right next to each other in the batting order: Law and Grace. They were in their proper order too, first Grace, batting in the fifth position, and then Law. For as Paul explained to the Galatians, God gave grace to Abraham before He gave Moses the law. And there they stood on the baseball diamond—Grace and Law—holding down opposite corners of the infield. Opposing batters would smash the ball to third, where Law would knock it down and throw it over to first for the out. Reformation theology in action: Law to Grace to retire the side. The apostle Paul never had to suffer through a long losing season at Wrigley Field, but he would have loved Chicago's theology. Law and Grace are not opponents; they are teammates working together for the salvation of God's people. The law leads to grace, which is to be found only in Christ.[1]

Paul has spent a considerable amount of time thus far in the letter of Galatians explaining why the Mosaic Law is inferior to the grace of Christ. However, Paul wants us also to realize that the law does have a purpose

---

1. Ryken, *Galatians*, 130–131.

Law and Grace: A Dynamic Duo (Gal. 3:15–25)

in God's plan. Law and grace actually work together rather than at cross purposes. They are a team working in tandem to accomplish salvation. Law and grace are a picture of spiritual truth in tension—not contradictory, but complementary. In the remainder of chapter 3, Paul is going to help us sort out this theological paradox. He is piggy-backing off his previous line of reasoning to show how God's original promise to Abraham of justification by faith is still in effect for all believers. He is also going to explain why God gave the law in the first place if it was never intended to provide salvation.

The Promise of Grace (3:15–18)

Paul opens by explaining the principles behind the way covenants worked in the days of the Old Testament. A covenant was simply a contract or a treaty between two parties. He begins by speaking in general terms about how covenants operated, "To give a human example, brothers: even with a man-made covenant, no one annuls it or adds to it once it has been ratified" (3:15). Covenants were binding agreements made between two parties that could not be broken or changed without the mutual consent of the people involved. If two parties agreed to the terms of a contract, then a third party could not come along years later and change the fine print of the agreement. This is the working principle that enables a society to function in an orderly way and God has been pleased to adopt the same principle in His dealings with men.[2]

The Scriptures record several covenants that God made with man down through the ages. In the Edenic Covenant, Adam and Eve were given conditions whereby they could live in the Garden (Gen. 2:16–17). After Adam sinned and broke the terms of their covenant with God, they were evicted from Paradise and a new covenant was given in light of man's disobedience. The Adamic Covenant included the curses pronounced against mankind for the sin of Adam and Eve, as well as God's provision for that sin (Gen. 3:14–19). After Noah emerged from the great flood, God spelled out another covenant to all humanity. God promised that He would never again destroy all life on earth with water. To ratify this covenant, He gave the rainbow as the sign of His promise (Gen. 9:9–17). These do not exhaust all the biblical covenants, but you get the idea that God never backs out of an agreement once He has committed. When a new covenant is introduced and overlaps with a previous covenant, the new provisions do not cancel

---

2. Phillips, *Exploring Galatians*, 100–101.

the older ones. Paul's point is that if human covenants are not alterable, then how much more binding is a promise when Almighty God makes a covenant, such as the case with Abraham?

"Now to Abraham and his Seed were the promises made. He does not say, 'And to seeds,' as of many, but as of one, 'And to your Seed,' who is Christ." (3:16). This is an interesting verse because it gives testimony to the verbal inspiration of the Bible, which teaches that every word is from God. Notice that Paul's argument is not just based around one word, but on the number of the word. This argument hinges on whether the word "seed" in the Abrahamic Covenant was originally singular or plural.[3]

Recall that God's promise to Abraham was that He would make from his descendants a great nation and that through Abraham's progeny all the nations of the world would be blessed (Gen. 12:1–3). The ultimate goal of the Abrahamic Covenant was to produce the lineage leading to the birth of Christ (Matt. 1:1). The definitive promise given to Abraham that would affect the entire world was not just the little plot of land known as Canaan, but the spiritual blessings of mankind having his enmity with God removed and being brought into an eternal relationship with God through faith in Christ. This is why Paul is very particular in pointing out that the promise of the seed was singular, not plural. The stress on seed, not seeds, was made simply to remind the readers that the blessing which would come from Abraham's lineage referred to a single individual, Jesus Christ. Therefore, fulfillment of the Abrahamic covenant did not depend on the nation of Israel but on the person of Christ.

The concept of "the Seed" goes back to Genesis 3:15, also known as the *protoevagelion*, or "the Gospel before the Gospel." This is the first prophecy in the Bible and it predicts the coming of a virgin-born Redeemer who would eventually crush the head of the Serpent. In this moment, God is speaking to Satan and He says, "And I will put enmity between you and the woman, and between your seed and her Seed; He shall bruise your head, and you shall bruise His heel." Notice here that "the seed of the woman" is singular, referring to an individual, just as it did in the Abrahamic Covenant. Satan would only deliver a glancing blow to this coming Redeemer, which occurred when Christ died on Calvary. However, it would be Jesus' resurrection from the dead that would destroy death and the works of the Devil (Heb. 2:9, 1 John 3:8). The cross and the empty tomb were the one-two punch that crushed the head of the Serpent.

3. Jeremiah, *Claiming Faith, Finding Freedom*, vol. 1, 97.

Law and Grace: A Dynamic Duo (Gal. 3:15–25)

Paul's argument goes even deeper when we examine the context in which God ratified His covenant with Abraham. According to the story in Genesis 15, Abraham was actually asleep when the covenant was sealed. Remember that the Lord asked Abraham to sacrifice a heifer, a ram, a goat, a dove, and a pigeon and split them in half. The reason for this was because it was customary in the ancient Near East for two parties making a covenant to walk between the slain animals and seal their agreement in blood. The symbolic act was like a handshake which said, "May what happened to these carcasses happen to us if we neglect to uphold our end of the agreement." After waiting for several hours, the text says that a deep sleep fell upon Abraham and then the Lord alone passed through the sacrifice as a flame:

> Now when the sun was going down, a deep sleep fell upon Abram; and behold, horror and great darkness fell upon him . . . And it came to pass, when the sun went down and it was dark, that behold, there appeared a smoking oven and a burning torch that passed between those pieces. On the same day the Lord made a covenant with Abram, saying: "To your descendants I have given this land, from the river of Egypt to the great river, the River Euphrates . . ." (Gen. 15:12, 17–18)

Why does God wait until Abraham is sawing logs to make his move? Because God was enacting a covenant with Himself. This was an act of grace in which Abraham could not play any part. Abraham did nothing to make a covenant with God, but God did everything to make a covenant with Abraham. God did not lay down any conditions for Abraham to meet, so it could not be revoked by anything Abraham did or did not do. No one and no thing could abrogate the Abrahamic covenant, even if Abraham or any of his seed failed. Thus, God's covenant with Abraham was unconditional and unilateral because God owned all the obligation of fulfilling the covenant.

The point that Paul is getting at here is that since God ratified the Abrahamic covenant before He gave the law to Moses, the law could not invalidate the original promise to Abraham. That is why Paul remarks, "And this I say, that the law, which was four hundred and thirty years later, cannot annul the covenant that was confirmed before by God in Christ, that it should make the promise of no effect. For if the inheritance is of the law, it is no longer of promise; but God gave it to Abraham by promise" (3:17–18).

Perhaps, an illustration will help. Suppose I were to promise my son that I will take him to watch a basketball game, and not just any game, but the greatest rivalry in college hoops—the UNC Tarheels versus the Duke Blue Devils in Chapel Hill. I give a promise, no strings attached, backed by the integrity of my character and pledged by my word. A promise is a promise. What if, a few weeks later, I was to add some conditions, rules, and laws that the child had to obey if he wished to get that present? First, he has to keep his room spotless and it must pass a weekly inspection. Second, he has to do the dishes and take out the trash every evening. Third, he has to read three chapters from the Bible every night before bed. Fourth, he has to keep a "B" average or above in his studies. On and on the list could go.

The result from such an abrogation of my original promise would mean that I would have perjured myself, broken my word, and gone back on my promise. I would have changed the ground rules. I would be making the attainment of the coveted basketball game hinge upon works, something that had to be done to earn the reward, and not my original unconditional promise. It would no longer be a gift but something to be earned.

What Paul wanted the Galatians and us to understand was that God does not behave like that. His character is such that it is impossible for Him to ever go back upon His promise once He has given it.[4] Salvation has and always will be through the finished work of Christ on the cross. Legalism is lethal because it undermines what Jesus said on the Cross, "It is finished" (John 19:30). Legalism implies that we must finish what Christ began by pleasing God through what we do. So the promise of grace was given to Abraham and is still offered today.

The Purpose of the Law (3:19–25)

Paul moves on to clear up the confusion about the real reasons why God gave the law. The law was never intended to achieve salvation as the Judiazers thought, but rather the law was given later to diagnose man's spiritual condition and point him to the redemption offered by the promised "Seed of Abraham." In fact, grace and law serve totally different purposes in God's kingdom. Examine the chart below to see the differences.

---

4. Phillips, *Exploring Galatians*, 105.

Law and Grace: A Dynamic Duo (Gal. 3:15–25)

Abrahamic Covenant (Grace)	Mosaic Covenant (Law)
A Promise of a seed and a nation	A Sign of God's chosen people
Permanent	Temporary
Unconditional	Conditional
Faith-based	Works-based
Fulfilled in Jesus Christ	Fulfilled by Jesus Christ

John MacArthur adds:

> The covenant with Abraham was an unconditional covenant of promise relying solely on God's faithfulness, whereas the covenant with Moses was a conditional covenant of law relying on man's faithfulness. To Abraham, God said, "I Will." Through Moses he said, "Thou shalt." The promise set forth a religion dependent on God. The law set forth a religion dependent on man. The promise centers on God's plan, God's grace, God's initiative, God's sovereignty, God's blessings. The law centers on man's duty, man's work, man's responsibility, man's behavior, man's obedience. The promise, being grounded in grace, requires only sincere faith. The law, being grounded in works, demands perfect obedience.[5]

Paul finds this a good place to pause and consider that the law has never been dispensed away with in God's economy. There is a great purpose in the law and a need for continuing to teach its precepts. I would even go so far as to say that the Gospel will not make sense without the law. So Paul identifies at least three reasons why the law was given.

First, we see that *the law was given to define sin*. In 3:19–20 Paul writes, "What purpose then does the law serve? It was added because of transgressions, till the Seed should come to whom the promise was made; and it was

---

5. MacArthur, *Galatians*, 82.

appointed through angels by the hand of a mediator. Now a mediator does not mediate for one only, but God is one."

A "transgression" is stepping across a boundary line, disobeying a clear command. The purpose of the law was to delineate what areas of life were forbidden territory. The law reveals to us not only that we missed the mark of God's holiness but that we deliberately stepped across a very clear line that God said, "Don't cross." In a parallel passage in Romans 7:7, Paul remarks, "What then shall we say? That the law is sin? By no means! Yet if it had not been for the law, I would not have known sin. For I would not have known what it is to covet if the law had not said, 'You shall not covet.'" So the law was given to educate people and show them that breaking the law would incur painful consequences.

Don't misunderstand this verse. The addition of the law did not mean that there was no sin in existence up to that point! Suppose you were driving through the country and found a peach tree loaded with ripe peaches. The tree was not near any house so you decide to stop and help yourself. You cross a rickety barbed-wire fence and load your arms with these luscious peaches. You bite into the first one and find its taste sweeter than you imagined. Then you notice a sign: NO TRESPASSING ALLOWED. What does that do to your appetite for the peaches? As soon as you realize that there is a prohibition in gathering these peaches, you find yourself looking around, perhaps feeling anxious that you might be caught. The sweet taste turns almost sour. That solitary commandment strikes fear in your heart. What if you had not seen the sign? Would you have been wrong to have taken the peaches for yourself? Certainly you would have been wrong. But with the sign you understood that you transgressed against the owner of the peach tree. A particular person was offended by your act.

Similarly, this is why God added the law, to help man better understand His character and the consequences that came with breaking His law. We look at God as He is revealed in the law; then we look downward to see ourselves and realize how bankrupt we are in our own moral character.

Secondly, we see that *the law was given to diagnose man's problem*. "Is the law then against the promises of God? Certainly not! For if there had been a law given which could have given life, truly righteousness would have been by the law. But the Scripture has confined all under sin that the promise by faith in Jesus Christ might be given to those who believe. But before faith came, we were kept under guard by the law, kept for the faith which would afterward be revealed" (3:21–23).

Law and Grace: A Dynamic Duo (Gal. 3:15–25)

In this analogy, the law is likened to a prison warden to keep us locked up in sin's penitentiary. We are the inmates and the law our jailer, refusing to let us go. The only thing that can free us from the law's condemnation is a sinless advocate who kept the law on our behalf. Paul reminds his readers that law and grace did not represent two different ways of salvation; man is not saved by faith and by works. Grace is no more opposed to law any more than the surgeon's scalpel opposes healing. The two systems worked together to bring salvation. The law was never intended to impart life, but to diagnose man's sin problem and condemn him to death. The problem was not with the law—it was perfect—the problem was with man's inability to keep the law no matter how hard he tried. Referring back to Romans 7:9–10, Paul says, "I was once alive apart from the law, but when the commandment came, sin came alive and I died. The very commandment that promised life proved to be death to me."

In other words, the law not only identified sin, but it intensified man's guilt. The law gave us God's standard of perfection but with no assistance or encouragement in keeping it. In fact, the more man tried to keep the law, the more evident it became that it was an impossible task. The law condemns us because it arouses within us a desire to do the very thing we know is wrong. Like the old limerick which says:

> There once was a man from Darjeeling,
> Who traveled from London to Ealing.
> It said on the door,
> "Please don't spit on the floor,"
> So he carefully spat on the ceiling.

In his book, *The Grace Awakening,* Chuck Swindoll illustrates the way the law works in this way:

> I remember when I was in my early teens, one of my first jobs was throwing a paper route. I threw the *Houston Press* for a couple of years during junior high school. It was a good job and kept me out of mischief, but it got tiring. After a long afternoon of folding about two hundred papers, throwing my route and turning toward home on my bike, I remember coming to the backyard of a large lawn at the corner across the street from our house. I thought to myself, *I'm tired . . . no need to go all the way down to the end of the street and around this big yard. I'll just cut across and be home in a jiffy.* It was a quick and easy shortcut. The first time I did that I entertained a little twinge of guilt as I rode my bike across that nice,

plush grass. You need to understand, this was a beautiful yard. To make matters worse our neighbor was very particular about it. I had watched him manicure it week after week. Still, I figured it wouldn't hurt just this once. Late the next afternoon I came tooling down the same street, thinking, *I wonder if I ought to use that same shortcut?* I did ... with less guilt than the first time. Theoretically, something told me I shouldn't, but practically, I rationalized around the wrong. In less than two weeks my bicycle tires had begun to wear a narrow path across the yard. By then, I knew in my heart I really should be going down and around the corner, but I didn't. I just shoved all those guilt feelings down out of sight.

By the end of the third week, a small but very obvious sign appeared near the sidewalk, blocking the path I had made. It read: "KEEP OFF THE GRASS—NO BIKES." Everything but my name was on the sign! I confess, I ignored it; I went around the sign and rode right over my path, glancing at the sign as I rode by. Admittedly, I felt worse! Why? The sign identified my sin, which in turn, intensified my guilt. But what is most interesting, the sign didn't stop me from going across the yard. As a matter of fact, it held a strange fascination. It somehow prodded me into further wrong.[6]

Third, we see that *the law was given to drive sinners to Christ*. "Therefore the law was our tutor to bring us to Christ, that we might be justified by faith. But after faith has come, we are no longer under a tutor" (3:24–25). Paul uses another analogy to show how the law was intended to move us to the point where we recognize our need for Christ. We go from the prison to the pedagogue. Notice that Paul refers to the Law as a "tutor," "guardian," or "schoolmaster." The Greek word used in the text is *paidagogs* from which we derive our English word "pedagogy." In the Greco-Roman world, well-to-do families would employ a slave in their family whose duty was to supervise the young boys on behalf of the parents. The pedagogues would take the boys to and from school, teach them manners, help them with their lessons, and inflict strict discipline if they stepped out of line.

The role of a tutor was only temporary. Eventually, when the boy grew to maturity, the pedagogue and the young man would part ways. As an instructor his purpose was only to take care of the boy until adulthood. While the tutor and the young man may remain close, the tutor no longer held any authority over the man.

Paul is saying that the sole purpose of the law was temporary. The law was like a tutor because it instructed and corrected man in God's ways until

---

6. Swindoll, *The Grace Awakening*, 25.

Law and Grace: A Dynamic Duo (Gal. 3:15–25)

Christ was revealed and the guardian was no longer needed. Once the law pointed us in the direction of Christ and we believed in Him for salvation, then we were free from the regulation of the law, just as the boy was free from the tutor when he came to maturity. John Stott put it this way, "We cannot come to Christ, to be justified until we have first been to Moses to be condemned. But once we have been to Moses and acknowledged our sin, guilt, and condemnation, we must not stay there. We must let Moses lead us to Christ."[7]

Remember when you were in grade school and the last day of school came around before summer break? That was the greatest day of the whole year because you could taste the freedom. As the saying goes, "No more lessons, no more books, no more teacher's dirty looks!" I remember back in college I had to take a required statistics class that was a total burden. I hate math anyway. No offense to you math teachers out there, but math is a tool of the Devil created to inflict pain on the human race. The workload for this one class was so much that it took hours of homework and study to stay ahead. I couldn't wait to get done with this class. Then I would never have to look at another statistics problem again.

The day of the final exam was one of the greatest days of my life. I could hardly wait to write down the last answer on my test. At that point the final grade didn't matter as long as the class was over. I remember after my exam I went directly back to the student bookstore. I strolled up to the counter, took out my fat statistics book, and put it on the counter along with my rented calculator. I said, "I'm here to sell back my book because I'm never doing statistics ever again." I sold my book and my calculator back to the student store, took my $10 and went and bought an ice-cream. It was total relief and freedom!

In a sense, that's what Paul is talking about here—shedding the fetters of something that used to rule your life and make existence one long drudgery. Grace frees us from this wearisome idea that we can somehow earn God's love by doing works and keeping commandments. Just think, because of Christ we don't have to sacrifice animals on altars, we don't have to make sure our food is kosher, and we don't have to keep the Sabbath laws. Each and every one of us should sit down and think of the lists we have made in our lives. Then we should tear them all to shreds because school is out and grace is here!

---

7. Stott, *The Message of Galatians*, 102.

CHAPTER 8

Who Do You Belong To? (3:26–29)

"To infinity and beyond!" That's just one of many catch phrases that have entered into our cultural lexicon from the wildly successful *Toy Story* films. I don't know about you, but they are some of my favorite animated movies. Besides the incredible CGI, engaging plot, and hilarious dialogue, the sub-text of the films is tied together by Christian themes. These may not be obvious to children, but "big kids" might pick up on them if they are looking carefully.

Throughout the series, Woody, the pull-string cowboy doll, constantly struggles with identity crisis. In the first movie, we are introduced to Woody's character and we quickly learn that he is one of Andy's favorite toys. In fact, Andy has inscribed his name in permanent ink on the bottom of Woody's boot. Anytime Woody begins to feel insecure or abandoned, all he does is turn over his boot to see the reminder that Andy loves him.

One of the most poignant scenes of the series comes in *Toy Story 2*. While Andy is away at summer camp, Woody is toy-napped by Al, a greedy collector who needs Woody to complete his Roundup Gang collection which he hopes to sell for a pretty penny. Woody is on his way to a museum where he'll spend the rest of his life behind glass. It's up to Buzz Lightyear and company to rescue Woody from being a collector's item and remind him what being a toy is all about.

By the time Buzz and the gang find Woody, he's already resigned to the fact that his best days are behind him. Woody shocks his friends, claiming that he actually wants to go to the toy collector's gallery. In a near-reverse from the first film, Buzz explains, "Woody you're not a collectible, you are a child's plaything. You are A TOY!" But Woody pleads that he is now living on borrowed time; any more damage and he could be thrown away. Buzz reminds Woody that he once told him life was only worth living if you're loved by a kid, and that's why he came to rescue Woody, because he believed those words. "I don't have a choice, Buzz," says Woody. "This is my only chance." "To do what, Woody?" asks Buzz, "To be looked at from behind glass and never be loved again? Some life." After they leave, Woody contemplates what Buzz said. Dejected, Woody sits down alone and then he looks at his boot. As he and scrapes off the new paint covering up the name of his owner "ANDY," the ole' cowboy changes his mind when remembers who he belongs to and what his purpose is.

We are not that different from Woody. We have an intrinsic need to know our true identity. Often times we forget who we belong to and we need a reminder that we have been "bought with a price" (1 Cor. 6:20). Paul finishes chapter three by reminding us what it means to be a child of God and to belong to the family of Jesus. Many times we take our salvation for granted, but Paul is here to inform us that being saved and justified by God is no small thing. God lavishes His grace upon us like a doting father provides for his children. God not only writes his name on our hearts, but we receive the following gifts.

A New Identity (3:26)

Researching your family tree can be a fun and rewarding hobby. For one Minnesota man, it was a life-changing experience. Marty Johnson knew he was the product of two young college students who had a brief affair. Neither parent was prepared to deal with raising a child, so Johnson was given up for adoption and grew up in a loving home in Minnesota. Years later as an adult, he started digging through past records and got in contact with his birth-mother. Then a letter arrived one day that said, "Welcome to the Ogike dynasty! You come from a noble and prestigious family." The letter went on to explain that Johnson was the next in line to inherit the position of village chief from his biological father, John Ogike, the current chief of Aboh village in Nigeria. Johnson flew to Nigeria to meet his new family. He went from having no knowledge about any blood relatives to a noisy celebration in the village. There he was united with brothers and sisters, numerous aunts, uncles, cousins, and of course, his father.[1]

In a similar way, Jesus is God's wonderful surprise letter declaring that we are His sons, heirs of God and co-heirs with Christ. "For you are all sons of God through faith in Christ Jesus" (3:26). For those in Christ,

---

1. "Adopted Minnesota Man Learns He Is A Prince."

our identity has been radically changed. Once we were the Devil's children, living in sin because that was our true spiritual heritage (1 John 3:10). By grace we have been transferred into the family of God and given a brand-new identity. John 1:12 says, "But to all who did receive him, who believed in his name, he gave the right to become children of God."

Notice there is a crucial limitation here as well. This change of identity is only for those who have "faith in Christ Jesus." Why is this important? Because often you will hear people thoughtlessly say, "We're all God's children," as if to imply that everyone on earth is a child of God. But that is not true! There isn't a single verse in the Bible that teaches such a thing. A more biblical way to say it would be that we're all God's creation, but only those who trust in Christ are truly God's children. Without faith in Jesus there is no entrance into God's family.[2]

A New Intimacy (3:27)

"For as many of you as were baptized into Christ have put on Christ" (3:27). If there was one thing the law could never do it was give us intimacy and oneness with God. The law only brought separation and distance. This verse does not refer to water baptism but spiritual baptism. The instant we place our faith in Christ, we enter into a living union with Christ (Rom. 6:3–4, 1 Cor. 12:13).

Paul uses the imagery of changing clothes when he says we have, "put on Christ." The believer has laid aside the dirty garments of sin and they are now clothed in the righteousness of Christ. Wiersbe adds, "But to the Galatians, this idea of 'changing clothes' would have an additional meaning. When the Roman child came of age, he took off his childhood garments and put on the toga of the adult citizen . . . The believer has an adult status before God—so why go back to the childhood of the law?"[3] Coming to Christ is like gaining a whole new wardrobe. You exchange the tattered rags of the old life for the beautiful robes of the character of Christ (Col. 3:8–15).

---

2. Pritchard, "Born Free: Seven Promises You Can Count On."
3. Wiersbe, *Be Free*, 86.

Who Do You Belong To? (3:26-29)

A New Institution (3:28)

"There is neither Jew nor Greek, there is neither slave nor free, there is neither male nor female; for you are all one in Christ Jesus" (3:28). The law divided people between Jew and Gentile, clean and unclean, slaves and freemen, male and female. The law only perpetuated ethnocentrism, racism, and religious snobbery. Tradition says that a devout Jewish male would pray every day, "Lord thank you that I am a Jew and not a Gentile, a man and not a woman, a freeman and not a slave."[4]

However, Paul hit the Galatians with an astounding thought. Slave and free walk hand in hand into the family of God. Jews no longer need to look down their noses at Gentiles. The battle of the sexes need not be fought anymore. Men and women are equals. The first century was a world of chauvinism, racism, and classism. However, the Church destroyed all cultural barriers and knocked down the walls of separation.

It is said that after the Civil War, General Robert E. Lee, a devout Christian, visited a church in Washington, D.C. During the Communion service, he was seen kneeling beside a black man. Later, when someone asked how he could do that, Lee replied, "My friend, all ground is level at the foot of the cross." What makes that ground so level? The awfulness of our sins, the terrible price Jesus paid to forgive them, and the love He has for all people. Prejudice cannot survive for those who have knelt at Calvary.[5]

A New Inheritance (3:29)

"And if you are Christ's, then you are Abraham's seed, and heirs according to the promise" (3:29). If you go back and study the original promise given to Abraham in Genesis 12:3, you'll see that God declared He would give him *property*, "to a land I will show you," *progeny* "I will make you a great nation," *protection*, "I will bless those who bless you, And I will curse him who curses you," and *prosperity*, "And in you all the families of the earth shall be blessed."

When Paul says that we are "heirs according to the promise," we must naturally wonder what part of Abraham's inheritance belongs to us. The Abrahamic Covenant contained physical and spiritual blessings. The

---

4. Ibid.
5. DeHann, "Level Ground."

material blessings promised to Abraham's physical descendants, the Jewish nation, included land, lineage, and the Lord's protection. These are unique to Israel alone and do not apply to the Church. This verse is not teaching replacement theology, that somehow the Church replaces or supplants Israel in God's sovereign program. All that God promised the Jewish people will be given to them in the future Millennial Kingdom.

Instead, Paul is referring to the fact that if we are in Christ, we inherit the spiritual blessings of Abraham. ". . . And in you all the families of the earth shall be blessed." This part of the Abrahamic Covenant refers to the coming Redeemer, Jesus Christ, who would atone for the sins of all mankind and be a universal blessing (1 John 2:2). When we trust in Christ, we inherit the same promise of justification by faith that Abraham received. In Romans 4:11, Abraham is referred to by Paul as "the father of all those who believe." Abe was an Old Testament prototype of justification by faith. Abraham exercised faith looking towards the cross of Christ. When we believe in Christ by looking backwards at the Cross, we are declared righteous in the same way Abraham was (Gen. 15:6). Philip Ryken explains, "We do not have to be biologically related to Abraham to claim his inheritance. All we need is faith in Jesus Christ. The true sons of Abraham are not identified biologically, but Christologically.[6]

Not too long ago I read about the amazing story of Max Melitzer, a 65 year old man who had been homeless for decades in Salt Lake City. Max and his brother lost touch with one another many years ago, but in 2010 his brother died and left him $100,000. The family hired a private investigator to look for Max and a year after his brothers' death, following a two month search, they found him in a Salt Lake City park. The investigator told him the good news and then took him out for a seafood dinner.[7]

For a whole year, Max wondered around Salt Lake City as a homeless, rich man. His needs were met, but he did not know it. The investigator who found him did not make him rich. He already was but didn't know it. The private investigator gave him the good news and spoke the truth that he needed to be reconciled to his inheritance. Due to nothing more than not knowing what belonged to him, Max missed approximately 365 nights of sleep in a king size bed, over 1,000 delicious meals, and perhaps 365 hot showers.

---

6. Ryken, *Galatians*, 124.
7. "Homeless Man, Max Melitzer Learns He's Rich."

Who Do You Belong To? (3:26-29)

How many believers walk around seemingly unfamiliar with all that they possess in Christ? The world is full of people like Max—people wealthy in Christ beyond imagination, but walking around in spiritual poverty. Don't forget whose child you are and the heavenly inheritance that has your name on it.

CHAPTER 9

Trading Sonship for Slavery (4:1–11)

A FEW YEARS AGO I was preparing for a sermon when the unthinkable happened and I encountered a serious computer problem. The Bible study program that I was running on my laptop prompted me to do an update of the software. Okay, no big deal. I had done this before. So I downloaded the updates thinking all was fine because I now had the most sophisticated version of the software.

However, after the update, every time I tried to start up the Bible program my computer would freeze up and, inevitably, I would have to shut down and restart the computer all over again. When I tried to reboot the Bible program, the same malfunction occurred. At this point, I was convinced that my computer was possessed by the Dark Lord himself. My computer had become a victim of Screwtape's treachery and apparently some evil spirit did not want me to finish the message. Then I recalled Jesus' words to His disciples when they ran up against a similar spiritual roadblock. Jesus did what they couldn't do and released a demon-possessed boy from bondage. When the disciples asked why their attempts to exercise the demon failed, Jesus explained with a sigh and a shrug, "This kind of thing can come out by nothing but prayer and fasting" (Mark 9:29). I prayed, but alas nothing happened immediately.

After an hour of dealing with this frustration, I called the Bible software manufacturer and explained to them the situation. It seemed like we went through every possible troubleshooting solution and yet the problem still persisted. The clock was ticking. Sunday morning was coming like a freight train and I had to finish this message. Beads of anxious sweat formed. Finally, the technician asked me, "Check your drives and other ports to make sure there is nothing else running."

Trading Sonship for Slavery (4:1-11)

As I eyeballed every possible seam, nook, and cranny on the machine, I noticed something. "There's an SD card in the drive." He said, "Remove the SD card and restart the Bible program." I did just that and, like magic, the program ran better than ever. How could my computer woes be caused to such a seemingly small thing? Never in a million years would I have thought of that solution. When I asked why taking out the card solved the problem, the technician explained that it was a "systems conflict."

He explained that a systems conflict occurs when a computer tries operate two contradictory programs. Apparently, the Bible program was receiving two different sets of commands; one set from the updated software and another set of instructions from the data on the memory card. He said, "When the Bible program booted up it was receiving conflicting information from two sets of data. These two opposing systems going on at once caused the program to crash."

It wasn't until later that I realized the afternoon's headache was actually a spiritual lesson in disguise. I would submit to you that there is an equally disastrous systems conflict that occurs in the spiritual realm between the programs of law and grace; if you try to mix the two you'll get confused, dysfunctional Christian living.

Law says "achieve," but grace says "receive." The law tells us we must earn our spot on the team, while grace tells us we are already accepted into the family. Under the heavy hand of the law we are told to "try harder." But under grace we are told to look at the cross where Jesus said, "It is finished." The law only leads to slavery, while grace makes us sons and daughters of the King.

You might say that the church in Galatia was undergoing a massive systems conflict. The believers in this particular church understood by the preaching of Paul that faith alone in Christ alone was all they needed to be saved. However, after a period of time they were deceived into believing the lies of false teachers who instructed them that along with grace they also needed works of the law. Thus, the Galatian Christians were walking contradictions, torn between two paradigms.

Paul has labored diligently to show the Galatians where they had gotten these two principles of law and grace mixed up. So far Paul has tried to use various illustrations to show the true purpose of the law and its temporary nature. In the preceding verses, he compared the law to a tutor or a custodian (3:24-25), which was only an interim instructor until Christ was revealed and then it was no longer needed. Paul is going to continue with this analogy to teach the Galatians that the law was meant for spiritual children who had not yet reached maturity. Therefore, if they desired to revert back to legalism they were thwarting their own spiritual development.

The Slavery of the Law (4:1–3)

Paul is continuing an analogy that he began in the previous section having to do with a child coming of age. His metaphor is meant to show that the law is a kind of bondage for people who are spiritual children, not mature adults who have freedom in Christ. "I mean that the heir, as long as he is a child, is no different from a slave, though he is the owner of everything, but he is under guardians and managers until the date set by his father" (4:1–2).

Paul explains that a child who is set to inherit his father's estate is no better off than a household slave until he reaches adulthood and outgrows the authority of the tutor who is placed over him. Remember that in this ancient culture it was common for families to assign capable and trusted slaves to act as guardians over boys and girls until they came into adulthood. These pedagogues would have full charge over the child's education, training, and welfare. The child was subservient to the slave and couldn't go anywhere or do anything without permission. Paul's point is that even though this child may one day inherit everything his father owns, as a minor he is still (for all practical purposes) on equal status with a slave.

Paul tells us that graduation from childhood to adulthood happened "on a date set by his father" (4:2). The ancient cultures all had different ceremonies to mark the coming of age of boys and girls. In the Greek culture, when the boys turned eighteen they would have a ceremony called *apatouria* where the boy's long hair would be cut off and offered to the god Apollo. Jewish boys were considered minors until the age of twelve. However, at his *bar mitzvah* the boy would officially be recognized as a man by his father.

Roman custom did not specify an age when a person became ready for adulthood. When the father deemed the heir ready, he celebrated this time by a festival known as *Liberalia* held on March 17th. At this time, the heir received his *toga virilis* (coat of adulthood). The boy burned his childhood toys at this festival. This boy, now a man, had authority over the slave that governed him as a child. This is likely the ceremony that Paul had in mind.

A person who operates under the law is no different than a child who is heir to an entire estate yet under strict guardianship. This is why Paul

Trading Sonship for Slavery (4:1–11)

expounds by saying, "In the same way we also, when we were children, were enslaved to the elementary principles of the world" (4:3). There is an interesting Greek word used in the text for "children." The word in the original language refers to an infant. In other words, Paul is saying that the law treated its practitioners as helpless babies. Everything has to be done for an infant. A child must be told what to eat, what to wear, what time to go to bed, and the result is that the child lives under the rule of a guardian who thinks for them.

Paul is arguing that legalism treats us no differently because it tells us what to eat, how to pray, when to work, what to wear, and how to worship. The law basically regulated every aspect of daily life so that it made those under it slaves to its endless lists and demands. He's essentially saying to the Galatians, "Hey, it's time to grow up and stop relying on the law to define every detail of life." Legalism is not a step forward into maturity, but a step backward into childhood. It is like a PhD candidate who goes back to grade school, a master artist resorting to finger paints, or a teenager putting training wheels back on his bicycle.

These verses reminded me of the days when I was learning to get my driver's license. Remember those long afternoons in the Driver's Ed car with the glaring sign on the roof telling everyone to stay as far away as possible? Or what about the awkwardness of learning how to parallel park, knowing that the instructor was watching your every move, just waiting for you to trade paint with car next to you? In Driver's Ed, you might be driving, but only under the strict supervision of the instructor. The Driver's Ed teacher tells you where to turn, constantly monitors your speed, reminds you to check your mirrors, and so on.

When I was in Driver's Ed, I always thought it was a unique form of indentured servitude because I basically acted as the teacher's personal chauffeur. No kidding. Our teacher probably got more errands done during our driving time than when he was off-duty. I would drive him across town to pick up the dry cleaning. Next, it was the post office. Then we would go through the drive-thru and he would get a cheeseburger and fries and eat while I had to endure the smell of that food filling the car. "By the way, don't eat and drive. It's too distracting," he'd say while he scraped the leftover melted cheese off the wrapper.

Strangely enough, legalism is like that overbearing and controlling driving instructor that only gives commands and never really lets you go where you want to go. At the end of the day, you've accomplished someone else's agenda and you're still not "on your own." John Phillips adds:

> Legalism lays down the Law. It says, "You must not do this, that, or the other things; you must not go here, there, or the other place. You must not wear that or style your hair like that; you must wear this. You must give this amount, support these meetings or those programs, restrict yourself to this circle of fellowship and boycott that group over there. You can believe only what we tell you what to believe and you are to attack everyone who dares to differ. You may read these books, but you mustn't read those books." The result is bondage. It is grown-up childishness."[1]

The Sonship of the Believer (4:4–7)

In 1987, all of America stopped to watch a real-life drama unfold in Midland, Texas. Eighteen-month-old Jessica McClure fell down an abandoned well and was trapped. Millions of Americans watched the story of baby Jessica unfold on television. Finally, to the relief of everyone, Jessica came out of the well on October 16, 1987 to cheers and national attention. In case you don't remember the details of the story, let me give you a summary of what happened: "After 55 grueling hours trapped at the bottom of a 22-foot well, eighteen-month-old Jessica clawed her way out of the bottom of the pit, inch by inch, digging her little toes and fingers into the side of the well. 'What a hero, that Jessica!'"

You may be thinking, "Whoa! That's not what happened! She didn't climb out! She was totally helpless down there. She was powerless to save herself. If she hadn't been rescued by those people she would have perished." You are exactly right! And you and I are in exactly the same situation. We cannot save ourselves by keeping the law, performing good works, or adding to what Jesus accomplished on the cross. The Bible says, "At just the right time, when we were still powerless, Christ died for the ungodly" (Rom. 5:6). We deserve no more applause for our salvation than baby Jessica got for being rescued.[2]

This is Paul's next premise in his theological argument. Just as baby Jessica's rescue had to come from an external source, so too our only hope for salvation is from outside of us through Jesus Christ. Having demolished

---

1. Phillips, *Exploring Galatians*, 115.
2. Alcorn, *The Grace and Truth Paradox*, 30.

Trading Sonship for Slavery (4:1–11)

any hint that the believer might rescue himself through the law, Paul has set the stage for the entrance of the long-awaited Deliverer. If the law only held us down, and if keeping it could never get us out of the pit of sin, then how could we be saved? He wanted the Galatians, along with us, to understand that the intervention of Jesus Christ into our universe was a premeditated work of God's grace.

First, our salvation is *a work of redemption by the Son of God*. "But when the fullness of time had come, God sent forth his Son, born of woman, born under the law, to redeem those who were under the law, so that we might receive adoption as sons" (4:4–5). Paul explains that just as there was an appointed date for a human father to recognize his son's coming of age, so too the Father in heaven set an appointed time to send His Son Jesus Christ into the world as our Redeemer. Notice the phrase, "when the fullness of time had come," which is used to describe the precise timing of Jesus' advent. This refers to the exact year, month, and day that the world was providentially prepared from before creation for the birth of the Savior. I like to imagine there was a day on God's calendar with a big star on it. This was the day selected in the counsels of the Godhead from eternity past when the second person of the Trinity would voluntarily take on human flesh, step out of eternity and into time, and shrink himself into the womb of Mary. Max Lucado wrote brilliantly of this moment:

> It all happened in a moment, a most remarkable moment. As moments go, that one appeared no different than any other. If you could somehow pick it up off the timeline and examine it, it would look exactly like the ones that have passed while you have read these words. It came and it went. It was one of the countless moments that have marked time since eternity became measurable. But in reality, that particular moment was like none other. For through that segment of time a spectacular thing occurred. God became a man. While the creatures of earth walked unaware, Divinity arrived. Heaven opened herself and placed her most precious one in a human womb. The omnipotent, in one instant, made Himself breakable. He who had been spirit became pierceable. He who was larger than the universe became an embryo. And He who sustains the world with a word chose to be dependent upon the nourishment of a young girl. God as a fetus. Holiness sleeping in a womb. The creator of life being created. God was given eyebrows, elbows, two kidneys, and a spleen. He stretched against the walls

and floated in the amniotic fluids of His mother. God had come near.[3]

These verses raise all kinds of provocative questions. For instance, have you ever wondered, "Why did Jesus come to earth when He did?" Why did He come then and not now? Why be born in first-century Palestine when there was no electricity or running water? What we can surmise from these verses is that in the centuries prior to Christ's entrance into humanity, there was no panic in heaven over the affairs of men. God's timing is always perfect. The idea conveyed is that the Heavenly Father worked in history to bring about just the right setting for His Son to be born.

Religiously, the law had fully accomplished its purpose in the Jewish world and run its course. For thousands of years the Jews had tried to live up to its impossible standards, but they continually failed. The philosophies and pagan religions of the Greek world were also bankrupt. These hollow traditions were powerless to change men's lives. Spiritual hunger was at an all-time high.

Culturally, the world was unified by the Greek language. By the time Jesus was born, Alexander the Great had made his march across the earth and established a common language. This is important because when it came time to spread the Gospel throughout the world, everyone could speak and read the same language.

Politically, the Roman Empire had created a time of peace and prosperity called the *Pax Romana*. The iron legions of Rome had secured relative peace and built an elaborate system of roads all over the Mediterranean making it easy for the Gospel to travel from one province to another.

This is a testament to the sovereignty of God. God moved the nations of the world around like pawns on a chessboard. He established kingdoms and toppled them like a kid playing with toy soldiers in a sandbox. He allowed roads to be paved and languages to be invented in anticipation of the advent of Jesus and the propagation of the Gospel.

Paul was also careful to point out the uniqueness of this Savior. He was, "sent forth by God, born of a woman." In one phrase Paul perfectly balances the humanity and deity of Christ. There never was a time when He was not, thus Jesus always existed with the Father and Holy Spirit in eternity past (John 1:1). Yet, when He entered the human race, He didn't come down from heaven in ethereal light as a fully mature adult. Just like every other person who walked the earth (besides Adam and Eve), He was

---

3. Lucado, *God Came Near*, 25–26.

Trading Sonship for Slavery (4:1–11)

incubated for nine months and took a short trip down His mother's birth canal. His conception was supernatural (Luke 1:35), but His delivery was totally ordinary.

Moreover, Jesus was also born "under the law" according to verse 4:4. Jesus came as a man living in submission to the Mosaic Law. He was born into Judaism, He was circumcised, He observed the Sabbath and the national festivals, He respected the dietary restrictions, and He memorized the Scriptures. Jesus was born "under the law" so that He could fulfill every minute detail on our behalf (Matt. 5:17). He fulfilled the moral law in His life and the ceremonial law in His death (Rom. 8:3–4).

The ultimate purpose for Christ's coming is also stated, "to redeem those who were under the law that we might receive the adoption as sons" (4:5). The word redemption means "to set free by paying a price" or "to buy back." In the days of antiquity you could go to a slave auction and, for the right price, purchase a slave off the auction block and make him your personal servant. Paul is saying that Jesus paid the price for our freedom by using His life as a ransom (Mark 10:45). Jesus purchased us out of the slave market of sin (Eph. 1:7) and spared us from the entire Mosaic Law (1 Peter 1:18–19). God not only created us, but He then paid the ultimate price to buy us back and set us free.

Many years ago, A.J. Gordon was the pastor of a church in Boston. One day he met a young boy in front of the sanctuary carrying a rusty cage in which several birds fluttered nervously. Gordon inquired, "Son, where did you get those birds?" The boy replied, "I trapped them out in the field." "What are you going to do with them?" Gordon asked. "I'm going to play with them, and then I guess I'll just feed them to an old cat we have at home," the boy explained. When Gordon offered to buy them, the lad exclaimed, "Mister, you don't want them. They're just little old wild birds and can't sing very well." Gordon replied, "I'll give you $2 for the cage and the birds." "Okay. It's a deal, but you're making a bad bargain."

The exchange was made and the boy went away whistling, happy with the coins jingling in his pockets. Gordon walked around to the back of the church property, opened the door of the small wire coop, and let the struggling creatures soar into the blue. The next Sunday he took the empty cage into the pulpit and used it to illustrate his sermon about Christ's coming to seek and to save the lost—paying for them with His own precious blood. "That boy told me the birds were not songsters," said Gordon, "but when I released them and they winged their way heavenward, it seemed to me they were singing, 'Redeemed, redeemed, redeemed!'" For all those who have been bought by the blood of the Lamb, they have same song.

Secondly, our salvation is *a work of adoption by the Spirit of God*. "And because you are sons, God has sent forth the Spirit of His Son into your hearts, crying out, "Abba, Father!" Therefore you are no longer a slave but a son, and if a son, then an heir of God through Christ" (4:6–7). Paul parts the veil of mystery that covers the Trinity and helps us understand how each member of the Godhead plays a different role in the plan of salvation. The Father sent the Son (John 3:16–17). The Son lived a perfect and blameless life under the law and gave Himself as the sin-bearer of the world (2 Cor. 5:21). Then the Son, upon returning to heaven, sent the Spirit to convict us of sin, regenerate our hearts, and take up abode in our hearts (John 7:38–39, 16:8–11).

God gives us proof that we are His sons and daughters because we have the indwelling Holy Spirit crying out in our hearts. Paul wants his readers to know that salvation means sonship—inclusion into the family of God. Adoption is the act of God whereby He gives to each of His children an adult standing. This means you can enjoy all the privileges and responsibilities that come with being in God's family. In the natural world, adoption only means that you bring someone who is not biologically related into your family and love them as your own. But no matter how much you care for that child, it's humanly impossible to place your DNA in that person. However, in the spiritual realm, the Bible says that God not only deposits His nature within us—which is regeneration (John 3:3)—but He also brings us into His family and adopts us as His own. God does two things at the moment of salvation. Not only does God give us life, but He also places us in His family and makes us recipients of an inheritance. He is our Father by way of the new birth and by adoption.

The word "Abba" is the Aramaic word for "Father." It is the most endearing word that could be used for a father. The English equivalent would be "Daddy." By receiving the Holy Spirit, it brings believers into a personal intimate relationship with our Heavenly Father, so much so that we can call Him "Daddy." Under legalism, the prime motivation for trying to keep rules and regulations was fear—fear of not measuring up, fear of failure, fear of God's wrath. A slave only lives in fear of the taskmaster's whip. But now there has been a total paradigm shift. Because of the Holy Spirit, our motivation for serving God is love. I like the way one pastor explained the impact of adoption:

Trading Sonship for Slavery (4:1–11)

When I was a child, my father brought home a 12-year-old boy named Roger, whose parents died from a drug overdose. There was no one to care for Roger, so my folks decided they would raise him as their own. At first it was difficult for Roger to adjust to his new home. Several times a day, I heard my parents saying to Roger, "No, no. That's not how we behave in this family." "No, no. You don't have to scream or fight or hurt other people to get what you want." "No, no, Roger. We expect you to show respect in this family." In time, Roger began to change. Did he have to make those changes to become part of the family? No. He was part of the family by the grace of my father. But did he have to work hard because he was in the family? You bet he did. It was tough for Roger to change, and he had to work at it. But he was motivated by gratitude for the amazing love he had received. Do you have a lot of hard work to do now that the Spirit has adopted you into God's family? Certainly. But not to become a son or a daughter of the Heavenly Father. No, you make those changes because you are a son or daughter. And every time you start to revert back to the old addictions to sin, the Holy Spirit will say to you, "No, no. That's now how we act in this family."[4]

The Squandering of Liberty (4:8–11)

I am reminded of a story from American history that I used tell my students when I taught high school history. On June 19, 1865, over two years after President Lincoln had signed the Emancipation Proclamation, General Gordon Granger rode into Galveston, Texas and read General Order Number 3: "The people of Texas are informed that in accordance with a Proclamation from the Executive of the United States, all slaves are free." For the first time, slaves in Texas learned that they were declared free by the president. Some were shocked, but many others celebrated. June 19 soon became known as "Juneteenth"—the day the slaves were set free in Texas.

Ignorance of the truth kept them in bondage, so too it is with Christians who live in legalism rather than grace. They are ignorant of the fact that God has declared them sons and they should never go back to being slaves. This is why Paul ends this section in 4:8–11 by lamenting of the Galatians regression back into the follies of legalism. Look at how *The Message* Bible paraphrases Paul's words:

4. Barnes, "How We Act in God's Family."

> Earlier, before you knew God personally, you were enslaved to so-called gods that had nothing of the divine about them. But now that you know the real God—or rather since God knows you—how can you possibly subject yourselves again to those paper tigers? For that is exactly what you do when you are intimidated into scrupulously observing all the traditions, taboos, and superstitions associated with special days and seasons and years. I am afraid that all my hard work among you has gone up in a puff of smoke![5]

Before their conversion, they were ignorant sinners who worshipped pagan, false gods. Christ had delivered them from the bondage of their slavery, but now they had "drunk the kool-aid" that the legalists were peddling to them. The Galatians were strapping themselves into a religious straightjacket and didn't realize it. The Judaizers convinced the Galatians to keep the Sabbaths and Old Testament feasts scrupulously lest any prescribed observance of the law be overlooked. Paul was afraid that all his labor was for nothing. He had every right to be disappointed with them. After all, he almost lost his life preaching the Gospel in their midst.

By the grace of God, we must remember what we once were before Christ found us and vow to never return to it. We must take hold of our freedom in Christ and conform our lives to His grace daily. A good example of this is John Newton. He was an only child and lost his mother when he was only seven-years-old. He put on the uniform of a sailor at the tender age of eleven and became involved, in the words of one of his biographers, "in the unspeakable atrocities of the African slave trade." He plumbed the depths of human sin and degradation. When he was twenty-three, on March 10, 1774, as his ship was in imminent peril of sinking in a terrible storm, he cried out to God for mercy and found it. Later on, he penned the words of the hymn "Amazing Grace" which has blessed so many over the years. However, in order to never forget how God had lavished His grace on a blasphemer and drunkard like himself, Newton had the words of Deuteronomy 15:15 etched across the mantelpiece of his study. "And thou shalt remember that thou wast a bondman in the land of Egypt, and the Lord thy God redeemed thee."[6]

By keeping God's grace at the forefront of our attention, not only will we be motivated to embrace Christian liberty, but we will always be

---

5. Peterson, *The Message*, Gal. 4:8–11.
6. Stott, *The Message of Galatians*, 110.

Trading Sonship for Slavery (4:1–11)

reminded of the great cost that Christ paid for our ransom. When you know you've been bought with a price, everything changes. We become what the most important person in our life thinks we are. How would your life change if you truly believed the Bible's astounding words about God's love for you? You're no longer an orphan, but you've been adopted by a Heavenly Father. You're no longer a slave, but a son or daughter of the King of Kings. You're no longer a prodigal, but an estranged loved one returned home to a party thrown in your honor.

CHAPTER 10

Velvet Steel (4:12–20)

It's an incredibly rare thing to find a leader who is admired and respected by both friends and enemies. Yet such was the case with two tremendous figures that were on opposing sides during the Civil War. Lee and Lincoln—the consummate southern gentleman and the rail-splitter—although they may have been fighting for different causes, both men exemplified a kind of leadership that was tough but tender.

In his day, Robert E. Lee was a marvel of unimpeachable character, humility, and sterling courage. He commanded his armies with integrity and an immutable fear of God. Those who have studied the lives of Lee's contemporaries—Grant, Sherman, McClellan, Pendleton—have noticed that many of the vices which flawed these men were conspicuously absent from the moral fiber of Lee. Perhaps there is no better example of Lee's humble heroism than one touching snapshot which occurred during the battle of Petersburg. Historian J. Wilkins Steven wrote:

> Lee found himself in an exposed position under intense fire. He ordered his men around him to seek shelter and then he stepped out into the open to pick up a baby sparrow that fallen from a tree. Returning the sparrow to its nest, Lee followed his men to shelter.[1]

Another writer said of Lee, "Never a general to hide safely far back behind the front lines, Lee frequently courted danger with an unflappable spirit of invincibility. He conducted his life securely under the providential hand of God, in whom he trusted with a whole heart."[2]

---

1. Wilkins, *Call of Duty*, 225.
2. Swindoll, *Elijah*, xii.

Velvet Steel (4:12–20)

Lincoln's courage and character were no less noteworthy. His battlefield was a different venue than Lee's, yet he faced incredible criticism and vitriol. The legacy of our nation's sixteenth president stands as a magnificent model of how a man should handle personal assaults on his character. Public criticism against him intensified during the last seven years of his life. One of his biographers writes:

> Abraham Lincoln was slandered, libeled, and hated perhaps more intensely than any man ever to run for the nation's highest office. He was publicly called just about every name imaginable by the press of the day, including a grotesque baboon, a third-rate country lawyer who once split rails and now splits the Union, a coarse vulgar joker, a dictator, an ape, a buffoon, and others. The Illinois State Register labeled him "the craftiest and most dishonest politician that ever disgraced an office in America." Severe and unjust criticism did not subside after Lincoln took the oath of office, nor did it come only from Southern sympathizers. It came from within the Union itself, from Congress, from some factions within the Republican Party, and, initially, from within his own cabinet. As president, Lincoln learned that, no matter what he did, there were going to be people who would not be pleased. As his enemies increased, so did the criticism against him. But Lincoln handled it all with a patience, forbearance, and determination uncommon of most men.[3]

The "grace under fire" attitude of Lincoln inspired the famous American historian and poet Carl Sandburg to describe the president as "velvet steel"—a title which I believe is also an apt description of Lee, and not to forget the apostle Paul.

Paul was not a battlefield general, nor was he a president, but he had the guts to stand on the frontlines of battle and lead the early Church through some of its toughest challenges. In my opinion, Paul was the epitome of velvet steel. He had the heart of a child, the mind of a scholar, and the hide of a rhinoceros. Thus far in his letter to the Galatian believers, he has been a prosecuting attorney, a skilled theologian, and a courageous freedom fighter. He has employed every kind of tactic in confronting this confused church—logic, sarcasm, clever analogies, and now parental scolding.

You'll recall that Paul hasn't really had much good to say about the Galatians. Earlier he called them "fools" and accused them of being "bewitched" (3:1). In fact, if you judged Paul on the basis of the first three

---

3. Phillips, *Lincoln on Leadership*, 66–67.

chapters, you would conclude that he was a brilliant intellectual with no heart.

However, something changes in Paul's approach midway through this epistle. By the time you get through these verses in this passage, he will have called the Galatians "brethren" (4:12) and "little children" (4:18). In this passage, you see "Paul the Pastor" revealed. Paul opens up his heart to the Galatians and pleads with them as a tender spiritual father to return to Christ and the simplicity of the Gospel. I am reminded of the country song that Holly Dunn sang years ago entitled "Daddy's Hands." The chorus of the song went like this:

> Daddy's hands were soft and kind when I was cryin'.
> Daddy's hands were hard as steel when I'd done wrong.
> Daddy's hands weren't always gentle, but I've come to understand
> There was always love in Daddy's hands.[4]

I think the theme of that song encapsulates Paul's role as the pastor of these wayward believers. In fact, any pastor worth his salt knows that sometimes he has to be confrontational and then other times he has to be compassionate. A pastor has to be velvet and steel at the same time or as Jesus said, "wise as a serpent and gentle as a dove" (Matt. 10:16). In this passage, we see how Paul the pastor kept this balance and how he loved the believers in Galatia.

A Pastor's Patience (4:12)

When Paul first visited Galatia, he did not come as an arrogant "I'm-better-than-you" legalist who had no sensitivity to the Gentile culture. He did not come to them as a Jew but as a Christian. That is why he wrote, "Brothers, I entreat you, become as I am, for I also have become as you are. You did me no wrong."

The best ministry always flows out of relationships. Pastoring is more than the impartation of knowledge or cold Bible doctrine. Ministry is about people. Paul knew that. He could never win them if they remained angry with him. How does he express his love without giving up his principles? He begins by reminding them of past blessings they had enjoyed together.

Essentially, he is inviting them to be free from legalism like he was. Paul had tried to carry around the ball and chain of rules and regulations

---

4. Dunn, "Daddy's Hands," MTM Music, 1986.

Velvet Steel (4:12–20)

under the Jewish law, but to no avail. Its yoke was oppressive and cumbersome; Paul wished this curse upon no man. He knew all about the bondage that the Galatians were getting into. Just a few years earlier he had come out of the prison into which they were now heading. Paul is pleading with them, "Don't go back into chains!"

These are the words of a parent who is in pain over their children's foolish decisions. If you think about all that Paul went through with this one church, it's amazing he didn't throw-up his hands and quit. I'm sure at times he felt like a broken record player, preaching the same message over and over again. I'm sure he wondered, "When is this actually going to get through to them?" But Paul's love for them kept him in the fight.

By the end of his career Paul knew a thing or two about developing patience as a pastor. He instructed young Timothy, "preach the word; be ready in season and out of season; reprove, rebuke, and exhort *with complete patience* and teaching" (2 Tim. 4:2). I'd argue that pastoral patience is more difficult than theological precision. For most pastors, it's easier to prepare and preach a sermon than to be patient with the flock. Dealing with the same people week in and week out requires a huge investment and it's physically and emotionally exhausting.

I have concluded that there are always going to be those people who you counsel with over and over and you never see any noticeable change in their life. You will preach your heart out and still people will be in the crowd yawning or folding up their Bibles as if to say, "Can we wrap this up please?" There will be people who you have invested considerable time and energy into that will, for no apparent reason, leave the church and go completely MIA.

Likewise, there is always going to be that one person who is a consistent nitpicker. Did you hear about the pastor who regularly received anonymous critical letters from someone who signed each note, "The Thorn"? Attached to the first note was an explanation that since the apostle Paul had a thorn in the flesh, this writer felt that his pastor should have one too. So he had appointed himself "The Thorn." This pastor wrote him back and signed it, "Sincerely, The Hedge Trimmer."

A Pastor's Perseverance (4:12–13)

In an attempt to arrest their hearts, Paul took the Galatians down memory lane. "You know it was because of a bodily ailment that I preached the gospel to you at first, and though my condition was a trial to you, you did not scorn or despise me, but received me as an angel of God, as Christ Jesus" (4:13–14).

Apparently, when Paul arrived in Galatia he was seriously afflicted by a debilitating illness. Bible scholars have speculated what ailment Paul was referring to here. Some think it was his infamous "thorn in the flesh," but no one can be certain (2 Cor. 12:7–9). Others have thought it might have something to do with failing eyesight as a result of the blinding light that he saw during his conversion experience on the road to Damascus (Acts 9:1–9). Still others have conjectured that Paul suffered from malaria. In that case, the disease would have weakened him and disfigured him so that he was disgusting to behold.

Whatever the case might have been, the people at Galatia accepted Paul with open arms and took care of his physical needs while he took care of their spiritual needs. The Galatians could have thrown Paul to the curb, but they took him in instead. Amazingly, Paul's sickness became a providential instrument to bring him to the Galatians so that they might receive the Gospel. This should be a reminder to you and me that we are not walking accidents. The circumstances of life are not left to time and chance. There is a Grand Weaver who "orders the steps of a righteous man" so that He puts us into situations to establish the Gospel.

J. Oswald Sanders once told the story of an indigenous missionary in India who walked barefoot from village to village preaching the gospel. After a long day, many miles, and much discouragement, he tried to speak up for the gospel in a particular village. They shouted him down and ran him out. Dejected and exhausted, he slouched down under a tree and fell asleep.

When he awoke the whole town was gathered to hear him. The head man of the village explained that they came to look him over while he was sleeping. When they saw his blistered feet they concluded that this must be a holy man and that they had been evil to reject him. His suffering had now bought him the currency of authenticity and influence, so the villagers asked to hear his message. According to Sanders, he preached the Gospel and the whole village believed.[5]

So it was with Paul and the Galatians. What I admire about the ministry of Paul is his never-say-die attitude. Even though he suffered tremendously, as long as there was air in his lungs he was going to be preaching the Gospel. He never lost sight of the fact that God called him to endure

---

5. Piper, *Let the Nations Be Glad*, 115.

hardship and be faithful to the Gospel ministry. This is a good reminder to you and me when we wish the Christian walk was easier and our burdens lighter. Just think—if we got our way and God removed the hardship from us when we first cried "Uncle!" then His character development program in us would be aborted too soon. Moreover, it could be our pain or that unplanned detour that God uses to guide us exactly to the people hungriest for the Gospel.

A Pastor's Principles (4:15–16)

There was quite a contrast in how Paul was first received in Galatia and how they were now treating him. Initially, they loved his preaching and teaching in those early days, but now they treated him with contempt. The honeymoon phase was over and the Galatians were treating Paul like the proverbial "red-headed stepchild." What was the source of their derision? The long and the short of it was that Paul stepped on their toes with the truth.

Feeling the sting of being slighted, Paul wrote in 4:15–16, "For I testify to you that, if possible, you would have gouged out your eyes and given them to me. Have I then become your enemy by telling you the truth?" Paul reminded the Galatians that at one time they loved him so much that they would have sacrificed their own eyes for his sake. Scholars tell us that was a common figure of speech, suggesting that the Galatians would have given up their most precious and irreplaceable organs if doing so would have helped him. Now they were giving him the cold shoulder. Perhaps more painful than his physical infirmity were the feelings of betrayal when Paul saw how the Galatians turned on him at the word of the Judaizers.

Paul was maligned because he was not willing to compromise the truth. He told the Galatians not what they wanted to hear, but what they needed to hear. Unwillingness to sugarcoat the tough stuff in the Bible always results in some people getting offended at the preacher. Sadly, we live in a world that cannot handle biblical truth and honesty. Naturally, shallow people are more attracted to the churches where the pastor gives positive, encouraging, self-help sermons and where there is never any mention of sin, depravity, or personal culpability.

But if a man will not preach the whole counsel of God's word, then you have to seriously question his motives. Is he looking for the approval of God or of men? You wouldn't go to a doctor who couldn't bear the thought of telling his patients a bad diagnosis. If you had a terminal illness, certainly you deserve the right to know. So why get mad at a faithful minister who correctly diagnoses a spiritual sickness? Any preacher who really loves his people is not worried about popularity but about giving them the truth no matter how bad it hurts.

Randy Alcorn in his book, *The Grace and Truth Paradox*, explains the temptation he faced to water-down the Gospel when he shared the offense of the Cross with his dying father:

> My father was the most resistant person to the Gospel I have ever known. He warned me never to talk to him about "that religious stuff" . . . At age eighty-four, Dad was diagnosed with terminal cancer . . . I arrived an hour before surgery, praying that in his pain and despair, with no easy way out my Dad would turn to Christ. Standing by his bed, I opened my Bible to Romans. I began reading in chapter 3, "There is none righteous, no not one . . . All have sinned and fallen short of the glory of God." Those weren't easy words to read. My tavern-owner father had always taken hot offense at being called a sinner. I wanted to gloss over this portion, quickly moving to the good news of God's grace, but I forced myself to keep reading verse after verse about human sin. Why? Because, I told myself, if I really love Dad, I have to tell him the whole truth. If God's going to do a miracle of conversion here, that's His job. My job is to say what God says . . . Finally, I looked Dad in the eyes and asked, "Have you ever confessed your sins and asked Jesus Christ to forgive you?" "No," he said in a weak voice. "But . . . I think it's about time I did." I will never forget that moment. The impossible took place right before my eyes: my father prayed aloud, confessed his sins and placed his trust in Christ . . . That morning in the hospital I wanted to minimize the truth of human sin. I wanted to pass truth and go directly to grace. Yet, without the bad news there can be no good news. Without the truth of God's holiness and the stark reality of our sin, Christ's grace is meaningless. The worst thing I could have done to my father was what I was tempted to do, water-down the Gospel."[6]

The reality is that when we try to soften the Gospel by minimizing sin, we keep people from Jesus and, conversely, when we try to harden the Gospel by minimizing grace, we also keep people from Jesus. It's not enough to offer grace or truth—we have to offer grace and truth. Paul wonderfully balanced both as a loving pastor to the Galatians. In the first three chapters

---

6. Alcorn, *The Grace and Truth Paradox*, 58–60.

he administered the spanking, but now he is wrapping his arms around the Galatians to let them know it was all out of a heart of love.

A Pastor's Protection (4:17)

Paul compared his faithfulness to the false loyalty of the Judaizers. He wanted the Galatians to see that the Judaizers were nothing more than wolves in sheep's clothing. Their true motives were not to glorify God, but to build-up their holy huddle and use the Galatians to glorify themselves. The Judaizers zealously courted the Galatians to persuade them to join their camp, but they were not interested in the truth; they were interested in a following. Eugene Peterson paraphrases Paul's warning in 4:17 like this:

> Those heretical teachers go to great lengths to flatter you, but their motives are rotten. They want to shut you out of the free world of God's grace so that you will always depend on them for approval and direction, making them feel important."[7]

Jesus condemned the methods of the Pharisees because they employed a similar tactic. He said, "Woe to you, scribes and Pharisees, hypocrites! For you travel across sea and land to make a single proselyte, and when he becomes a proselyte, you make him twice as much a child of hell as yourselves" (Matt. 23:15).

The Judaizers wanted to isolate their converts and indoctrinate them into their endless lists of rules and regulations. Through flattery and ego-stroking they wanted the Galatians to become their groupies with the hopes they would fawn over them and wait on the edge of their seat in anticipation over the next word that dropped from their lips. So they courted the baby believers in Galatia and buttered them up in order to make them their slaves.

By the way, this is the exact tactic that the cults of today use. The Jehovah's Witnesses or the Mormon missionaries will show up on your doorstep and tell you they are Christians. In reality, they use the same terms evangelicals do—Jesus, salvation, faith, sin—however, they've changed the definitions radically. Slowly but surely, they try to get you to replace your Bible with theirs and convince you that they alone have a corner-market on the truth. Warren Wiersbe writes:

> One of the marks of a false teacher is that he tries to attract other men's converts to himself, and not simply to the truth of the Word

7. Peterson, *The Message*, Gal. 4:17.

or to the person of Jesus Christ. It was not the Judaizers who originally came to Galatia and led them to Christ; it was Paul. Like the cultists today, these false teachers were not winning lost sinners to Christ, but were stealing converts from those who were truly serving the Lord.[8]

Paul saw through the Judaizers feigned friendship and warned the Galatians sternly because he was zealous for their souls, but only to lead them to freedom in Christ. "But it is good to be zealous in a good thing always, and not only when I am present with you" (4:18). Paul wanted the Galatians to follow Jesus Christ for the right reasons. The Galatians had zeal for grace when Paul was with them, but when he left they became vulnerable to the legalists. They were like kids who misbehaved when the teacher left the room, shooting spit-wads and flying paper airplanes. As long as Paul was around they weren't as likely to succumb to the legalists peer pressure. So he exhorted them to grow up and act consistently, even if he wasn't there to keep an eye on them.

One of the most fitting descriptions of the pastor's role in the Scriptures is that of a shepherd (1 Peter 5:1–4). Imagine Paul in the role of shepherd here fighting for the lives of his sheep who have wandered off into a precarious place. The caring pastor is like that shepherd who carefully watches over the sheep and does everything in his power to drive off enemies and point out potential dangers along with way.

When you study the life of a shepherd, you learn that his rod and staff served many purposes, one of which was to defend the flock against predators (Ps. 23:4). The rod was essentially an oak club about 3 or 4 feet long. On the end was a round head into which the shepherd pounded hard bits of metal. This rod became a versatile weapon to ward off wild animals. If a shepherd was really good with the rod, he could fling the rod out like a missile and strike a scavenger lurking in the distance. In his fascinating memoir of shepherding life, *A Shepherd's Look at Psalm 23*, Phillip Keller explained one such instance:

> I could never get over how often, and with what accuracy, the African herders would hurl their knob-kerries at some recalcitrant beast that misbehaved. If the shepherd saw a sheep wandering away on its own, or approaching poisonous weeds, or getting too close to

---

8. Wiersbe, *Be Free*, 99.

danger of one sort or another, the club would go whistling through the air to send the wayward animal scurrying back to the bunch.[9]

Paul has done a similar thing here. He has flung out a javelin of truth to protect his flock and hopefully guide them back to the safety of the fold. Martin Luther added:

> A preacher must both be a soldier and a shepherd. He must nourish, defend, and teach. He must have teeth in his mouth and he must be able to bite and fight. Even if I preach correctly and shepherd the flock with sound doctrine, if I neglect my duty, if I do not warn the sheep against the wolves, what kind of builder would I be if I were to pile up masonry and then stand by while another tears it down.[10]

A Pastor's Passion (4:19-20)

Paul expressed his passion for the Galatians when he concluded this paragraph with these tender remarks, "My little children, for whom I am again in the anguish of childbirth until Christ is formed in you!" (4:19). Don't overlook Paul's language when he refers to them as "little children." What's astounding is that this is the only place in any of Paul's writings that he uses this term. We would expect this title from John, the apostle of love (1 John 2:1, 12-13, 18, 28, 3:7, 3:18, 5:21), but not necessarily from Paul and not in the middle of Galatians which is largely a letter of correction and rebuke!

The metaphor that Paul is using in association with these believers is that of childbirth. Paul travailed to bring them into the Kingdom, like a mother does in the heat of labor to bring her child into the world. His first labor with the Galatians had evidently ended in a miscarriage. But he didn't give up. Paul labored with them again in the truth of the Gospel. He was feeling the labor pains all over again because they had fallen into such error and it was going to be difficult to bring them back to simplicity in Christ. It was like a second birth for Paul.

The main goal was that "Christ be formed in them" or that they would take on the shape of Christ like a fetus takes shape within the mother's womb. He desired metamorphosis from the inside-out, not a cosmetic change on the outside like the legalists were trying for. What Paul wanted

---

9. Keller, *A Shepherd's Look at Psalm 23*, 88.
10. Luther, *Table Talk*, ccciii.

for his people more than anything else was for them to become the hands and feet of Jesus. John Stott commented on this verse like this:

> What should matter to the people is not the pastor's appearance, but whether Christ is speaking through him. And what should matter to the pastor is not the people's approval, but whether Christ is being formed in them. The church needs people who, in listening to their pastor, listen for the message of Christ and pastors who, in laboring among the people, look for the image of Christ."[11]

Paul ends by bemoaning the fact that the pen and ink couldn't contain the full pathos of his heart. "I wish I could be present with you now and change my tone, for I am perplexed about you" (4:20). The trouble with letters is that they can't convey the tone of the writer's voice or the twinkle in their eye. Paul wanted to be there in person to deliver this message of tough love. If there is one thing we have learned from this passage, it's that love is willing to do and say the difficult things. Being gentle doesn't mean that we are soft on sin. Love necessitates that we tell the truth even when others may not want to hear it. Paul never gave up on the Galatians because Christ never gave up on him, and He'll never give up on us either (Phil. 1:6).

As a youngster I took a trip to Dollywood and I noticed a fascinating machine in one of the candy stores. You could drop a penny inside this machine, turn a hand crank, and the penny would go through a series of gears and presses. As you turned the crank, this penny would be flattened and elongated until the original image of Lincoln was totally erased. Then at the end a die came down and pressed a new image into the copper. When the penny came out of the machine, it had a different logo and an inscription that read, "Dollywood—Great Smoky Mountains."

For some reason, that elaborate penny-defacing machine reminds me of the truth of Galatians 4:19, "until Christ is formed in you." God wants to take our lives and radically remake them over again so that the old man is removed and the image of His Son replaces what once was there (2 Cor. 5:17). Like that penny, which was hard pressed on both sides, the process will be painful and cause discomfort. He will use trials, burdens, and even our own failures to erase those features which are unlike Him. Once we are malleable, Jesus will chisel away at us. At times it may seem like God is being most unloving, but love never leaves us the same way it found us. When we are tempted to doubt His love, we must remember that He is a Heavenly Father with a heart of velvet steel.

11. Stott, *The Message of Galatians*, 119.

CHAPTER 11

A Tale of Two Sons (4:21–31)

It's amazing the spiritual lessons God can teach you if you have your eyes and ears open. One day God turned a moment in a shopping mall into a classroom of instruction. I am convinced that little boys can make a game out of almost anything—sticks, a rubber ball, a length of rope—you name it and little boys can put their imagination to work. It was obvious their mother had left these two boys unsupervised and in this moment of freedom they had found endless fun running around the food court like wild Indians.

Try to picture two rambunctious boys planning to race each other on the escalators. The challenge was to see who could reach the top floor the fastest. The two escalators were side-by-side, one went up and one went down. From what I could tell from my vantage point one kid was going to just simply ride the escalator to the top, while his comrade was going to get on the other escalator coming down and try to run up it, fighting against the flow of the machine.

On your marks... get ready... set... go! I watched the two carefully as they propelled themselves toward the escalators like they'd been shot out of a rifle. At first it looked as if boy number one, who climbed on the escalator going up, was going to lose the race. But the laws of physics took over. As you can imagine, boy number one's journey to the top was quite effortless. In fact, he spent most of his ride laughing at the other kid who was stumbling up the steps.

Meanwhile, boy number two was trying to run up the escalator and was having quite a difficult time. With every step forward he took, it was like the escalator pulled him three steps back. Pretty soon he ran out of breath and just quit trying. Deflated and sucking wind, he let the escalator take him down to the bottom. He had proven the truth of Isaiah 40:30, "Even youths shall faint and be weary, and young men shall fall exhausted."

After some reflection I realized that the little race on the escalator was an illustration of the difference between law and grace. Law is like the kid running up the escalator which is moving down. Law is the way of self-effort, exertion, and performance. Law relies on the power of the flesh to achieve salvation. Going the way of the law is exhausting and not much fun. In fact, you end up getting nowhere. Grace, on the other hand, is like the first kid gliding up the escalator with ease. Grace is the way of resting in Christ's finished work on the Cross. Grace isn't achieved but received. Grace is about enjoying the ride, and relying on the power of the Holy Spirit to take you through life.

This distinction between law and grace, flesh and Spirit, is a central theme in Galatians. Paul has been trying to get the Galatians to see the vast difference between these two contradictory approaches to the Christian life. In the last section of chapter four Paul digs into the Old Testament and uses another illustration from the life of Abraham to teach a lesson to the Galatians dabbling in legalism. Paul reminds his readers of the story of Abraham's wife, Sarah, and her handmaiden, Hagar, and the two sons which were born from these women, Ishmael and Isaac.

Admittedly, this is not an easy read. In fact, many scholars and commentators believe this to be one of the most cryptic passages in the New Testament. However, we can zero in on what Paul meant to teach in this complicated passage by keeping it to the overall context of the message of Galatians. Recall that in this middle-third of the letter, Paul is laying the theological foundation for the superiority of grace over the law. He is still demolishing the idea that legalism is a legitimate way of obtaining God's favor. So in order to show the futility of that reasoning, Paul has saved his knock-out right hook for last.

The Allegory (4:21–27)

Paul uses the historical event from Genesis as an allegory to describe the difference between two different ways of living—bondage through the law and the flesh, or freedom through grace in Christ. By the way, in case you forgot, an allegory is simply a story where the characters, places, and events have hidden meanings. It's a story that can be read on two different

A Tale of Two Sons (4:21–31)

levels—the literal and the symbolic—just like *Pilgrim's Progress* or *The Chronicles of Narnia*.

Paul begins in 4:21–22 by reminding us of Abraham's *two sons—Isaac vs. Ishmael*. "Tell me, you who desire to be under the law, do you not listen to the law? For it is written that Abraham had two sons, one by a slave woman and one by a free woman. But the son of the slave was born according to the flesh, while the son of the free woman was born through promise."

It will be impossible to understand the meaning of Paul's allegory if you don't first have a working knowledge of Abraham's story.

- *Abraham, age 75*: The saga of Abraham began when God called him out of Ur and promised to make him the father of a great nation (Gen. 12:1–3). Both Abraham and his wife Sarah desired children, but much to her disgrace, Sarah was barren and well past the age of childbearing.

- *Abraham, age 82*: Fast-forward seven years and there's still no heir. Abraham came to the conclusion that his chief servant, Eliezer, would be his heir. However, the Lord affirmed His original promise in Genesis 15:2–4 that a son was coming.

- *Abraham, age 85*: The biological clock on Sarah had long been broken. So she got impatient and devised a plot to get around her infertility. At the advice of Sarah, Abraham had a one night stand with Hagar, Sarah's Egyptian handmaiden, in order to produce a son through her (Gen. 16:1–3). This action was legal in that time period, but completely out of the will of God. Abraham was supposed to wait on God, but he took matters into his own hands.

- *Abraham, age 86*: This is where things began to get really interesting. Hagar bore Abraham a son and named him Ishmael. However, Abraham should have known that having two women under one tent was just asking for trouble. Sarah's plan backfired. She became green with envy that she could not be a mother (Gen. 16:4). Hagar taunted her elderly counterpart. If looks could kill, Sarah would have been a murderer by the way she eyed Hagar. What went on in Abraham's household would have been perfect fodder for reality television.

- *Abraham, age 99*: Abraham was content to allow Ishmael to be the heir to all that God had promised. However, Ishmael was never to be the son of promise. So after a long period of silence, God renewed his original promise to Abraham that he would have a son through Sarah and that his name should be called Isaac (Gen. 17:19). When Sarah heard this news, she laughed. Thus, the name Isaac means "laughter."

- *Abraham, age 100:* The birth of Isaac was nothing less than supernatural. Abraham and Sarah were prime candidates for Rascal scooters, dentures, and adult diapers. Yet these two senior citizens would be raising kids when other people their age were sitting in nursing homes. The Lord allowed Abraham and Sarah to get well past the age of being parents so that there would be no question that Isaac was the son of Promise (Gen. 21: 2, 5). The birth of Isaac was supposed to be a joyous occasion and, initially, it was. However, it created a whole new set of problems in the home. For fourteen years Ishmael has been the only son. Now there was competition between these two sons for the love and affection of Abraham.

- *Abraham, age 103*: When Isaac turned three-years-old, the family feud became volatile. According to the custom of the day, when a child turned three-years-old a big celebration was in order to mark the weaning of that child. By this time, Ishmael was seventeen and at his younger sibling's party he began to mock and scorn Isaac (Gen. 21:8–10). Two wives plus two sons equals more drama than a middle school girl's locker room. Abraham is forced by Sarah to make a choice between her and Isaac or Hagar and Ishmael—reluctantly, he sent Hagar and Ishmael away (Gen. 21:14).

Next, Paul points out that the two sons and two mothers actually point to *two systems—flesh vs. faith.* "But the son of the slave was born according to the flesh, while the son of the free woman was born through promise" (4:23). Sarah's scheming got Abraham into all kinds of trouble. Instead of waiting on God she got impatient, devised her own plan, and operated in the power of the flesh. When the plan boomeranged, it proved the high cost of living outside the will of God. If they would have only waited, Abraham and Sarah could have escaped major turmoil and heartache.

Paul's point in referencing this story is to illustrate a deeper meaning than just an example of a dysfunctional family. The two wives and the two sons represent two separate spiritual realities—living by the flesh or living by faith.

A Tale of Two Sons (4:21–31)

Ishmael	Isaac
Son of the flesh	Son of the Promise
Product of human works	Product of faith in God
Outside of God's will	Fulfillment of God's will
Natural conception	Supernatural conception
Man's way	God's way
Legalism	Grace
Brought curse and scorn	Brought blessing and joy

John MacArthur has observed, "The conception of Ishmael represents man's way, the way of the flesh, whereas Isaac represents God's way, the way of promise . . . The one is the way of legalism, the other the way of grace. Ishmael symbolizes those who had only a natural birth and who trust in their own works. Isaac symbolizes those who have had spiritual birth because they have trusted in the work of Jesus Christ."[1]

Next in the allegory we need to notice the *two symbols—law vs. liberty*. "Now this may be interpreted allegorically: these women are two covenants. One is from Mount Sinai, bearing children for slavery; she is Hagar. Now Hagar is Mount Sinai in Arabia; she corresponds to the present Jerusalem, for she is in slavery with her children. But the Jerusalem above is free, and she is our mother" (4:24–26).

Paul goes with his interpretation by explaining that Sarah and Hagar are symbols of two different covenants—Hagar is an emblem of the law and works, while Sarah is a picture of grace and faith. Notice that Paul pairs Hagar with Mt. Sinai, the place where Moses received the law from God. Then he associates the law with the city of Jerusalem where the practicing Jews still believed that keeping the law made them right with God. Paul is trying to get across that the way of Hagar is like that of the legalists who also operate in the flesh and are in bondage to the law.

---

1. MacArthur, *Galatians*, 124.

Free at Last

The text makes it clear that Hagar was a slave (4:22, 24), so her son Ishmael was also a slave. Ishmael's birth was contrived by human works and scheming. Paul's allegory is trying to show the Galatians that since Hagar's offspring was a slave boy then in a similar way, when you choose the way of Hagar, or living by human effort under the law, you are choosing bondage.

On the other hand, Sarah was free (4:22). Sarah's son Isaac was a product of faith in God and he was born free. Sarah had nothing to do with the conception of Isaac because he was a miracle from God. Paul connects Sarah with "Jerusalem above" which is a term for God's Heavenly Kingdom. Paul is arguing that when you operate in faith, the natural result is freedom, just as Sarah produced a free son when she finally believed God. Moreover, living by faith is the way of heaven, unlike earthly Jerusalem which is governed by rules and regulations.

Hagar	Sarah
Slave woman with a slave son	Free woman with a free son
Ishmael, conceived through the flesh	Isaac, conceived by faith
Represents works of the law	Represents grace
Legalism	Liberty
The way of Mt. Sinai (Earth)	The way of Mt. Zion (Heaven)

Paul is confronting the Galatians to choose liberty or legalism, works or faith, law or grace, heaven or earth—because they cannot have both. All of humanity is either going the way of Hagar or Sarah. Likewise, everyone is either a son or a slave—Ishmael or Isaac. Hagar and Ishmael stand for all those who want to help God out by doing good works to earn salvation. Sarah and Isaac stand for all those who believe God's promise and are saved by faith alone. Picture Abraham as the father of two vast streams of humanity. What started as a purely personal family problem comes to signify the

A Tale of Two Sons (4:21–31)

great division of humanity into two groups—those who trust in God alone for salvation and those who trust in their works to help them earn salvation. All the religious systems of the world boil down to just two systems. They are either riding the escalator or trying to climb it by sheer effort.

The Applications (4:28–31)

Like any good teacher, Paul doesn't just wax eloquent about abstract spiritual principles and leave his audience scratching their heads thinking, "Okay, so what?" He always has his feet planted firmly on planet earth. So he ends this most interesting Old Testament illustration with a few significant practical applications.

Paul's first application is that *believers are children of promise*. "Now you, brothers, like Isaac, are children of promise" (4:28). Paul applies the truth of Isaac's physical birth to our spiritual birth. Isaac was supernaturally conceived and in a similar way, so too believers are born-again by a miracle of God. Abraham and Sarah could do nothing to produce the birth of their son except believe God and let Him do the impossible. Similarly, mankind can do nothing to produce his spiritual birth except place faith in Christ and allow the Holy Spirit to birth in him a new nature (John 3:3). Isaac's birth was done apart from human effort on the principle of faith, just like our spiritual birth is by grace through faith (Eph. 2:8).

The next application is not so cozy for Paul points out that *believers are candidates for persecution*. "But just as at that time he who was born according to the flesh persecuted him who was born according to the Spirit, so also it is now" (4:29). Paul makes a connection between the persecution that Isaac endured as the favored son of promise and the ridicule that true believers will receive from those outside the faith. Ishmael hated Isaac and mocked him. In the same way, the Judaizers would revile the Galatians who did not practice the legalism they did. David Jeremiah makes an insightful comment on this verse:

> Paul had once been involved on the giving end of that persecution as the leading persecutor of the early church. But when Paul became a follower of Christ, he himself became the object of persecution at the hands of his former colleagues. His bitterest enemies were the Jewish legalists of whom he was a celebrated leader. They now chased him down, spread lies about him, and stirred up the people

against him. They would have put him to death on more than one occasion if God had not intervened to protect and deliver him.[2]

In *The Calling*, Brother Andrew writes of his efforts to get the Gospel into communist China in spite of intense opposition. Through a clandestine operation, Andrew and his comrades were planning to smuggle one million Bibles into China. Wanting to be sure that the Chinese Christians he was working with understood the immensity of the task at hand and were willing to accept the incredible risk, Andrew sent Joseph, a close friend and Chinese team member, to meet with five key house church leaders.

Joseph asked them, "Do you know how much space one million Bibles takes up?" They all replied, "We have already prepared storage places." "Do you know what would happen to you," Joseph continued, "if you were caught with even a portion of the Bibles?" One of the Chinese pastors stepped forward and said, "Joseph, all five of us have been in prison for the Lord. All together we've spent seventy-two years in jail for Jesus. We are willing to die if it means that a million brothers and sisters can have a copy of God's Word." With tears in his eyes, Joseph folded up his long list of questions and put it away.[3]

Whether it's risking our life or our reputation, serving the Gospel requires courage. God never promised that His work would be safe. Jesus said, "A servant is not greater than his master. If they persecuted Me, they will also persecute you." (John 15:20). If you are living a godly life, then you will be persecuted in some way, shape, or form. But persecution can actually help you grow stronger spiritually. Persecution reminds us that we are children of God. "Indeed, all who desire to live a godly life in Christ Jesus will be persecuted" (2 Tim. 3:12). Persecution also causes us to cling more tightly to Jesus and remember that this world is not our home (Matt. 5:11–12).

Lastly, Paul wants us to dig in our heels and remember that *believers are not to compromise the principle of grace.* "But what does the Scripture say? 'Cast out the slave woman and her son, for the son of the slave woman shall not inherit with the son of the free woman.'" (4:30). Paul is quoting from Genesis 21:10. When Sarah saw Ishmael mocking Isaac, she demanded that Abraham cast Hagar and Ishmael out of the family because there was no way all of them could co-exist under the same tent.

Paul is telling the Galatians that bringing the works of law back into their lives is like Abraham bringing Hagar and Ishmael back into the tent.

2. Jeremiah, *Claiming Faith, Finding Freedom*, vol. 2, 33.
3. Brother Andrew, *The Calling*.

A Tale of Two Sons (4:21–31)

You cannot mix law and grace any more than Hagar and Ishmael could live peaceably with Sarah and Isaac. Paul laid it out in simple terms that they were not to tolerate the teaching of the Judaizers; they were to put them out of the church. They were to give no room for such false teaching.

Moreover, Paul argues that all believers need to realize that they are called to freedom, "So, brothers, we are not children of the slave but of the free woman" (4:31). The Judaizers were trying to reconcile the incompatible systems of law and grace, yet the two cannot be made to co-exist anymore than oil and water. The law panders to the flesh and prides itself on human performance. Grace, on the other hand, denies that man can ever do anything to merit God's favor. Wiersbe writes, "We must keep in mind that legalism does not mean the setting of spiritual standards; it means worshipping these standards thinking that we are spiritual because we obey them. It also means judging other believers on the basis of those standards ... The old nature loves legalism because it gives the flesh a chance to look good."[4]

There is an old story of an aspiring artist who was commissioned to do a large sculpture for a famous museum. At last, he had the opportunity to create the masterpiece that he had always dreamed about. After chiseling away at it for years and polishing the figure into life-like realism, the project was finally finished. However, when he completed his masterpiece, he discovered to his horror that the sculpture was much too large to be taken out through a door or a window. The only way to get the statue out of the artist's studio was to destroy the walls of the building which kept it, and that was not possible. Tragically, the masterpiece that the artist created was forever captive to the room in which it was created.

This is also the fate of all human attempts at salvation. Nothing a person does to earn God's favor can ever leave this Earth where man's masterpieces of good works were created. Thus, a line in the sand must be drawn. The whole of humanity is divided by which side of the Cross they are on. The Ishmaels of this world trust in themselves. The Isaacs of this world trust in God alone for salvation. The Hagars of the world look to the flesh while the Sarahs of the world trust God in faith. One path leads to Sinai and bondage. The other forks off and leads to Zion and freedom. So when we distill all the hundreds of religions and cults of the world down to their basics, we find out there are only two religions to speak of—the religion of human achievement and the religion of divine accomplishment. Which one are you trusting in?

---

4. Wiersbe, *The Wiersbe Bible Commentary: New Testament*, 569.

CHAPTER 12

Standing Firm in Liberty (5:1–6)

BORN A SLAVE ON a Virginia farm, Booker T. Washington (1856–1915) rose to become one of the most influential African-American intellectuals of the late 19th century. In 1881, he founded the Tuskegee Institute, a black school in Alabama devoted to training teachers. Washington also served as an adviser to Presidents Theodore Roosevelt and William Howard Taft. In his autobiography, *Up from Slavery*, he tells an interesting story about when the news of emancipation reached his plantation.

Every morning of his young life, Washington and all of the other plantation slaves were awakened by the crow of a rooster. Long before daybreak, the unwelcome noise would fill the sod shanties, reminding Washington and his fellow workers to crawl out of bed and leave for the cotton fields. The rooster's crow came to symbolize their dedicated life of long days and backbreaking labor.

But then came the Emancipation Proclamation. Abraham Lincoln pronounced freedom for all slaves. The first morning afterward, young Booker was awakened by the rooster again. Only this time his mother was chasing it around the barnyard with an ax. The Washington family fried and ate their alarm clock for lunch. Their first act of freedom was to silence the reminder of slavery.[1]

Are there any roosters stealing your sleep? The message of Galatians is that freedom has been declared and it's time to cut ties with the traditions, rules, and religions of our past life. For five chapters Paul has been swinging his ax at legalism, cutting down anything that might threaten the gospel of grace. Chapter five marks the beginning of a new section in the letter. The first section (1–2) was personal, the second section was doctrinal (3–4),

---

1. Miller, *Into the Depths of God*, 135.

Standing Firm in Liberty (5:1–6)

and in the last two chapters Paul is going to get practical. Paul's focus now turns to explain what a grace-based Christian life looks like.

A Declaration of Liberty (5:1)

"For freedom Christ has set us free; stand firm therefore, and do not submit again to a yoke of slavery." This verse is perhaps the cornerstone of Galatians. Paul uses one of his favorite expressions, "stand firm," which is found throughout several of his other letters (1 Cor. 15:1, 16:13; Eph. 6:11; 2 Thess. 2:15). It's important to notice how the Bible uses different word pictures to describe the posture we are to take depending on the situation. For example, we are to "flee temptation" (2 Tim. 2:22), "resist the Devil" (James 4:7), "walk in the light" (1 John 1:7), and when it comes to grace, we are to stand with our feet firmly planted. In other words, Paul is saying, "Dig in your heels and defend your freedom because there are spiritual marauders who are trying to take it from you." John Phillips writes:

> Paul's great rallying cry would bring to mind the Roman way of waging war. When faced by wild, undisciplined enemy hoards, the Romans simply locked their shields together, planted their feet firmly in the ground, and presented to the charging enemy an iron wall of steel and resolution. This is the kind of stand we must take against error.[2]

When I was a kid learning how to play basketball, I had a coach who taught us the "triple-threat position." I can still hear his voice echoing through the gymnasium, "You can't be an athlete and have your legs stiff as a board. You've got to get low." The triple-threat position was achieved by spreading your feet shoulder-length apart, then bending at the knees in a half crouching position, like you were sitting in an invisible chair. This was the primary stance for playing defense—sliding the feet to stay with an opponent. It was also the mode of attack on offense. From the triple-threat position you could dribble, pass, or shoot. Whatever the game situation called for, you were ready to move when you got the ball.

This is the kind of readiness that Paul was exhorting the Galatians to take in the defense of their liberty. If believers do not to take a firm stand on the grace principle, then they can easily revert to legalism. It is not enough to float along just singing "Amazing Grace." Christians must persist in their

---

2. Phillips, *Exploring Galatians*, 143.

understanding and application of grace. It takes attentiveness to sustain our freedom in Christ or else legalism will creep back into our Christian lives if we are not on our toes spiritually.

Not only is there a military picture in this verse, but there is also an agricultural picture. Notice that Paul writes, "and do not submit again to a yoke of slavery." A yoke was a harness that farmers placed upon the shoulders of beasts of burden to control them as they plowed a field. Under a yoke, the only option is to submit to the will of the master. The yoke of works is a terribly oppressive taskmaster. It seeks to govern every aspect of life from what you wear, to what you eat, to what you see and where you go. It seems that humanity's default position is to try to work for our salvation, expecting a ticket into heaven for having our good outweigh our bad.

Jesus said in Matt. 11:28–30, "Come to me all who labor and are heavy laden and I will give you rest. Take my yoke upon you and learn from me, for I am gentle and lowly in heart, and you will find rest for your souls. For my yoke is easy and my burden is light." In context, Jesus was talking to people who were tired of trying to keep the oppressive religion of the Pharisees. Christ wants us to be yoked to Him—not rules and moral systems we've invented. When we are joined to Christ, we find that His precepts are freeing. His grace is not a license to do whatever we want but the power to become what we ought.

I have always been fascinated by slave stories and the extent to which many of the slaves in the American south went in order to escape their plantations. For example, Henry "Box" Brown was a 19th century Virginia slave who perhaps devised the most ingenious method ever of escaping the bonds of servitude. He shipped himself to Philadelphia in a wooden crate.

Brown was born in 1815 in Louisa County, Virginia. In 1830, Brown found himself working in a Virginia tobacco factory in which whippings, beatings, and hangings became everyday occurrences. With the help of several abolitionist friends, Brown concocted a plan to ship himself in a box, three feet long and two feet wide, to Philadelphia where an abolitionist by the name of James McKim had agreed to receive the box. The box, labeled "dry goods," was lined with cloth and had a single hole cut in the top for air. The first leg of Henry's journey began by wagon on March 23, 1849. The total trip took twenty-seven hours and He was transferred numerous times between railroad, steamboat, wagon, and ferry. When the box arrived at the headquarters of the Philadelphia Anti-Slavery Society, Brown emerged from the box and recited a psalm.

Standing Firm in Liberty (5:1-6)

There was a man who was not willing to submit to the yoke of slavery! Freedom is one of the most expensive commodities in the world and when you don't have it, you'll do almost anything to obtain it. Every human being who can fog up a mirror longs for freedom. Yet those who have it often forget its true value. Freedom isn't cheap. Paradoxically, salvation is infinitely costly but absolutely free. Have we become so familiar with the Gospel that we fail to appreciate what our salvation cost the Savior? We can value His sacrifice by standing firm in our freedom and not devaluing the Cross with human works.

The Dangers of Legalism (5:2-6)

Paul moves on to explain the disastrous consequences of choosing to go back to the law. He uses circumcision as an example because that was the particular issue troubling the Galatians. When believers try to seek God's favor through works and performance, we forfeit several benefits that Jesus offers us through His grace. Paul outlines a few of these losses.

First, we see that *legalism deprives us of Christ's sacrifice*. "Look: I, Paul, say to you that if you accept circumcision, Christ will be of no advantage to you" (5:2). The pressing issue in Paul's day was whether it was necessary for Christians to adopt the Mosaic Law in order to be truly saved. The Judaizers taught that Christians had to first become Jews; this meant that the Gentile men had to be circumcised. By going through this outward ritual, this changed the basis of salvation from grace to works. Thankfully, circumcision is not an issue like it was in the first century, but we have replaced that tradition with other grace-killers.

I heard a story about a wealthy religious man who employed a gardener who was a true believer in Christ. The gardener tried to convince the wealthy man that adding good works could not improve man's standing with God, but he would not listen. One day the gardener had a brilliant idea. He knew of an apple tree on the man's estate that never bore any fruit. On a bright, sunny morning near harvest time the rich man was walking through the orchard and was utterly surprised to see this barren tree finally bearing fruit. However, when the owner went to examine the tree he noticed that the gardener had tied each piece of fruit on to the branches with string. The gardener left a note on the trunk, "Religion without Christ is like a dead tree on which fruit is merely tied on."

Works cannot make us alive to God. Paul reminds us that if you make salvation conditional, then that implicitly means that Christ's sacrifice wasn't enough. Trying to add works to grace is an affront to the Cross and an insult to Christ. The sacrifice of Jesus was perfect and complete, but it is of no value to a person who trusts in something else to save him besides the blood of Christ.

The second danger is that *legalism makes us debtors to the law.* "I testify again to every man who accepts circumcision that he is obligated to keep the whole law" (5:3). The law is not a cafeteria line where you can say, "I'd like a helping of circumcision, but I don't want any sacrifices. I'm going to hold off on the feast days, but I'll take an extra helping of the dietary restrictions." Paul says, "The law doesn't work that way." The law is an all-or-nothing proposition. Remember what James said, "For whoever keeps the whole law but fails in one point has become accountable for all of it. For he who said, 'Do not commit adultery,' also said, 'Do not murder.' If you do not commit adultery but do murder, you have become a transgressor of the law" (2:10–11). In other words, if a person were to perfectly keep the totality of the law in thought, word, and deed for his whole life and then break only one command in his final breath, then he would forfeit salvation. Wiersbe writes:

> Imagine a motorist driving down a city street and deliberately driving through a red light. He is pulled over by a policeman who asks to see his driver's license. Immediately, the driver begins to defend himself. "Officer, I know that I ran that red light—but I have never robbed anybody. I've never killed anybody. I've never cheated on my income tax. The policeman smiles as he writes the ticket, because he knows that no amount of obedience can make up for one act of disobedience. It is one law and the same law that protects the obedient man and punishes the offender. To boast about keeping part of the law while at the same time breaking another part is to confess that I am worthy of punishment.[3]

Third, *legalism divorces us from grace.* "You are severed from Christ, you who would be justified by the law; you have fallen away from grace" (5:4). Paul warns that believers who choose the way of legalism also negate the gift of grace. I don't think Paul was suggesting that the Galatians could lose their salvation, but what he meant was that they had robbed themselves of all the good things Jesus could do for them. A person who is trying to work for God's favor cannot ever experience grace because grace

---

3 Wiersbe, *The Wiersbe Bible Commentary: New Testament*, 571–572.

Standing Firm in Liberty (5:1–6)

is not merited, earned, or achieved. Moreover, they could never expect to experience true Christian growth if they decided to estrange themselves from Christ.

Some time ago, I was watching a TV show about dumb criminals and the ridiculous things they do to get caught red-handed. They had one man on the program who robbed a convenient store and made off with a little over $100 from the cash register. When the police finally caught up with him, they discovered that the handgun he used to rob the store was a very rare Smith and Wesson pistol that was worth $10,000. The criminal was holding a fortune in his hand and didn't know it! He lost it all because he was truly ignorant of the treasure he already possessed.

Those who choose legalism over grace have forfeited the riches that they have in Christ for the poverty of legalism. Martin Luther gave an interesting illustration of this verse. He imagined that all believers are aboard the "ship of grace," bound for heaven. However, rather than relying on grace to get them to their final destination, the legalist jumps overboard and decides he will tread water, splash in the waves, and find his own way.[4] If you spurn the grace of God for that which cannot save you, then you have bolted from the sphere of God's grace to flounder in a sea of works.

Another danger is that *legalism deadens the work of the Spirit.* "For through the Spirit, by faith, we ourselves eagerly wait for the hope of righteousness. For in Christ Jesus neither circumcision nor uncircumcision counts for anything, but only faith working through love" (5:5–6). Legalism tries to achieve sanctification by working hard at doing the "right" things. The legalist relies on rituals, outward practices, and self-righteousness to make himself more pleasing to God. This reduces life to a series of checklists. So if you do the right things and follow the prescribed behaviors, then it gives you the false assurance that you have done something to move one rung higher on the ladder towards God. However, there is a glaring problem with this way of life. How much is enough? The legalist never knows if he has met the gold standard. When does one finally arrive at "holiness"?

In one of his books, Philip Yancey writes about the extremism of one monk that never knew when to draw the line in his pursuit of holiness. High on a mountainous spur in northern Syria Simeon Stylites stood, squatted, sometimes sat, and occasionally lay. He was there for over forty years during the fifth century. He attracted so many admirers in the first few years that he felt obliged to seek refuge on a pillar which grew, as the

---

4. George, *The New American Commentary: New Testament*, 359.

years went by, to reach forty-five feet. He lived at that final height for thirty-five years. He even prostrated himself before God 1,224 times a day. While this is an extraordinary example of legalism and asceticism gone wrong, you understand that this man's ultimate motivation for living on top of a column came from a performance standard which said, "I can be holy by doing more drastic things."[5]

Only the indwelling presence of the Holy Spirit can produce the character of Christ. Each day the working of the Holy Spirit changes our nature to be less like ourselves and more like Christ. It's an incremental transformation that won't be achieved until the day we see Christ face-to-face. When Paul writes that we are "waiting for the hope of righteousness," he is referring to the future coming of Christ in which believers will be ultimately freed from the presence of sin and given a glorified body (Rom. 8:32; Phil. 3:20–21; 1 John 3:2). Grace-oriented believers look for perfection in heaven and not on earth; not in time, but in eternity.

Paul also notes that the in the Spirit-filled life, the motivation for good works is totally different than that of legalism. The little phrase, "faith working through love," means that those who have been filled with the Spirit will be actively displaying their faith in Christ through acts of charity—not because they "have to," but because they "want to." The motivation for works in legalism is tied to a sense of duty and fear, but under the direction of the Spirit the motivation is out of love for God and others. Even though we are not saved by good works, we are saved to do good works (James 2:18). Thus, the difference between legalism and Christian liberty is relationship. In legalism, the works are done from a set of unforgiving obligations. But, in liberty, works are done because there is a relationship with a loving God.

How else could you explain the behavior of a man like Henri Nouwen except that he had been radically shaped by grace and the Spirit of God? Nouwen was a professor at Harvard University who struggled with whether he was in the right place of his calling. On a trip to St. Petersburg, Russia, he visited the Hermitage Museum in order to see a particular painting—Rembrandt's portrayal of the prodigal son. In that painting, Rembrandt captures the moment when the son is returning home and the father is rushing out to meet him.

Nouwen studied the painting, not for ten minutes, or even for an hour. He sat before the painting for several hours. He poured over every stroke of color, every wrinkle on the father's skin, every hint of unmitigated delight

---

5. Yancey, *What's So Amazing About Grace*, 199.

Standing Firm in Liberty (5:1-6)

at the sight of his son, every mark on the son's downtrodden but hopeful face, and every ray of sunlight in the painting which appeared as real as if it beamed through the canvas. After uninterrupted concentration, he got up as a changed man. The gospel of grace had broken through to him. He returned home, resigned his position at Harvard, and until his sudden and seemingly untimely death, worked at a home for the mentally retarded in Toronto, Canada. This great writer and intellectual devoted his life to loving those who were in such special need.[6]

The best that legalism can produce is a Simon Stylites balancing on a pillar like a circus clown. Meanwhile, "faith working through love" can result in a Henri Nouwen, a Katie Davis, a Steve Saint, or a George Mueller giving themselves sacrificially in response to the grace they experienced. Under the law, the boundaries are clearly defined—don't do this, don't eat that, read only this, don't wear that. There is no risk involved. Just blindly follow the rules like a mindless robot. Can anything be more lifeless, predictable, or boring?

The alternative is grace which involves an element of adventure. When you're trusting in God and following the lead of the Spirit, there is no telling where you might end up. In the end, living by grace is a much more rewarding proposition because it allows the freedom to grow and mature. When grace is experienced, it fosters faith which is then displayed by acts of love. Those who've experienced amazing grace are eager to do good. When they perform deeds of charity, faith is nurtured and the cycle repeats. Such is the genius of grace. Grace not only frees us, but it gives us the desire to use our freedom for others.

---

6. Zacharias, *Recapture the Wonder*, 154.

CHAPTER 13

Facing Off Against False Teachers (5:7–12)

IN THE MOVIE *The Hurt Locker* the audience gets a dramatic and intense glimpse into the lives of three men who are part of an exclusive team of bomb specialists during the Iraq war, also known as an Explosive Ordnance Disposal unit. The job of this team is to locate and diffuse landmines, bombs, and other IEDs planted by terrorists who are fighting against American forces. Watching the film, you understand that for the guys strapping on their bulky protective suits, every day on the front lines is a life or death proposition. One wrong step, a slip of the fingers, a lapse in judgment, or cutting the wrong wire can lead to instant death and a big crater in the ground. In order to successfully diffuse a bomb, they need courage, a steady hand, and an intuitive mechanical knowledge of the explosive device. It doesn't hurt to be a little crazy and an adrenaline junkie too.

During one memorable scene, Sargent William James is called in to handle a bomb threat in a residential area. As he approaches the detonation site, James unearths what appears to be just a single bomb. However, as he dusts off the rubble he notices a wire running from the explosive device. As he pulls the wire upward, James discovers to his horror that the wire happens to be connected to half a dozen other bombs buried under the sand. He is now surrounded by bombs, a situation which would make even the most highly-trained specialist become paralyzed with panic. Undaunted, James goes to work with steely, cool resolve as he tries to find a kill switch or lynchpin to diffuse the homemade rig.

I won't spoil the movie for those who haven't seen it, but I mention that scene as an illustration of where Paul was in the midst of the Galatian controversy. The church he started had been infiltrated by false teachers who undermined his teaching by planting several theological landmines. Some of the Galatians had become casualties while others were venturing

Facing Off Against False Teachers (5:7-12)

into no man's land. Paul was there trying to prevent the whole thing from blowing up. As the faithful pastor started poking around, he uncovered more grace-killing lies than he originally thought were there. Once he diffused the lie which said, "Grace isn't enough," he found another which said, "In order to be a Christian, you must be circumcised," and still another said that "Works make you more acceptable to God."

The situation was a tenuous one. But the experienced apostle put his finger on the main problem and devised a solution. The Galatians needed to grow up in the grace of Christ and oust the false teachers from the Church with the weekly garbage. It would be like diffusing a time bomb by cutting off its power source. With the Judaizers gone, the lies would stop and the Church could move forward. In this passage, we will see Paul come out with some strong language against the false teachers who were destroying the Church and standing as rivals to liberty. False teachers plagued the church in Paul's day and according to the Scriptures they will continue to multiply as we move closer to the end times (Matt. 24:5, 1 Tim. 4:1-2, 2 Peter 2:1, 1 John 2:18-19). Paul outlines several characteristics of false teachers that can be applied universally to the Church any time the truth is being eroded by lies.

False Teachers Capture Weaker Believers (5:7-8)

"You were running well. Who hindered you from obeying the truth? This persuasion is not from Him who calls you." Ever watch the Discovery Channel or any of the nature programs where they show the cheetahs hunting on the African plains? Which gazelle is the one that always gets picked off? It's the straggler at the back of the pack. It's the one with a gimp leg or the fawn that is separated from its mother. Predators usually go for the easiest kill. It works that way in the spiritual realm as well. The Judaizers swooped in and preyed on susceptible new converts in Galatia that weren't mature enough to discern between truth and falsehood.

Paul must have been a sports fan because he commonly used pictures from the athletic field. His readers would have been familiar with the Olympic Games which featured sprints, so he compares the Christian life to a footrace in 5:7. The Galatians had started off so promising, but somewhere along the way false teachers got them off track. These young Christians were going to be disqualified if they didn't get back on course. The danger of false teachers is that they kidnap good-hearted, growing believers, indoctrinate them, and then we never see them darken the door of a doctrinally sound church again. This is why we must be in the Word, continually feeding ourselves on the truth so that we can differentiate fact from fiction. When you know the truth, you can lovingly tell false teachers, "Get lost!"

Several years ago I got a phone call from a friend of mine that I watched grow up in the faith. He attended Bible College for a few semesters and even taught some Sunday school classes. It looked like he was off to a promising start. He was on fire for God and had a genuine zeal for soul-winning. But something happened along the way. He called to inform me of the new church he and his wife had recently joined. When he said the name of the church, I shook my head because I knew it wasn't good. "Hope you like wearing shackles," I thought to myself.

He proceeded to tell me how the church was so wonderful. After criticizing other churches in the area for being "too liberal," he began to extol this new church as having a corner-market on the truth. The preacher didn't allow the women to wear pants. He described it as "old-fashioned" preaching that focused mostly on sin, hell, and judgment. The choir sang from a particular hymn book with the songs he liked. Finally, he tried to convince me that the translation of the Bible that I studied from was inferior. He said I needed to re-evaluate my methods or I would be headed down a slippery slope.

Sadly, my friend had gotten entrapped in a very legalistic church and like Paul warning these Galatians, I could see him veering off course. My friend was still a young Christian and his convictions hadn't yet solidified. He was easy prey for a spiritual huckster. False teaching and legalism can put you on a "detour" from which you never return. In reality, it goes both ways. Legalism and liberalism can pull believers from opposite directions into error. Truth without love is legalism and love without truth is liberalism, but biblical Christianity is a balance of truth and love.

False Teachers Contaminate the Church (5:9)

"A little leaven leavens the whole lump." Paul uses another metaphor, this time from the kitchen. In the Old Testament, yeast or leaven is generally a picture of sin. Leaven is a perfect illustration for sin, because if sin is left alone it will slowly grow and grow until it permeates completely, just like a small amount of yeast causes a batch of dough to ferment and swell. Paul

Facing Off Against False Teachers (5:7–12)

is trying to get the Galatians to take the false teachers seriously because all it takes is one little seed of a lie mixed with the truth to contaminate the purity of the church.

William Hordern tells a story that illustrates how a single comma can change the entire meaning of a message. Back in the days when messages were sent by telegraph, there was a code for each punctuation mark. A wealthy woman touring Europe cabled her husband to ask whether she could buy a beautiful bracelet for $75,000. The husband relayed the message back, "No, price too high." The cable operator, in transmitting the message, missed the signal for the comma. The woman received the message which read, "No price too high." She bought the bracelet and the husband sued the telegraph company. After that the users of Morse code spelled out punctuation. One "small" error can be costly.[1]

Ben Franklin put it like this, "For want of a nail the shoe was lost. For want of a shoe the horse was lost. For want of a horse the rider was lost, and for want of the rider the battle was lost." Minor issues can become major problems. This is why we cannot compromise on the truth of the Gospel. The doctrines of the Bible stand or fall as a line of dominoes. Compromise on one and the others will be sure to topple as well.

False Teachers Face a Certain Condemnation (5:10)

In case you think the con artists in the Church are getting away with it, think again. Paul tells us, "I have confidence in the Lord that you will take no other view, and the one who is troubling you will bear the penalty, whoever he is." The Bible reserves some the strongest language of judgment for false teachers. The reason is because those in leadership have a greater level of influence. James 3:1 is a warning to all those who aspire to be teachers or preachers, "Not many of you should become teachers, my brothers, for you know that we who teach will be judged with greater strictness." With greater influence there is greater responsibility and the greater potential to lead many astray. False teachers will be judged by the content of the message and the motivation of their heart. Every idle word spoken can be and will be evaluated at Jesus' final job performance review (Matt. 12:36–37).

Some of you may remember what happened to Jim Bakker, who sat atop the world of televangelism during the 1980s. Bakkar hosted the weekly health and wealth preaching hour, PTL, which later became known as "Pass

---

1. Hordern, *A Layman's Guide to Protestant Theology*, 15–16.

the Loot" after a sex and money scandal brought Bakkar down. It was also discovered that PTL was merely a front for defrauding thousands of gullible people out of millions of dollars. Bakkar was convicted and given forty-five years in prison. His wife, Tammy Faye, divorced him. He went from being a millionaire to making eleven cents an hour scrubbing toilets in a North Carolina prison. However, Bakkar revealed in his tell-all confession, *I Was Wrong*, that while in prison he realized that he was not truly born again and that the Holy Spirit revealed to him the error of his name-it-and-claim-it Gospel. After his salvation he later wrote in bitter repentance:

> I had influenced so many people to accept a 'prosperity message,' now I felt that I had a responsibility to tell my friends what I had been learning from my studies of the Bible. I wrote a simple, straightforward letter and sent it to some of the people who had written me in prison. In the letter, I told of the verses I had used improperly and what I had discovered by studying the true meaning of those verses. I apologized for preaching a gospel that emphasized earthly prosperity rather than spiritual riches. I wrote, 'I ask all who have sat under my ministry to forgive me for preaching a gospel emphasizing earthly prosperity. Jesus said, 'Do not lay up for yourselves treasure on earth.' He wants us to be in love only with Him.'[2]

Whether on earth or in eternity, God will bring false teachers into judgment. While we should never tolerate false doctrine, I think our hearts should pity those who deliberately misconstrue the Word of God for personal gain. One day they will have to stand before Jesus and give an account for their deception. Can there by anything more fearful than standing before the Lord with no excuses and nowhere to hide (Heb. 10:31)?

False Teachers Criticize Teachers of Grace (5:11–12)

"But if I, brothers, still preach circumcision, why am I still being persecuted? In that case the offense of the cross has been removed" (5:11). Paul was being hotly criticized for preaching the cross of Christ. If he wanted to preach an easy message which pandered to the flesh, he could have diluted the Gospel and added works. But because he endured persecution, Paul proved that he did not add anything to the message of grace. The reason why Paul suffered for his message is because the Gospel is a tremendous

---

2. Baaker, *I Was Wrong*, 540–541.

Facing Off Against False Teachers (5:7–12)

insult to man's ego. The Cross says you cannot do anything to save yourself and you bring nothing to table to offer God (except your sins). In 1 Cor. 1:23, Paul says that the cross of Christ is "a stumbling block to the Jew and folly to the Gentiles." The Gospel is a scandalous message because it utterly exposes man in all his depravity, sin, and helplessness. John Stott adds:

> Persecution is a mark of every true Christian preacher. Down the centuries of the Christian church . . . Christian preachers who refuse to distort or dilute the Gospel of grace have had to suffer for their faithfulness. The Gospel is grievously offensive to the pride of men. It tells them that they are sinners, rebels, under the wrath and condemnation of God, they can do nothing to save themselves or secure their salvation, and that only through Christ crucified can they be saved. If we preach this Gospel, we shall arouse ridicule and opposition."[3]

The fires of persecution haven't cooled since the days of Paul. Take, for example, the amazing story of Umar Mulinde, a former Muslim who converted to Christianity. Umar was raised as a radical Shiite Muslim and was taught to hate all Jews and Christians. Then one night Umar's sleep was disturbed by a haunting dream. Umar described his dream like this:

> I was in the midst of a fire crying, and I saw the people who were with me in this fire were the fellow Muslims from my mosque. But as I was crying at the climax of the scene, somebody shining on the right side told me that Islam is leading you to this torture. Repent, be born again, you shall survive.

At first Umar ignored the dream, and prayed to Allah that he would get rid of the nightmares. But Umar experienced the same dream again. After the second time Christ appeared, Umar said he went to the closest Christian church he could find where the Gospel was explained to him and he gave his life to Christ. However, leaving Islam led to some major life-threatening problems for Umar. On Christmas Eve 2011, two Muslims attacked him with acid. The horrific assault ate away at some of his skin and led to the loss of an eye and an ear. Umar now has to wear a special mask to hide his disfigurement. However, despite his unexpected suffering, Umar didn't quit serving Christ. After answering the Lord's call into ministry, Umar started a church in Uganda and became a pastor.[4]

---

3. Stott, *The Message of Galatians*, 137.
4. "Muslim Extremists Throw Acid on Church Leader," *Voice of the Martyr's*.

Free at Last

Few Westerners understand this kind of opposition, but there are courageous brothers and sisters around the world who don't mind taking a beating for Jesus' sake. Make no mistake about it—standing up for Jesus doesn't give you a free pass from hardship. In many ways it paints a red bulls-eye on your back. What we should remember is that the broken bones actually result in more positives than negatives. Persecution fuels the growth of our faith (1 Peter 4:12–19), brings us into a more intimate fellowship with Christ (Phil. 3:10), displays the authenticity of the Gospel (Phil. 1:12–14), turns enemies into friends (Rom. 12:20–21), and prepares for us a great reward in heaven (Matt. 5:11–12).

Paul's words in 5:12 are some of the most pungent in all of his writings. "I wish those who unsettle you would emasculate themselves!" Ouch! Can you imagine the shockwave that coursed through the congregation in Galatia when they first gathered to read Paul's letter and they came to this verse? In no uncertain terms Paul is telling the Judaizers to go all the way with their legalistic traditions and castrate themselves. You can practically feel the scorn and sarcasm dripping off Paul's pen. When it came to defending his converts from cultists, Paul was as vicious as a mother bear protecting her cubs. I like the way John MacArthur clarifies Paul's harsh rebuke:

> Paul was so passionately opposed to the heresy of the Judaizers that he wished they would even mutilate themselves . . . Paul was not expressing a crude and cruel desire for the Judaizer's punishment. God would take care of that (5:10) . . . His point was, "If the Judaizers are so insistent on circumcision as a means of pleasing God, why don't they go ahead and castrate themselves as a supreme act of religious devotion. If, like the pagans, they believe human achievement can earn divine favor, why don't they go to the pagan extremes of self-mutilation, like the Cybelene priests?"[5]

There is no doubt that the Galatians would have understood Paul's punchline. Galatia was just down the road from the city of Phrygia where there was a temple dedicated to the worship of the goddess Cybele. The priests in this temple showed their dedication to this fertility goddess by castrating themselves. Thus, the priests in this city were voluntary eunuchs. The approval from God that the legalists were attempting to achieve through their traditions was the same kind of self-salvation the pagans were trying to procure for themselves through pagan rituals. Both were man's attempt to climb the ladder of works into heaven and both are equally deceptive.

5. MacArthur, *Galatians*, 142.

Facing Off Against False Teachers (5:7–12)

A trip to the Holocaust Museum in Washington D.C. will leave you with images that you can never dislodge from your mind. I visited as a college student thinking that I was ready since I had been exposed to works like Elie Wiesel's *Night* and Steven Spielberg's *Schindler's List*. I was woefully unprepared for the visceral and emotional afternoon I spent watching films, reading stories, and examining artifacts of the worst humanity is capable of. My mouth dropped in shock as I looked up at a thirty-foot pile of gunnysacks made from human hair. I stood silent in railcars with scratch marks along the walls were prisoners tried to escape by clawing with their fingernails. The gaunt specters of men and women clothed in dirty uniforms that swallowed their emaciated figures were plastered everywhere. All of them were people with jobs, families, and lives that were violently ended.

In one section of the museum there was displayed a replica of the iron gate which guarded the entrance to Auschwitz. The twisted and rusty letters spelled out what seemed to be a cruel taunt to tall those that entered—"Arbeit Macht Frei." A placard explained the meaning of the German phrase, "Work Makes Free." I also learned that this phrase was used to adorn the entrances of other concentration camps like Dachau and Sachsenhausen. What made this sign so unusually tortuous was that it promised a false hope to all the prisoners. It was a lie that promised people a liberation that would only come through exhausting labor, suffering, and death. In other words, the people who entered those camps came to realize that no one was getting out alive and their only ticket to release was through work which ended in death.

I submit that story to you because I think that the phrase "Arbeit Macht Frei" is a lie that is smuggled into every one of the world's religions, except Christianity. There are so many who have entered into the iron gates of man-made religion under the assumption that their works will gain them freedom. There are millions of sincere practitioners from faiths near and far that think if their good deeds outweigh their bad deeds, they have earned a ticket into heaven. "Arbeit Macht Frei" is the hope of every false religion—good works equal spiritual freedom.

The Gospel stands in contradiction to that lie. It says that we have been given freedom by the death of another. We did nothing to aid in our emancipation. Christ paid the debt He did not owe for those who could not pay. So we are left with two irrevocable choices—a cross with three nails or prison bars with the inscription, "Arbeit Macht Frei."

CHAPTER 14

Risky Business (5:13–15)

IN THE MARINERS' MUSEUM in Newport News, Virginia, there's a special display for a rickety, home-made aluminum kayak. This tiny, makeshift boat seems oddly out of place in the midst of displays for impressive Navy vessels and artifacts from significant battles on the sea. But a bronze plaque tells museum visitors the story behind this kayak's heroic makers.

In 1966, an auto mechanic named Laureano and his wife Consuelo decided that they could no longer live under the oppression of Cuba's totalitarian regime. After spending months collecting scrap metal, they pieced together a boat just barely big enough for two small people. Then Laureano jury-rigged a small lawn mower engine on the back of the kayak.

After months of planning, on a moonless September night, sitting back to back and wearing only their swimming suits, they set out in the treacherous Straits of Florida. They had only enough water and food for a couple of days. Finally, after they had floated in open water for over 70 hours, the U.S. Coast Guard found and rescued the couple just south of Alligator Reef Light in the Florida Keys. Was it worth the risk to find freedom? Laureano thought so. Years later he said:

> When one has grown up in liberty, you realize it is important to have freedom. We lived in the enormous prison which is Cuba, where one's life is not worth one crumb. Where one goes out into the street and does not know whether or not one will return to one's home, because the political police can arrest you without any warning and put you in prison. Before this could happen to us, we thought that going into the ocean, and risking death or being eaten by sharks, is a million times better than to stay suffering under political oppression.[1]

---

1. From a plaque and display in the Mariners' Museum in Newport News, Virginia.

Risky Business (5:13-15)

When freedom is at stake, the potential benefits usually outweigh the risks. Thomas Jefferson once remarked, "I prefer dangerous freedom over peaceful slavery." Freedom is risky business. There are hazards involved. Just think back to when you first got your driver's license and dad (or mom) turned over the car keys to you. When you're behind the wheel with no chaperone for the first time, the possibilities seem endless. Finally, you could drive with the tunes you liked blaring into the stratosphere and no one would complain. You could have exceeded the speed limit, stayed out past your curfew, or driven to another state without your parents knowing. Maybe some of you guys borrowed your dad's truck and all you could think about was seeing if it could handle a mud hole or if it was faster than your buddy's sports car.

Do you remember the Christmas classic *Home Alone*? The film tells the story of how eight-year-old Kevin McCallister gets left at home by himself during the Christmas holiday. His family accidently forgets him at home as they rush to make a flight and they don't realize he's missing until they are halfway across the Atlantic bound for Paris. With free reign of the house and no adult supervision, Kevin goes crazy. He eats ice cream for breakfast, lunch, and dinner. He pillages his brother's secret stash of goodies that he was never allowed to touch. He stays up late watching gangster movies. He jumps on the bed and sleds down the stairs outside into the snow. Obviously, Kevin couldn't handle the freedom and many Christians can't either.

Living by grace is risky too. There are many pastors who wouldn't dare preach the fullness of God's grace because they are afraid of what it might do to their church people. They might get the wrong idea and use grace as a license to push the envelope and walk as close to edge of carnality as possible.

Long ago, Paul recognized the inescapable tension that Christian liberty created between the baser impulses of the flesh and higher calling of the Spirit. In fact, he warned the Galatians that freedom was risky business. The Gospel of grace that he preached granted believers freedom from the law, but it also opened the door to other pitfalls and grey areas. Living the grace-filled life is like balancing on a razor's edge between legalism and liberalism. Fall to either side and you commit error. John MacArthur likened legalism and liberalism to two parallel streams that run between heaven and earth:

> The stream of legalism is clear, sparkling, and pure, but its water run so deep and furiously that no one can enter it without being drowned or smashed on the rocks of its harsh demands. The

stream of liberalism, by contrast, is relatively quiet and still, and crossing it seems attractive. But its waters are so contaminated with poisons and pollutants that to try to cross it is also certain death. Both streams are uncrossable and deadly, one because of impossible moral and spiritual demands, the other because of moral and spiritual filth. But spanning those two deadly streams is the Gospel of Jesus Christ, the only safe passage from earth to heaven.[2]

The next verses help us understand how to keep this tension in check so that we don't go to one unhealthy extreme or the other.

Exploiting Liberty through License (5:13)

Paul begins by explaining the limits of Christian freedom. "For you were called to freedom, brothers. Only do not use your freedom as an opportunity for the flesh . . ." (5:13). Even though as liberated Christians we are free from the restrictions of the law, we are not free to do whatever we want. Grace does not give us a license to sin by suddenly removing God's moral guardrails. The word "opportunity" has an interesting context. It comes from a Greek word that is a military term which refers to a base of operations for an attack upon an enemy. This is a vivid picture and a clear warning—we should never use our freedom as a beachhead, springboard, or entry point to indulge the flesh.[3]

Paul addressed this same issue in Romans. After describing the great abundance of grace that has been shown to us in Christ, he asks the question, "What shall we say then? Are we to continue in sin that grace might increase?" (Rom. 6:1). In other words, since God has given us grace, can I not do more sinning to receive more grace? Will my indulgence in sin not simply open the floodgates of grace to pour forth upon me in greater measure? Paul's answer: "May it never be! How shall we who died to sin still live in it?" (Rom. 6:2).

The main problem with grace-abusers is that they view grace merely as hell insurance. The problem is you can "ask Jesus into your heart" without truly repenting. Praying "the sinner's prayer" is not like getting a one-time inoculation. Salvation does indeed happen in a moment, and I believe that once you are saved you are always saved. The mark, however, of someone who is saved is that they maintain their confession of faith until the end of

---

2. MacArthur, *Galatians*, 145.
3. Jeremiah, *Claiming Faith, Finding Freedom*, vol. 2, 63.

Risky Business (5:13-15)

their life. Salvation is not a prayer you pray in a one-time ceremony, but it's a posture of repentance, grace, and faith that you begin in a moment and maintain for the rest of your days. Grace is intended to produce radical lifestyle change because it is based on a sacred trust. In one of his books, Max Lucado brings this to light by telling a personal story:

> My father had a simple rule about credit cards: own as few of them as possible and pay them off as soon as possible. His salary as a mechanic was sufficient, but not abundant, and he hated the thought of paying interest. He made it a point to pay the balance in full at the end of each month. You can imagine my surprise when he put a credit card in my hand the day I left for college. Standing in the driveway with car packed and farewells said, he handed it to me. I looked at the name on the plastic; it wasn't mine, it was his. He had ordered an extra card for me. His only instructions to me were, "Be careful how you use it." Pretty risky, don't you think? As I was driving to college it occurred to me that I was a free man. I could go anywhere I wanted to go. I had wheels and a tank of gas. I had my clothes. I had money in my pocket and a stereo in my trunk, and most of all, I had a credit card. I was a slave set free! The chains were off. I could be in Mexico before nightfall! What was to keep me from going wild? . . . Grace fosters an eagerness for good. Grace doesn't spawn a desire to sin. If one has truly embraced God's gift, he will not mock it. In fact, if a person uses God's mercy as liberty to sin, one might wonder whether the person ever knew God's mercy at all. When my father gave me his card, he didn't attach a list of regulations. There was no contract for me to sign or rules for me to read. He didn't tell me to place my hand on the Bible and pledge to reimburse him for any expenses. In fact, he didn't ask for any payment at all. As things turned out, I went a few weeks into the semester without using it. Why? Because he gave me more than a card; he gave me his trust. And where I might break his rules, I wasn't about to abuse his trust. God's trust makes us eager to do right. Such is the genius of grace.[4]

Another problem with those who take advantage of grace is that they usually have a flawed understanding of freedom. The world defines freedom as "the liberty to do whatever you want without the fear of repercussions or consequences." How many times have you heard, "As long as I'm not hurting anyone, then it's okay?" However, freedom is not the absence of restraint; instead, it's finding the right restraints which enable us to reach

---

4. Lucado, *In the Grip of Grace*, 81–83.

our maximum potential. Christian freedom is not available so that we can do what we want but so that we can become what God wants us to be.

When I was in third-grade I noticed that I couldn't read what the teacher wrote on the blackboard anymore. A trip to the eye doctor revealed that I was nearsighted. At the age of ten I had come under the bondage of myopia. Still to this day, I am a slave to blurry vision and thus my freedom is restricted. However, the optometrist presented me with a solution called corrective lenses. If I wanted freedom from nearsightedness, I had to become a slave to wearing eyeglasses.

Were there risks involved? You bet. Other kids could call me names like "four eyes." I might not like having to be extra careful when playing sports. I could lose them, step on them, or sit on them, and that could get expensive. But the benefit of submitting to this new way of life was 20/20 vision. The days of squinting were over. As long as I submitted to wearing glasses I could see and, therefore, be free to realize my maximum potential. So in order to become free to see, I actually gave up some freedom to make room for glasses.

In a similar way, the liberty of grace is not intended to restrict our freedom from enjoying life, but to maximize it. The Christian life begins by changing masters. Before Christ, we were slaves to sin. In fact, we couldn't say "no" to it. But after we met Jesus we gave up our old life of sin and submitted ourselves to the Lordship of Christ so that we could experience life to the fullest. Because Christ is our new master, we have a newfound ability to resist sin and be free from its power. This is how the proper use of grace releases us to become what God wants us to be—free from the flesh and legalism.

Expressing Liberty through Love (5:14–15)

If grace were a highway, you might say that it has two forks. The first divergence we already drove down. Remember, it had no speed limits, rules, or guidelines to aid the drivers. There was absolute freedom on this road to drive however you wished. While it may have been a blast for a short time, we found out that it eventually goes nowhere. It was a clever diversion that became a dead end. That was the way of liberalism which abused and misunderstood grace.

Now we are ready to take the other fork in the road which leads us to the place where God wants us to go. God has given us freedom for a higher purpose other than joyriding. We are freed to help others to freedom. We

Risky Business (5:13–15)

are saved to serve. Notice how this is smuggled into the tail of 5:13, "Only do not use your freedom as an opportunity for the flesh, *but through love serve one another.*"

There is an irony in Paul's use of the word "serve." In the original language it's actually the Greek word for a slave. Paul could have used another term to describe the same idea which would have softened the language and perhaps made his audience more comfortable. But he speaks in great contrast. You have been a slave to sin. Now you are free in Christ. So take on a new form of slavery. Lovingly serve others by meeting their needs because Christ has met you at the most important point of need in your life. Paul explains what will happen if we roll up our sleeves and start serving.

First, *loving service perfects the law.* "For the whole law is fulfilled in one word: 'You shall love your neighbor as yourself'" (5:14). The Galatians wanted to keep the law, so Paul was obliged to help them by reducing the Ten Commandments to one word—love! This was a revolutionary principle that Paul also explained in Romans 13:8–10. The amazing truth is that love encapsulates all the laws God ever gave. Jesus explained it like this in Matt. 22:37–40:

> You shall love the Lord your God with all your heart and with all your soul and with all your mind. This is the great and first commandment. And a second is like it: You shall love your neighbor as yourself. On these two commandments depend all the Law and the Prophets.

Then in John 13:34–35, He said:

> A new commandment I give to you, that you love one another: just as I have loved you, you also are to love one another. By this all people will know that you are my disciples, if you have love for one another.

Love is the central hub of the wheel from which all the commandments of the law emanate. It makes perfect sense that if you love your neighbor, you won't commit adultery. If you love your neighbor, you won't steal his property. If you love your neighbor, you won't bear false witness about him. The bottom line is that if you have love, then you don't need a system of laws to tell you what to do.

Watchman Nee told the story about a Chinese Christian who owned a rice paddy next to one owed by a communist man. The Christian irrigated his paddy by manually pumping water out of a canal and into his fields.

This process took hours every day because the pump was operated by human elbow grease. Every day after the Christian pumped enough water to fill his field, the communist would come out, remove some boards that kept the water in the Christian's field, and let all the water flow down into his field. That way he didn't have to do the painstaking labor of pumping water.

This continued for weeks and the Christian became exhausted, so he prayed, "Lord if this keeps up, I'm going to lose all my rice, maybe even my field. I've got a family to care for. What can I do?" In answer to his request, the Lord brought him to this verse, "the law is fulfilled in one word, you shall love your neighbor as yourself." The next morning he arose much earlier and in the predawn hours of darkness he started pumping water into the fields of his communist neighbor. Then he replaced the board and pumped the water into his own rice paddy. In a few weeks both fields of rice were doing well and the communist was converted to Christ.

Which law told the Good Samaritan to bind up the wounds of the dying man on the road to Jericho? Which law compelled the God of the universe to stoop down and wash the grimy feet of His disciples? A person can keep the law without loving. But one cannot love without the law being fulfilled in them.

Secondly, *loving service protects the church*. In 5:15 Paul makes the remark, "But if you bite and devour one another, watch out that you are not consumed by one another." A lack of love can turn a church into a pack of wild animals—Christian cannibals! The Epistle of James takes up this same idea, "What is the source of quarrels and conflicts among you? Is not the source your pleasures that wage war in your members?" (4:1).

If we could peek through the keyhole of the front door of the church in Galatia, we might see something akin to a no-holds-barred wrestling match. The legalists and the grace-lovers were at each other's throats about how to interpret Scripture and which Old Testament laws needed to be observed. It was a cantankerous bunch of believers that gave Paul a real headache. But all the conflict could be squelched with a good dose of *agape* love.

In one of his books, Chuck Swindoll writes of a church that had a vibrant ministry and was having a powerful impact on their community. But then a disagreement began to form. While it seemed small and insignificant at first, it grew and grew until the church was sharply divided. When it became apparent that the issue could not be solved in an agreeable manner, half of the congregation left to form their own church. Today, while both churches still exist, neither has the outreach ministry that they did before. Would you like to know what the disagreement was over? After

Risky Business (5:13–15)

their services, the church would have a time of fellowship with coffee and light refreshments. The disagreement was over whether the coffee should be served by the back door or in the fellowship hall. An issue that small and petty destroyed what had been a great ministry.

It's amazing how small disagreements and selfish controversies can get blown out of proportion. Satan is well-versed in using small wedges to splinter, divide and separate the body of Christ. Selfish living breeds a stench among the church and ruins our testimony to the world. The only antidote is to evict the little egos which want to dominate and control and let the Spirit of God move in. "Love covers a multitude of sins," 1 Peter 4:8 reminds us. Love helps us overlook the faults of others and accept them because, frankly, we are pretty unlovable at times too. Love won't let us hold grudges and it frees us to let things go that don't matter. Most importantly, love is the best advertisement to the world that Jesus is our Master. When love-deprived people get a taste of *agape*, it makes them thirsty for more.

That's what Doug Nichols learned. In 1967, Doug was doing missions work in India when he contracted tuberculosis and was committed to a sanitarium for several months. In the TB sanitarium, Doug found himself in a lonely, confusing, and troubled place. He did not know the language of the other patients, but he wanted to share the Good News of Jesus with others.

All Doug had in the sanitarium were a few gospel tracts in their language, Parsee. He tried to pass them out, but nobody wanted them. Then one night Doug woke up at 2:00 AM, coughing so violently that he could not catch his breath. During this coughing fit, Doug noticed a little old emaciated man across the aisle trying to get out of bed. He was so weak, he could not stand up. He began to whimper. He tried again, but to no avail.

In the morning, Doug realized that the man had been trying to get up to use the bathroom. The stench in the ward was terrible. The other patients were angry at the old man for not being able to contain himself. The nurse cleaned up the mess and then slapped the man. The next night, again, Doug saw the old man trying to get out of bed. But this time Doug got out of bed and carried him to the toilet (just a hole in the floor) and then brought him back to his bed. The old man kissed Doug on the cheek and promptly went to sleep.

Early the next morning, Doug awoke to a steaming cup of tea beside his bed. Another patient had kindly made it for him. The patient motioned that he wanted one of those gospel tracts. The next two days, one after another patient asked, "Could I have one of those tracts too?"[5]

5. Cordeiro, *Jesus: Pure and Simple*, 59–60.

CHAPTER 15

The War Within (5:16–21, 24–26)

In 1885, author Robert Louis Stevenson was recovering from an illness that left him bedfast for many weeks. One night, Stevenson was plagued by a powerful nightmare in which he was being transformed into an evil creature. Stevenson's loud ravings and convulsions awoke his wife, who understandably became alarmed and awoke her husband from the bad dream. When he emerged from that nightmarish fantasy and regained his senses, Stevenson had the basic plot for his next novel. In just a matter of days, Stevenson put the pen to paper at a feverish pace and wrote *The Strange Case of Dr. Jekyll and Mr. Hyde*.

Published in 1887, the classic science-fiction tale of a spilt-personality disorder still endures as one of his most studied, allegorized, and re-created works. The reason for its popularity is because the main character, or should I say characters, are so compelling. The story is told through the eyes of an attorney and friend of Dr. Jekyll; a friend who becomes increasingly worried about the strange behavior and long periods of isolation of Dr. Jekyll. Readers first learn that Dr. Jekyll is a handsome, respected, and wealthy man in the London upper crust. In the prim and proper days of the Victorian age, Jekyll was a stand-out citizen, well known for his charity and decency.

However, as you get into the story, you find out that Dr. Jekyll has a dark-side to his personality. Even though, on the outside, he is an upstanding and moral man, Jekyll lives in silent desperation. Jekyll finds himself torn between two worlds. On one side is the moral restraint placed upon him by society and on the other side is his corrupt nature which desires to partake in uninhibited pleasure and evil. Jekyll is a man in conflict between goodness and morality and the baser passions of humanity.

The War Within (5:16–21, 24–26)

In an attempt to free himself from the struggle of good and evil that goes on inside him, Dr. Jekyll devises an artificial solution to his problem. In his secret laboratory, Dr. Jekyll develops a potion that allows his depravity to take over and manifest through the personality of Mr. Hyde. When the transformation is complete, not only is Mr. Hyde a hideous, slinking creature, but he also has no moral compass. Through Mr. Hyde, Dr. Jekyll is free to do anything he pleases without the repercussions of guilt from his conscious. When Mr. Hyde is in control, the beast is unleashed and he commits terrible acts of violence.

However, as Dr. Jekyll continually drinks the potion, he finds himself unable to control Mr. Hyde who grows stronger and stronger until Dr. Jekyll transforms into Mr. Hyde without even drinking the potion. Jekyll becomes terrified and unable to control Mr. Hyde from taking over at will. The evil side of Dr. Jekyll gains more and more power over the moral side of the good doctor. As a last resort, the conflicted doctor faces a choice to either kill himself, thus killing Hyde, or give in totally and become the monster he both hates and loves.

As the book draws to a close, two individuals investigating the crimes of Mr. Hyde find him dead of an apparent suicide. They find a letter that Dr. Jekyll composed before his final transformation into Mr. Hyde. He ends the letter with this statement, "I bring the life of that unhappy Henry Jekyll to an end." Therefore, the mystery is solved by the letter which explains that Dr. Jekyll and Mr. Hyde are one and the same man.

The story of Dr. Jekyll and Mr. Hyde is a good illustration of the battle that every Christian faces between two contradictory natures—the flesh and the Spirit. Up to this point in Galatians, Paul has dealt with the theme of Christian liberty with respect to the external oppression of legalism and its demands to regulate behavior through works. However, there is an equally dangerous enemy lurking much closer than we might think. Like Jekyll and Hyde, the Christian is a walking civil war who must daily referee the tug-of-war between the old sinful nature and the new nature created by the regeneration of the Holy Spirit. Paul highlights this war within and how the believer can experience victory over the flesh.

The Spirit versus the Flesh (5:16–18)

We might assume that upon conversion we would instantly experience a radical life-change. But it doesn't always work that way. Some people think,

"If I come to Christ, all my problems will be solved. I'll never struggle again." Think again! If you come to Christ, your problems are just starting. As a lost person, you sin because that's your nature. As a Christian, you have a new nature that pulls you toward God while the flesh remains with you until you die. The flesh hangs around and arises every morning to do battle against the work of the Spirit. In one sense, Christians have conflicts that the unsaved never know about. This is the war that Paul is writing about:

> But I say, walk by the Spirit, and you will not gratify the desires of the flesh. For the desires of the flesh are against the Spirit, and the desires of the Spirit are against the flesh, for these are opposed to each other, to keep you from doing the things you want to do. But if you are led by the Spirit, you are not under the law (5:16–18).

The Holy Spirit is mentioned at least fourteen times throughout the book of Galatians. Paul has already mentioned that the Spirit is evidence of our salvation (4:6). Now he commands us to "walk in the Spirit." The original language has the Greek word for "walk" in the present tense which indicates that this action is supposed to be a continual way of life. So to "walk in the Spirit" means to habitually live in obedience and under the direction of the Spirit's leading. As Eugene Peterson has wonderfully commented, "The Christian life is a long obedience in the same direction."

Walking in the Spirit is much like running with the wind. I'm a runner, so I'm used to dealing with the elements. In the summer, the blacktop radiates heat like a hot griddle and will cause you to get dehydrated in a hurry. In the winter, the cold will cause your hands and ears to freeze up like popsicles. In the spring, as the season changes, one thing I hate dealing with is the wind. Have you ever tried to run against the wind? A head-on collision with a gust will stymie your pace and even steal your next breath. However, there are times when you are running along and the wind will come from behind and propel you forward. Not only is a cool breeze refreshing, but it seems to make your next stride longer. When the wind is to my back, it's like nature is helping you take that next step.

So it is when I walk in the Spirit (which Jesus likened to the blowing wind in John 3:8). Under the guidance and direction of the Holy Spirit I find the strength to say, "No," to the sinful flesh and move forward in faith. However, if I try to buck the Spirit and do my own thing, indulging the flesh, I find it to be like running against the wind. Progress in my spiritual life is halted and the journey gets tiresome. I have learned there is a difference between walking in the Spirit and having the Spirit. Every Christian has the Spirit, but the Spirit does not have every Christian. So we have to be deliberate about handing the reigns of control over the Spirit.

When we walk in the Spirit, we deprive the flesh an opportunity to do its dirty work. The "flesh" is the willing instrument of sin—our inheritance from rebellious Adam. The Greek word for "flesh" in the New Testament is *sarx*, a term that can often refer to the physical body. However, when it is used by Paul, he is referring to the fallen, depraved, Adamic nature that we inherit at birth. One writer defined the flesh like this:

> The flesh is a built-in law of failure, making it impossible for the natural man to please or serve God. It is a compulsive inner force inherited from man's fall, which expresses itself in general and specific rebellion against God and His righteousness. The flesh can never be reformed or improved. The only hope for escape from the law of the flesh is its total execution and replacement by a new life in the Lord Jesus Christ."[1]

Forget the overused excuse for succumbing to temptation, "Well, the Devil made me do it." The Devil didn't have to push too hard because we are all pre-programmed with a propensity to gratify self through sin. That doesn't diminish the reality of temptation, but nonetheless spiritual failure is always an inside job. That is why the Bible says we have to intentionally take up arms against the flesh because it's never going away and it will always be there trying to trip you up. Take note of the following Scriptural profile of our ever-present enemy:

- In Matthew 26:41, Jesus warns, "Watch and pray that you may not enter into temptation. The spirit indeed is willing, but *the flesh is weak."*

- In John 6:63, Jesus declares, "It is the Spirit who gives life; *the flesh is no help at all."*

- In Romans 7:18, Paul underscores our struggle, *"For I know that nothing good dwells in me, that is, in my flesh.* For I have the desire to do what is right, but not the ability to carry it out."

- Romans 8:8, pulls no punches either, "So then they that are *in the flesh cannot please God."*

- In Romans 13:14, Paul instructs us to *"make no provision for the flesh, to fulfill its lusts."*

---

1. Bubeck, *The Adversary*, 28.

Obviously, there is not much good we can say about ourselves. Even if we are "religious," that can become a beachhead for the flesh to invade. If the flesh doesn't try to indulge in the repulsive side of life, it will indulge in the religious side. Notice Paul's comment in 5:18, "But if you are led by the Spirit, you are not under the law." There is a double antagonism in this war within—between the flesh and the Spirit, grace and law. The legalists trying to keep the law are only giving the flesh something to sink its teeth into. The flesh doesn't mind dressing up on Sunday morning, carrying a big Bible, or praying aloud. The flesh loves to puff us up with pride so that we, like the Pharisees, can look at our accomplishments and say, "Look at what I did. Jesus is so lucky to have me on His team."

Paul's point is that the path to holiness isn't in doing, but in being led and directed by the Spirit. The only way we can become what God wants us to be is by cooperating with the Spirit and crucifying the flesh. Consequently, the flesh cannot be totally eradicated, only managed and kept in check. The only way to overcome the flesh is to hand over control of your life to the Holy Spirit. Sanctification involves the arduous, life-long process of hating, starving, and outsmarting the old nature.

However, the Spirit of God doesn't work in a vacuum, but in conjunction with the Word of God and prayer. When we fill our lives with these things, the flesh has no room to breathe and it is starved out. Since there are two natures vying for dominance over you, the nature you feed the most is the one that is going to grow and overtake the other. A poet described the Christian struggle like this:

> Two passions beat within my chest,
> The one is foul, the other blessed.
> The one I love, the other I hate;
> The one I feed will dominate.

The Vices of the Flesh (5:19-21)

In his book, *Glorious Mess*, Mike Howerton tells the following story about a childhood experience of playing "mud football." After a huge downpour, he and his neighborhood buddies found a gully filled with two inches of standing water. Howerton describes what happened next:

> We had a blast. Every tackle would send you sliding for yards and yards. The ball was like a greased pig, which meant tons of

The War Within (5:16–21, 24–26)

fumbles and gang tackles and laughter. I remember tackling one of [my friends] and watching him skim across the surface of the water for something like four miles and thinking, "I might be in heaven." When he got up, I noticed something stuck on his shoulder. I peered closer, wondering, "What is that?" Now, there was a huge, concrete sewage runoff drain right next to the gully. And apparently during heavy rains, all sorts of things got backed up, and I don't know if the apartment complex immediately next to the school burst a pipe or what, but I do know we didn't really pay attention to the flotsam in the gully until I noticed that something on Craig's shoulder. I peered closer and suddenly realized it was a soaking piece of toilet paper. In that same instant I realized the smell surrounding me was a bit more pungent than a typical mud football game ought to smell. I yelled out, "We're playing in POOP WATER!" And we bolted for home as fast as we could. Talk about an instant of mental transformation . . . Sometimes in life we need our thinking transformed. Sometimes we think we're having fun until we realize we're rolling around in sewage.[2]

Ignorance is not always bliss, especially when it comes to sin. Paul's graphic list which enumerates the works of the flesh is something akin to Mike's disturbing revelation. At one time in a sinner's past, these actions—fornication, drunkenness, blasphemy, materialism—may have been fun romps in the mud. However, after coming to Christ and understanding the nature of sin, a believer now looks at these sins for what they really are—spiritual sewage. As a rebellious sinner, what we once thought of as acceptable, normal, and even enjoyable now becomes repulsive and shameful under the conviction of the Holy Spirit.

Paul's list is not exhaustive, but it is certainly descriptive. Here he lists seventeen (or sixteen depending on what version of the Bible you're reading) specific sins so that no one is mistaken about the types of behavior that are contrary to the Spirit of God. Some commentators have even broken them up into their various groups—*sexual sins* (sexual immorality, impurity, sensuality), *spiritual sins* (idolatry, sorcery), and *social sins* (enmity, strife, jealousy, fits of anger, rivalries, dissensions, divisions, envy, drunkenness, orgies, and things like these). *The Message* Bible renders this list in a different light:

> It is obvious what kind of life develops out of trying to get your own way all the time: repetitive, loveless, cheap sex; a stinking accumulation of mental and emotional garbage; frenzied and

---

2. Howerton, *Glorious Mess*, 101–102

joyless grabs for happiness; trinket gods; magic-show religion; paranoid loneliness; cutthroat competition; all-consuming-yet-never-satisfied wants; a brutal temper; an impotence to love or be loved; divided homes and divided lives; small-minded and lopsided pursuits; the vicious habit of depersonalizing everyone into a rival; uncontrolled and uncontrollable addictions; ugly parodies of community.[3]

Don't be thrown off by the last phrase in 5:21, "... those who do such things will not inherit the kingdom of God." Paul is not saying that anyone who has ever committed one of these will be excluded from heaven. If this were so, we'd all be doomed. This warning does not refer to the occasional falling into temptation and sin. Instead, he is talking about making these behaviors a habitual and continual pattern of life (1 Cor. 6:9, Eph. 5:5, Rev. 22:14–15). While it is true that all of us fall into these sins at one time or another, true Christians feel the conviction of the Holy Spirit and eventually turn their hearts back toward God in repentance. Paul is simply delineating two mutually exclusive patterns of life—one path that leads to eternal destruction (the flesh) and the other which leads to eternal life (the Spirit).

You may be asking yourself, "Why does Paul give us this long list?" Is it so we can skim through it and feel good about ourselves when we don't see our pet sins? Not exactly. I think it is here as a graphic reminder to you and to me that the potential for wickedness and evil is still within your heart and mine. The old nature is something we will battle until the day we die. Though the flesh may be dormant and under control, if given the chance it will rear its ugly head and manifest itself in one of the hideous forms.

I am reminded of the origin of the phrase "loose cannon." You will often hear people say, "That guy is a loose cannon!" What they mean is that particular person is unpredictable and liable to cause damage if not kept in check by some restraint. The term comes from the old wooden warships that carried heavy steel cannons in the hull of the ship. These huge metal beasts had to be fastened down with ropes and secured to the deck lest they become detached and cause all kinds of damage.

Victor Hugo once told a story about a ship that was being tossed about in a storm. The sailors heard an awful racket in the bowels of the ship. When they made it down into the cannonade they discovered that the violent rocking of the ship in the storm caused a cannon to come loose and it was rolling back and forth, slamming into the walls. The sailors panicked because if they

---

3. Peterson, *The Message*, Gal. 5:19–21.

could not secure the cannon, it would blast through the hull of the ship and cause the vessel to sink. The flesh is like a loose cannon inside every one of us. If it is not properly restrained, it will cause our ship to sink.

The Victory of the Spirit Over the Flesh (5:24–26)

In J.R.R. Tolkien's classic fantasy, *The Hobbit*, there was no creature seemingly more invincible than Smaug, the mighty dragon—that is until the unlikely hero, Bilbo Baggins, found one small chink in Smaug's thick armor. That information, in the hands of a skilled marksman named Bard, was all it took to seal the doom of the presumptuous dragon. Unaware of his weakness and underestimating his opponents, Smaug failed to protect himself. An arrow shot through the beast's underbelly pierced his heart, and the dragon was felled.[4]

That's an exciting fairy tale with a happy ending. But when it's a Christian leader felled, the ending is tragic. The Evil One knows too well the weak spots of the most mighty Christian warriors, not to mention the rest of us. He isn't one to waste his arrows, bouncing them harmlessly off the strongest plates of our spiritual armor. His aim is deadly, and it is at our points of greatest vulnerability that he will most certainly attack.

We are in battle—a battle far more fierce and strategic than any Alexander, Hannibal, or Napoleon ever fought. We must realize that no one prepares for a battle of which he is unaware, and no one wins a battle for which he doesn't prepare. Skip ahead just a few verses by going to the end of this passage and you will see Paul's simple two-step strategy for gaining victory over our most intimate foe.

First, Paul underlines the importance of *crucifying the flesh*, "And those who belong to Christ Jesus have crucified the flesh with its passions and desires" (5:24). Three times in Galatians we are reminded that the Christian believer should be following Christ in His crucifixion (2:20; 5:24; 6:14). Notice that the action of crucifixion that this verse describes is something that is not done to us but by us. In other words, this means willfully and deliberately putting to death the old way of life. John Stott explains:

> Every follower of Christ is to behave like a condemned criminal and carry his cross to the place of execution . . . We must not only take up our cross and walk with it, but we must actually see that the execution takes place. We are actually to take the flesh, our

---

4. Alcorn, *The Purity Principle*, 90.

willful, wayward self, and (metaphorically speaking) nail it to the cross. This is Paul's graphic description of repentance, of turning our back on the old life of selfishness and sin, repudiating it finally and utterly.[5]

If we take into consideration the nature of death by crucifixion, the applications of this verse are startling. Crucifixion was a capital punishment so horrendous that it was reserved only for the most debased and hated criminals. Insurrectionists, thieves, murderers, runaway slaves, and enemies of the state were the kinds of delinquents who hung on the cross. In fact, citizens of the Roman Empire were exempted from this kind of torture because it was so shameful. Yet if we are going to have victory over the flesh, then we must treat it with the same contempt as Rome treated its lawbreakers. Don't misunderstand me—I'm not advocating self-mutilation, but according to the verse we can have no soft place in our hearts for sin. We must look upon it with the same abhorrence as we would a Hitler or a Dahmer.

My daddy has an unequalled hatred for snakes. Growing up, I personally witnessed him decapitate, crush, and run over countless numbers of slithering serpents. He would say, "The only good snake is a dead one." I thought my father was serious about exterminating the legless reptiles until I watched a Jack Russell Terrier fearlessly take on a copperhead. My neighbors had a pet Jack Russell named Dixie and on one hot summer day I watched her from my driveway. A snake was baking in the afternoon sun and when the dog became aware of its presence, she went nuts barking, circling, and showing her disdain. Then, in one ninja-like move, the dog lunged forward, slung the snake up in the air with her snout, caught it midair, and shook it back and forth like a ragdoll.

I couldn't believe my eyes. The little dog couldn't have weighed more than fifteen pounds, but she tore into that copperhead like it was a chew toy. After the pup had her way, she laid the carcass down and trotted off like it was business as usual. Here's the point: if we are going to put the flesh to death, we must attack it with the same ferocity and malice. There can be no peaceful coexistence between the Spirit and the flesh.

Secondly, Paul notes the significance of giving *control to the Spirit*. "If we live by the Spirit, let us also keep in step with the Spirit. Let us not become conceited, provoking one another, envying one another" (5:25–26). Paul has in mind the idea of "follow the leader." As the Spirit directs our lives, we follow. As we discovered earlier, the typical word for "walk" which

---

5. Stott, *The Message of Galatians*, 150.

The War Within (5:16–21, 24–26)

we see in Paul's writings means "to conduct your life." But here he utilizes a rather unique word. It means "to stand in a row" as if at attention before the commanding officer or to "walk in a straight line" as if you are in military formation. The word infers that the one who is living by the Spirit will be marching to the Spirit's drumbeat. If you keep in step with God, you'll be out of step with the world. Notice that Paul tells the believer to do the walking. That is, he is to hear the Spirit's urgings and obey the Spirit's promptings. He is to be sensitive to the Spirit's direction and follow after Him. This is not a passive sort of life like the "let go and let God" mentality which so many have embraced. It is instead, an active seeking to follow after the Holy Spirit in total obedience and delight.

So what does this look like in everyday life? We can walk in the Spirit by staying in the Word of God regularly. "All Scripture is inspired by God and profitable for teaching, for reproof, for correction, for training in righteousness, that the man of God may be adequate, equipped for every good work" (2 Tim. 3:16–17). The Holy Spirit uses the Word of God to speak to us, teach us, give us new direction, inspire us, motivate us, discipline us, correct us, equip us, and strengthen us. The Spirit brings the written word to life through His revealing, illumining power. Think of a tea bag in hot water. If you merely dip the tea in the hot water and quickly pull it out, you will have little of its flavor. But if you take the time to steep it in the hot water, soaking it thoroughly, the contents of the tea bag permeate the water. If we steep our minds in the Word, its contents soak in more thoroughly, permeating every part of our lives.

Another vital step to walking in the Spirit is daily prayer. In Romans 8:36, we are told that we need the Holy Spirit to help us pray because we are weak. How many times have you started to pray and then threw in the towel after about two minutes? Guilty on all accounts. Due to our pride, we may not like to admit that we really don't know as much as we think we do. The truth is, we are more like the disciples than we realize—snoozing on our backs when we ought to be wrestling on our knees (Matt. 26:43).

We read throughout the Gospels that Jesus would regularly slip off to some quiet place for prayer (Mark 1:35, Luke 5:16). There He would refresh His soul in the Father's presence, communing with Him and pouring His soul out before the Father. Do you recall the occasion in the Garden of Gethsemane when Jesus prayed concerning the cup of God's wrath which He was about to endure? Three times Jesus prayed for God to allow an easier path, but He also said, "Yet not as I will, but as You will" (Matt.

26:39). The Lord completely submitted to the Father's will. When He arose from prayer, He was at peace and ready to face the agonies ahead. It was in prayer that the assurance of divine direction came. The same is true for us. 19th century clergyman, Henry Ward Beecher, said, "The first hour of the morning is the rudder of the day." Don't miss that; the rudder determines the direction. What you do before 8:00 AM charts the course for the rest of your day. If you find yourself spiritual life bored, tired, and disillusioned, I suspect you might have a rudder problem.

Crucifying the flesh and giving control to the Spirit is a gradual process of dying to self. Gaining victory over the flesh does not happen overnight. It takes months, or years in some cases, to see sinful habits starved out. Moreover, we must renew this attitude of ruthlessness against sin continually. Jesus said, "If anyone would come after me, let him deny himself and take up his cross *daily* and follow me" (Luke 9:23). As long as you inhabit this fleshly body, life will be a battleground. Every day we must make the decision to execute the flesh; it is not a one-time proposition.

Think of your life like a $100 bill. Most of us think of dying to ourselves as the one big moment where we hand over our $100 bill to Jesus. In a certain sense, that's true. Conversion does happen at a definite moment in space and time when we are forgiven, justified, and brought from death into life. However, following Jesus and becoming remade into His likeness is more than that. Instead of thinking of our lives as a $100 bill that we give to God and that's the end of the matter, we should define dying daily like this: we give God our $100 bill, He accepts it, and then He says, "This is mine, but I want you to cash it out for pennies and give me one penny back each day." That's daily death.[6] C.S. Lewis expressed it this way:

> Christ says 'Give me All. I don't want so much of your time and so much of your money and so much of your work: I want you. I have not come to torment your natural self, but to kill it. No half-measures are any good. I don't want to cut off a branch here and a branch there, I want to have the whole tree down. I don't want to drill the tooth, or crown it, or stop it, but to have it out. Hand over the natural self, all the desires which you think innocent as well as the ones you think wicked—the whole outfit. I will give you a new self instead. In fact, I will give you Myself: my own will shall become yours.'[7]

---

6. Idleman, *Not a Fan*, 168–169.
7. Lewis, *Mere Christianity*, 196–197.

CHAPTER 16

The Fruit of the Spirit (5:22–23)

THE HAMPTON COURT PALACE near London is home to the world's largest grapevine. Planted in 1769, "The Great Vine," as it is called, is a fruit-bearing marvel. The vine is protected from the harsh elements by a glass greenhouse. The parent root which feeds the massive vine is 12 feet in diameter, and some of the branches are over 120 feet long. Despite its age, the vine still produces anywhere from 485 to 700 pounds of fruit. Although some of the branches are 120 feet from the main root, they still bear the sweet and delicious fruit because they are connected to the life-giving vine.

No one can bear spiritual fruit without being connected to Christ, the Vine. Fruitfulness is not primarily a matter of what we accomplish. It's the result of being in close fellowship with Him. Thus, there is a night-and-day difference between the works of the flesh and the fruit of the Spirit. When you think of "works," words like "effort," "strain," "labor," "toil," and "exertion" come to mind. But fruit comes from being connected to a source of life. How many times have you seen an apple tree strain to produce apples? Never. When did a grape vine sweat to make a cluster of juicy grapes? It doesn't because it just flows from the life of the sap. In the same way, the fruit of the Spirit is produced because we abide in Christ and He abides in us. Jesus taught this principle in John 15:4–5:

> Abide in me, and I in you. As the branch cannot bear fruit by itself, unless it abides in the vine, neither can you, unless you abide in me. I am the vine; you are the branches. Whoever abides in me and I in him, he it is that bears much fruit, for apart from me you can do nothing.

When we walk in the Spirit, not only do we have victory over the flesh, but we exhibit the character of Christ. The fruit of the Spirit is the outward evidence of an inward life-change produced by the Holy Spirit. This process is gradual as the Spirit progressively works to transform us. Fruit doesn't grow overnight and neither does spiritual character. In order to help us do a spiritual inventory, Paul listed a nine-fold flavored fruit that can be understood in three categories: The *upward fruit* is what we experience in our relationship with God; the *outward fruit* is what we experience in our relationship with others; and the *inward fruit* is what we experience in our personal character.

Upward Fruit:

Love

The first and greatest of all virtues is love (1 Cor. 13:13). God is love (1 John 4:8). Love is the reason Jesus left the glory of heaven to live as a penniless carpenter on earth (John 3:16). The bloody cross of Calvary is an advertisement by which God declares to sinners, "This is how much I love you" (Rom. 5:8). Love is sacrificial, submissive, and selfless (John 15:13). Paul wrote, "If I have prophetic powers and understand all mysteries and all knowledge and if I have all faith, so as to move mountains but have not love, I am nothing" (1 Cor. 13:2). Love is the badge of the believer and the measuring stick of whether we are truly His disciples (John 13:35).

Imagine trying to capture Niagara Falls with a Dixie cup, or transferring Mt. Everest stone by stone into a child's sandbox, or putting the Milky Way into a mason jar. When we try to comprehend God's infinite love filling our cramped hearts, we arrive at such wonderful absurdities. There is no way to exhaust God's "no-strings-attached" love. He cannot love us any more than He already does and He cannot love us any less than He already does. The result of having our heart flooded by God's boundless love is that there's no way we can remain the same. "We love because He first loved us," 1 John 4:19 says. When we taste God's love, it explodes out of our lives like soda escaping a shaken aluminum can. Therefore, the key to giving love is living as you are loved by God.

The Greek word for love in the text, *agape*, doesn't refer to warm, fuzzy feelings but to a deliberate attitude of goodwill and charity to others. Love gives freely without looking at whether the other person deserves it, and it gives without expecting anything back. The kind of God-like love that Paul is talking about is content with taking great risks and shouldering great cost—like the Good Samaritan wiping the bloody wounds of the stranger

The Fruit of the Spirit (5:22–23)

on the road to Jericho and picking up the tab for his hotel bills (Luke 10:25–37). Love that comes from Jesus busts down barriers, melts hard hearts, and leaves witnesses scratching their heads in bewilderment.

Romanian pastor, Richard Wurmbrand, who endured unimaginable persecution and torture for his faith under the communist regime, once retold an ancient story that was found inscribed on a wall in the catacombs of Rome. A rich man named Proculus had hundreds of slaves. The slave named Paulus was so trustworthy that Proculus made him the steward over his whole household. One day Proculus took Paulus with him to the slave market to buy some new workers. Before the bargaining began, they examined the men to see if they were strong and healthy.

Among the slaves stood a weak, old man. Paulus urged his owner to buy this slave. Proculus answered, "But he is good for nothing." "Go ahead, buy him," Paulus insisted. "He is cheap. And I promise that the work in your household will get done even better than before." So Proculus agreed and purchased the elderly slave. And Paulus made good on his word. The work went better than ever.

But Proculus observed that Paulus now worked for two men. The old slave did no work at all, while Paulus tended to him, gave him the best food, and made him rest. Proculus was curious, so he confronted Paulus, "Who is this slave? You know I value you. I don't mind you protecting this old man. But tell me who he is. Is he your father who has fallen into slavery?"

Paulus answered, "It is someone to whom I owe more than to my father." "Your teacher then?" "No. Somebody to whom I owe even more." "Who then?" "This is my enemy." "Your enemy!" "Yes. He is the man who killed my father and sold us, the children, as slaves." Proculus stood speechless. "As for me," said Paulus, "I am a disciple of Christ, who has taught us to love our enemies and to reward evil with good."[1]

While the world says that love is a feeling, God says that love is a decision. Heaven's love chooses to look past a layer of mud, evil, and sin to find a barren heart thirsty for a drink from God's endless ocean of love. It's the kind of love that made Jesus choose the nails of Calvary and if we are to be like Him, it will require that we extend a compassionate hand.

---

1. Wurmbrand, "Love Pardons the Enemy."

Free at Last

Joy

Everything that brings us laughter, pleasure, and fulfillment was created by God. This means that God is the fountainhead of everything beautiful and awe-inspiring—from supernovas to giggling babies—they are all bite-size tastes of the goodness of God. "In God's presence," says the psalmist, "is fullness of joy and at his right hand are pleasures evermore" (Ps. 16:11). C.S. Lewis remarked that "joy is the serious business of heaven." Lewis Smedes explained, "To miss out on joy is to miss out on the reason for your existence." Christian philosopher, Dallas Willard, wrote that God is "the most joyous being in the universe." Then he illustrated that truth with the following story:

> While I was teaching in South Africa some time ago, a young man ... took me out to see the beaches near his home in Port Elizabeth. I was totally unprepared for the experience. I had seen beaches, or so I thought. But when we came over the rise where the sea and land opened up to us, I stood in stunned silence and then slowly walked toward the waves. Words cannot capture the view that confronted me ... I realized that God sees this all the time. He sees it, experiences it, knows it from every possible point of view, this and billions of other scenes like and unlike it, in this and billions of other worlds. Great tidal waves of joy must constantly wash through His being ... We pay a lot of money to get a tank with a few tropical fish in it and never tire of looking at their beauty and marvelous forms and movements. But God has seas full of them, which He constantly enjoys ... We are enraptured by a well-done movie sequence or by a few bars from an opera or lines from a poem. We treasure our great experiences for a lifetime, and we may have very few of them. But He is simply one great inexhaustible and eternal experience of all that is good and true and beautiful and right.

Willard concludes, "All of the good and beautiful things from which we occasionally drink tiny droplets of soul-exhilarating joy, God continuously experiences in all their breadth and depth and richness."[2]

It stands to reason then that God has never had a bad day. God doesn't get the blues and He has never felt the doldrums of a rainy Monday morning. "Wait!" you object, "What about the Cross? That wasn't a day of celebration and ticker-tape parades for Jesus." I can't deny that. Jesus suffered more

---

2. Willard, *The Divine Conspiracy*, 62–64.

The Fruit of the Spirit (5:22-23)

than any human could imagine when He became sin for us was forsaken by His Father. However, there is this perplexing verse over in Hebrews 12:2 which reads, "looking to Jesus, the founder and perfecter of our faith, *who for the joy that was set before him endured the cross*, despising the shame, and is seated at the right hand of the throne of God." You may need to read that again. Joy in the jaws of death!

How could Jesus face the hell of the cross with joy? He was able to look past the darkness of Friday afternoon to the glory that waited on Sunday morning. In other words, He measured the short-term suffering in light of the eternal glory that awaited Him upon completing the Father's plan. Because He had an eternal perspective, Jesus knew that victory was inevitable and when you know you're going to win it gives purpose to the pain.

This teaches us that unlike happiness, joy is gladness that is completely independent of the good or bad things that happen in the course of the day. In fact, joy denotes a supernatural gladness given by God's Spirit that actually seems to show up best during hard times. Joy outshines the doom and gloom of this world because we know that all things are working to accomplish God's good plan (Rom. 8:28). Joy springs from viewing the day's events from eternity's perspective and knowing that if you have Christ, nothing can stand against you (Rom. 8:31).

In John 15:11, Jesus says: "These things have I spoken unto you, that *my joy* might remain in you, and that your joy might be full." Perhaps you've thought of Jesus only as a "man of sorrows" and never thought of Him as the wellspring of joy. But remember that Jesus was not a crusty recluse. He performed His first miracle at a wedding when He changed water into wine (John 2:1–12). He was so full of life that His enemies called Him "a wine bibber and a glutton" (Luke 7:34). Jesus could be seen playing with the little children (Mark 10:13–16). His presence was like sunshine on a cloudless day.

Are you joy-impaired? If your attitude is more like Eeyore than Christ, then it's obvious something is missing. You can become a joyful person. With God's help you can get plugged into His bottomless resources of joy. The first step is taking responsibility for your joy and deciding to view life through the lens of God's eternal perspective. Life is filled with ups and downs, but you have a choice: which are you going to focus on—the good or the bad? The more you bathe your mind in the Word of God, the more positive and joyful you're going to be. Joy flows downhill from the source.

But, joy is also a decision (Phil 4:11). You are as joyful as you choose to be. So choose the joy of Christ today. He has more than enough to spare.

Peace

In his devotional book, *By the Still Waters*, Vance Havner tells of attending a small service in a little church on a cold February night. The people were local farming folk, and a time was given for sharing testimonies. The last to speak was a humble, plainly-dressed, elderly woman who rose and simply said: "I praise the Lord for a deep, settled peace. The world did not give it to me, and the world can't take it away." "That testimony lingers with me," wrote Havner. "I think of scholars and sages ransacking libraries and perusing heavy philosophies, searching for the secret of peace, while the plain, farm-woman had been enjoying it through the years."

When you're at peace, you have an inner confidence that things are not running wild—regardless of the storms that might be raging in life. But far too often, peace is like an elusive butterfly. Even Christians chase after it and find it just out of reach. Perhaps the rarest of all virtues, real peace comes only when we decide to take God at His word and trust that He is truly sovereign over everything (Eph. 1:11). If you could look through the keyhole of heaven's door, you'd notice that the throne is occupied by the Heavenly Father who never sleeps nor slumbers. Why worry, fret, or pop anxiety meds when He's got the whole world in His hands?

In John 14:26–27, before Jesus went to the cross He promised the disciples that the Holy Spirit would soon arrive. He said, "I'm leaving you well and whole. That's my parting gift to you. Peace. I don't leave you the way you're used to being left—feeling abandoned, bereft. So don't be upset. Don't be distraught" (MSG). While writing from prison, Paul spoke of a peace "that passes all understanding" (Phil. 4:7). God's peace is ample, available, and absolutely life-changing.

So what is true peace? It's not a hippy's charm on a necklace. Nor is it the pie-in-the-sky promise of a utopian society. Peace is when you have internal tranquility amidst external calamity. It's not the absence of turmoil but the presence of calmness even while in a place of chaos. It is a sense of wholeness and completeness that is content knowing that God controls the events of the day. Peace comes from knowing that even though you are in a storm, Jesus is in the boat with you.

The Fruit of the Spirit (5:22–23)

Remember the story from the Gospels where Jesus was sleeping in the boat during the storm and the disciples were panicking? There is no greater study in contrasts—the Savior was snoring while the disciples were sounding the S.O.S. In Mark's telling of the story, there is a critical detail that only he mentions. "And leaving the crowd, they took him with them in the boat, just as he was. *And other boats were with him*" (Mark 4:36).

Did you catch that last part? When the disciples and Jesus left the shores of Galilee, there were other boats that launched out with them, but only one boat had Jesus in it. We don't know what happened to the other boats during that terrible tempest on the Sea of Galilee, but we do know that the boat which carried Christ made it to the other side. Safety is not the absence of danger; safety is the presence of Jesus. The one thing you can be sure of if you're with Jesus when a storm comes up is that you'll be with Jesus when the storm subsides. If He doesn't calm the storm, then He will ride it out with you. As Corrie Ten Boom said, "If you look at the world, you'll be distressed. If you look within, you'll be depressed. If you look at God, you'll be at rest."

Today, choose one thing that distracts and disturbs you. Intentionally give it to God. Release your grasp on it and let it go. Who knows? In its place, you might find that elusive butterfly of peace resting in your open hand.[3]

Outward Fruit:

Patience

There is an old rhyme which says: "Patience is a virtue, possess it if you can. Found seldom in a woman, never in a man." Mark Twain quipped, "All good things arrive unto them that wait—and don't die in the meantime." Patience has almost gone extinct in our digital age of instant text messages, microwavable dinners, one-click online shopping, and on-demand television. If an internet video is buffering, we get fidgety. If traffic isn't moving, then our road rage is escalating. If our packages don't arrive on the due date, then everything is thrown off kilter. Needless to say, patience is in short supply these days.

There is an old joke about a preacher who was praying and asked God, "How long is ten million years to you?" God replied, "one second." The

---

3. Swindoll, "Peace That Exceeds Understanding."

next day the preacher asked God, "God, how much is ten million dollars to you?" And God replied, "A penny." Then, finally, the next day the preacher asked God, "God, can I have one of your pennies?" And God replied, "Just wait a sec." I know that story is silly, but at least it's right about one thing: there is no short-cut to getting patience.

The Greek word used here in the text for patience is a descriptive one. It figuratively means "taking a long time to boil." Think about a pot of boiling water. What factors determine the speed at which it boils? The size of the stove? No. The pot? Not always. The utensil may have an influence, but the primary factor is the intensity of the flame. Water boils quickly when the flame is high. It boils slowly when the flame is low. Patience "keeps the burner down low."[4]

The King James Version renders this quality as "longsuffering." It is the ability to endure ill treatment from life or at the hands of others without lashing out or paying back. This is the quiet willingness to accept irritating and painful situations. The next time some guy cuts you off in rush hour traffic, remember that God is testing your patience. When you're insulted by your condescending boss and you want to snap back, just hold your tongue and remember that it's God's way of using life's sandpaper to smooth out the rough edges. When you've been waiting in line at the DMV for an hour and the line hasn't moved and you feel the urge to complain, realize it's a patience-stretching moment.

Jesus spoke of the need for patience when He said in the Sermon on the Mount, "You have heard that it was said, 'An eye for an eye and a tooth for a tooth.' But I say to you, do not resist the one who is evil. But if anyone slaps you on the right cheek, turn to him the other also" (Matt. 5:38–39). I don't think Jesus was advocating pacifism here, nor is He saying that we should be everyone's personal doormat. Instead, He's advocating that we be like the pot of water which takes a long time to boil over. Let's face it, people are going to annoy you, insult you, and rub you the wrong way. You could get even. You could retaliate. You could give as good as you get. But what kind of witness is that? Patience is the higher road. It absorbs the small stuff, defers to strike back, and wins others over by an attrition of kindness.

No one treated Abraham Lincoln with more contempt than did Edwin Stanton who denounced Lincoln's policies and called him a "low, cunning clown." Stanton nicknamed Lincoln, "The Original Gorilla," and said that the famous explorer, Paul Du Chaillu, was a fool to wander about in

---

4. Lucado, *A Love Worth Giving*, 15.

The Fruit of the Spirit (5:22–23)

Africa trying to capture a gorilla when he could have found one so easily in Springfield, Illinois. Lincoln never said in anything in reply. Amazingly, when Lincoln was elected as president, he made Stanton his war minister because he felt that Stanton was the best man for the job. He treated him with every courtesy. The years wore on.

Then the fateful night came in 1865 when an assassin's bullet struck down Lincoln in Ford's Theatre. In a room off to the side where Lincoln's body was taken, stood Stanton all night. As he looked down on the silent, rugged face of the president, Stanton said, choking back tears, "There lies the greatest ruler of men this world has ever seen." Lincoln's patience conquered in the end.[5]

Kindness

"The greatest thing a man can do for a Heavenly Father," said Henry Drummond, "is to be kind to some of His other children." And Frederick William Faber commented, "Kindness has converted more sinners than zeal, eloquence, or learning." Someone else has suggested that "if you want to surprise someone these days, just be kind to them." Interesting, don't you think? Kindness isn't something we expect from others or ourselves anymore. Just think for a moment. When was the last time someone held the door open for you? What about a simple "Thank You" to the cashier or bag boy? What about picking up a piece of trash in the parking lot that wasn't yours?

A few years ago my nephew and I went out for lunch at one of our favorite hang-outs. It was a local sports bar where they have more big-screen televisions per square inch than the electronics store. We had a single mission that day—hot wings and March Madness basketball. We ordered our food, watched the games, and piled up the chicken bones and moist towelettes. With my lips burning, I took a bathroom break. When I returned, I was greeted by our stunned waitress who said, "Here's your ticket, but you don't need to pay. Someone has decided to pick up your tab." I was just as shocked as she was. "What?" I exclaimed, "Who would do that?" She pointed, "There here goes." I turned to notice a stranger leaving the restaurant, he lifted his hand as be backed out the door and said, "Jesus loves you. Now pass it on."

Incredible! A random act of kindness that hit me like a freight train. I never forgot that feeling of bewilderment, awe, and warmth. Pretty soon I

---

5. Green, *1,500 Illustrations for Preaching*, 258–259.

was looking for ways to bless others. What that free lunch from an anonymous guy taught me was that kindness is contagious. Once you are on the receiving end of kindness, it makes you want to share it with other people just to see their mouth drop open in astonishment.

No wonder then that Paul lists kindness among the fruits of the Spirit. The Greek term for kindness (*chrestotes*) appears ten times in the New Testament and it may also be translated "gentleness." Kindness is simply showing spontaneous and unconditional goodwill, generosity, or consideration toward another. It could take the form of anything from good manners, to offering your seat to someone standing up in a crowded place, or to putting coins in someone's expired parking meter. If you catch the fever, kindness can be a lot of fun because you never know what opportunities may pop up where you can surprise someone with a helping of grace.

In Ephesians 4:32, we read, "Be kind and compassionate to one another, forgiving each other, just as in Christ God forgave you" (Eph. 4:32). Moreover, in Colossians 3:12 we are to be "clothed in kindness," among other things. In both of these verses, the idea is that we make kindness a continual way of life. Being kind is a risk. We could be misunderstood or taken advantage of, but it is worth it. When we take the time to help someone else, we're allowing God to work through us. Who knows the ripple effect our kind acts will cause! Imagine what a kindness revolution could do?

Goodness

Driving down the highway one day I got behind an eighteen wheeler. As I was merging over to pass the big rig a pebble or some projectile came flying out from under the truck's back tire and it laser-beamed by windshield. I noticed that it left a small indention—no bigger than a button—in the glass. I didn't really think much of it since the car was several years old and had many dings already. This new mark would just add to the car's character. The next morning, I went out to get in the vehicle and overnight the small pit had spider-webbed into a hairline crack that extended all across the front glass. Apparently, the fluctuating temperature changes caused the fracture to appear quickly. Since it can be dangerous to drive with a cracked windshield, I had to replace it.

All it took was one pebble to begin the cracking process and the elements did the rest. If a single piece of pea gravel traveling at high speed can do that kind of damage, then imagine what character flaws can do over

The Fruit of the Spirit (5:22–23)

time to the integrity of a person. Nineteenth-century clergymen Phillips Brooks maintained, "Character is made in the small moments of our lives." The man who embezzles thousands of dollars from his company probably started with stealing bubble gum from the corner convenience store. Like my cracked windshield, compromised integrity finds its source in our deep flaws and worsening conditions promote further deterioration. John Maxwell observes:

> Think of integrity as having benefits similar to that of a house's foundation during a huge storm. If the foundation is sound, then it will hold up against the raging waters. But when there are cracks in the foundation, the stress of the storm deepens the cracks until eventually the foundation—and then the whole house—crumbles under the pressure. That's why it's crucial to maintain integrity by taking care of the little things. Many people misunderstand that. They think they can do whatever they want when it comes to the small things because they believe that as long as they don't have any major lapses, they're doing well. But that's not the way it works . . . Anytime you break a moral principle, you create a small crack in the foundation of your integrity. And then when times get tough, it becomes harder to act with integrity, not easier. Character isn't created in a crisis; it only comes to light. Everything you have done in the past—and the things you have neglected to do—come to a head when you're under pressure.[6]

Integrity, moral excellence, and honesty are really what Paul has in mind when he lists "goodness" among the fruit of the Spirit. Without this fruit, no Christian's witness can be accepted as genuine. Integrity is completeness or soundness. You have integrity if you complete a job even when no one is looking. You have integrity if you keep your word even when no one checks up on you. You have integrity when it would be easy to cheat, but you take the high road. Integrity is rock-like. It won't crack when it has to stand alone, and it won't crumble though the pressure mounts. Integrity keeps one from fearing the white light of examination or resisting the exacting demands of close scrutiny. It's honesty at all costs because we know that God is watching.

Moreover, integrity is your best friend. It will never betray you and it will keep you on the right track. When we pass the integrity test, God can promote us to the next level in His program. Think of Joseph not taking advantage of the scantily clad Miss Potiphar when the opportunity presented

---

6. Maxwell, *Becoming A Person of Influence*, 21.

itself. "How then can I do this great wickedness and sin against God?" he said (Gen. 39:9). Joseph got an A+ in God's gradebook. Even though he was falsely accused and spent some time in prison, God promoted him to prime minister of Egypt. What about Daniel not stuffing himself with the choice meats of Nebuchadnezzar? His tender conscience couldn't be violated. Later, he was thrown into a lion's den, but an angel protected him. Kings came and went in Babylon, but Daniel stayed in high places of government despite the regime changes. All because he lived out his namesake, "God is My Judge."

It is said that as the great Michelangelo painted the magnificent frescoes on the ceiling of the Sistine chapel—lying on his back for endless hours to finish every detail with great care—a friend asked him why he took such pains with figures that would be viewed from a considerable distance. "After all," the friend said, "Who will notice whether it is perfect or not?" "I will and God will," replied the artist, "that is enough."

Inward Fruit:

Faithfulness

Faithfulness is enduring loyalty, steadfast courage, stick-to-itiveness, and persistence. God isn't interested in us being famous in the world's eyes, but in us being faithful in His eyes. Someone has defined faithfulness as "love hanging on." I think that's a good way to describe this trait. Faithfulness says, "Even though there is discouragement and disappointment, I will not let go. I will not quit. I will keep on attending, giving, and serving because God has called me to be faithful." This is teaching a Sunday school class year after year, even if your class is just a few members or most of them are children. This is praying for lost loved ones who are far away from God. It's tithing every week when you'd rather take a vacation to Hawaii. It's volunteering to do a job when everyone else ducks out and looks for a place to hide. The Bible is full of things we are to remain faithful in doing:

- 1 Corinthians 4:2 reminds us that God is looking at how we handle His money, "it is required of stewards that they be found faithful."

- 1 Thessalonians 5:17 says we are to be committed to old-fashioned knee work, "pray without ceasing."

The Fruit of the Spirit (5:22-23)

- 2 Thessalonians 2:15 challenges us to stay faithful to sound doctrine, "stand firm and hold to the traditions that you were taught by us, either by our spoken word or by our letter."

- In marriage, we are admonished to stay faithful to our spouse, "let each one of you love his wife as himself, and let the wife see that she respects her husband" (Eph. 5:33).

- James 1:3-4 tells us to remain faithful to God during trials and adversity because "you know that the testing of your faith produces steadfastness. And let steadfastness have its full effect, that you may be perfect and complete, lacking in nothing."

- As a church body we are told not to "neglect to meet together, as is the habit of some, but encouraging one another, and all the more as you see the Day drawing near" (Heb. 10:25).

- In Mark 13:35, Jesus tells us to be faithful in looking for His return, "Therefore stay awake—for you do not know when the master of the house will come, in the evening, or at midnight, or when the rooster crows, or in the morning."

- Revelation 2:10 says we are to be "faithful unto death and then we'll receive the crown of life."

There is no better example of this trait than Polycarp who was faithful to the end. Polycarp lived in the city of Smyrna, located in modern day Turkey, during second century AD. Polycarp was an old man in his eighties and probably the last surviving person to have known an apostle, having been a disciple of John when he was killed for his faith. According to *Foxe's Book of Martyrs*, Polycarp was arrested on the charge of being a Christian, which in the days of the Roman Empire was a dangerous thing since Christianity was outlawed. Amidst an angry mob, the Roman proconsul took pity on such a gentle old man and urged Polycarp to proclaim, "Caesar is Lord." If only Polycarp would make this declaration and offer a small pinch of incense to Caesar's statue, he would escape torture and death. To this Polycarp responded, "Eighty-six years I have served Christ, and He never did me any wrong. How can I blaspheme my King who saved me?" Steadfast in his stand for Christ, Polycarp refused to compromise his beliefs and thus he was burned alive at the stake.

Don't get me wrong, I'm not saying you have to die a martyr's death to prove your allegiance to Jesus. But faithful Christians will get the job done no matter the cost. How can we take such bold risks and make difficult sacrifices? Because we know the eternal reward outweighs the temporary price tag (Mark 9:41, 2 Cor. 4:17, Rev. 22:12). Not only that, but one day we long to hear the sweet words from our Savior, "Well done, good and *faithful* servant. You have been faithful over a little; I will set you over much. Enter into the joy of your master" (Matt. 25:21).

Gentleness

Three young men hopped on a bus in Detroit in the 1930s and tried to pick a fight with a lone man sitting at the back of the vehicle. They insulted him. He didn't respond. They turned up the heat of the insults. He said nothing. Eventually, the stranger stood up. He was bigger than they had estimated from his seated position—much bigger. He reached into his pocket, handed them his business card and walked off the bus and then on his way.

As the bus drove on the young men gathered around the card to read the words: *Joe Louis. Boxer*. They had just tried to pick a fight with the man who would be the Heavyweight Boxing Champion of the World from 1937 to 1949, the number one boxer of all time according to the International Boxing Research Organization (second on the list is Muhammad Ali). It was said of Joe Louis that he could knock out a horse with one punch. Here was a man of immense power and skill, capable of defending his honor with a single, devastating blow. Yet he chose to forgo his status and hold his power for others—in this case, for some very fortunate young men.[7]

That story is the epitome of the eighth attribute mentioned in this list. It is often translated, "gentleness" or "meekness" in our English Bibles. Meekness is a fruit of the Spirit that seems very much lost in our aggressive, self-centered culture. Because people associate it with weakness, or being a push-over, most today do not admire others for being meek. A modern English dictionary or thesaurus makes it clear why meekness is associated with weakness. Notice its synonyms as listed in the *Reader's Digest Oxford Complete Word Finder*: tame, timid, mild, bland, unambitious, retiring, weak, docile, acquiescent, repressed, suppressed, spiritless, broken, and wimpish. Sounds like a description for a pale-faced, effeminate altar boy with the fortitude of a wet noodle. In a world dominated by the

---

7. Dickson, *Humilitas*, 25.

The Fruit of the Spirit (5:22–23)

strong—ruthless dictators, calloused drug traffickers, and cut-throat corporate executives—no one wants to be the wimp everyone takes advantage of.

We are told that Jesus was gentle, lowly, and meek (Matt. 11:29). But at the same time, when we study His heroics in the Gospels, we learn that He was certainly not a limp dishrag either. Jesus was strong enough to drive the money changers out of the temple with a homemade bullwhip (John 2:13–17), yet tender enough to entertain small children (Mark 10:13–16). He was fearless enough to command the winds and waves. He turned the raging Sea of Galilee into a glassy pond (Mark 4:35–41), yet He was humble enough to stoop and wash the grimy feet of His disciples (John 13:1–11). Jesus often stood toe-to-toe with the Pharisees and lashed them with scathing words of judgment and condemnation (Matt. 23:1–38), yet He stood at the grave of Lazarus and wept tears of sorrow (John 11:35). What a stunning contrast of toughness and tenderness.

I think it's safe to say that we have misunderstood the true meaning of meekness, especially in relationship to Jesus' example. Perhaps, the best description we should adopt is "strength under control." Picture a wild stallion that has been broken and is now tamed. That stallion still has as much power as when he was wild, but now that power is bottled up for the master's use. There is a wonderful cooperation between a powerful horse and its rider. An animal of tremendous size and strength, seven or eight times the weight of a man, submits itself to its master's control. A horse may race, leap, turn, prance, or stand motionless at the rider's slightest command. That's strength under perfect control and that defines the Christian concept of meekness.

2 Timothy 1:7 gives us a clue into how the Spirit passes on this characteristic of controlled strength to those He inhabits, "For the spirit that God has given us does not make us timid; instead, his spirit fills us with power, love, and self-control" (TEV). Contrary to popular opinion, we aren't being more spiritual by letting people walk all over us. Moreover, meekness is so important that Jesus mentioned in His foundational teaching, the Sermon on the Mount: "Blessed are the meek, for they shall inherit the earth" (Matt 5:5). The meek are among those so favored that they will share in Jesus' future rule over the planet. When we willingly place ourselves under the control of God, we are following the example of Jesus while He lived on this earth. He submitted His power to the Father's will (John. 5:30; 6:38; Heb. 10:9). So there is actually great strength in meekness. It's the power of God's

Spirit working through us when we yield to Him. If you think meekness is weakness, try being meek for a week.

Self-control

At lunchtime on May 15, 2001, CSX Locomotive No. 8888 eased down the tracks in a rail yard outside Toledo, Ohio. The engine known as "Crazy Eights" picked up speed as it pulled 47 freight cars, two of them loaded with toxic chemicals, south toward Columbus. The two tank cars contained thousands of gallons of the hazardous material—molten phenol acid—a toxic ingredient of paints and dyes that's harmful when it is inhaled, ingested, or comes into contact with the skin. The locomotive reached a speed of 51 miles per hour as it barreled along the tracks for nearly two hours. However, there was one major problem—no one was in the driver's seat. It was a classic runaway train situation.

When news of the unmanned behemoth became public, the Ohio State Highway Patrol assisted in evacuating the area around any railroad crossings to make sure no one got in the way. At first, railroad workers tried to derail the train. Just north of the college town of Bowling Green, the railroad workers laid down a steel wedge designed to derail a locomotive in just such an emergency. The Crazy Eights blew right through. It motored past factories, through cornfields and sugar-beet farms, and through the bog land known as the Great Black Swamps. By the time Locomotive 8888 passed the Whirlpool plant north of Findlay, TV news helicopters were following overhead.

Back in Toledo, supervisors began rolling out Plan B: Catch the train from behind. So the crew of a northbound train farther down the line was ordered to uncouple its locomotive and wait on a side track for the runaway to pass by. After Crazy Eights flew by, the second engine built up speed and snuck up behind the runaway. In a daring maneuver, the second engine latched on to the rear car of the speeding demon and the engineer applied the brakes ever so gently. By the time the train reached the rail yard in Kenton, OH, it was slowed to 11 miles per hour. In a last ditch effort, Jon Hosfeld, a 31-year CSX veteran who was waiting at a railroad crossing, jumped aboard the train, entered the locomotive and pulled its brake. Disaster was averted.

If this story sounds familiar, then perhaps you saw the 2010 special-effects laden film *Unstoppable* which brought the real-life drama to the

The Fruit of the Spirit (5:22-23)

silver screen. You may be wondering how the train became unmanned in the first place. According to one article, while Crazy Eights was leaving the yard in Toledo, the senior engineer was preparing "to make a routine repair—to climb out of his slowly moving locomotive and fix a track switch. For reasons still unknown, he applied the throttle instead of a brake system. Panicked, the engineer tried to jump back on the train. But he lost his footing on rain-slicked steps and was dragged 80 feet before he let go." [8]

Like that runaway train, people without self-control are a hazard to themselves and everyone around them. When it comes to spiritual living, self-control is a necessity because without it a believer will never be able to apply the brakes when temptation comes screaming down the tracks. This quality may also be translated as "temperance" and it refers to the mastery of one's desires, impulses, and appetites.

We see a good example of self-control implied in Proverbs 25:28: "Whoever has no rule over his own spirit is like a city broken down, without walls." The picture is that of an ancient city in which the walls have toppled over and has nothing to stand in the way of an invading enemy. So the person who has no restraint against the baser passions of the flesh—greed, sensuality, anger, etc.—doesn't stand a chance in this pressure cooker world. The Bible has much to say about this particular quality and the behaviors that accompany it:

- *People with self-control watch their words.* They put their minds in gear before opening their mouths: "Be careful what you say and protect your life. A careless talker destroys himself" (Pro. 13:3).

- *People with self-control also restrain their reactions.* How much can you take before you lose your cool? "If you are sensible, you will control your temper. When someone wrongs you, it is a great virtue to ignore it" (Pro. 19:11).

- *People with self-control also stick to their schedule.* If you don't determine how you will spend your time, then others will decide for you: "Be very careful, then, how you live—not as unwise but as wise, making the most of every opportunity, because the days are evil" (Eph. 5:15–16).

- *People with self-control know how to manage their money.* The self-controlled learn to live on less than what they make and know the

---

8. Worden, "Pennsylvania Man Lived the Drama that Inspired 'Unstoppable'"

value of a budget is that it tells your money where you want it to go rather than leaving you wondering where it went! "In the house of the wise are stores of choice food and oil, but a foolish man devours all he has" (Pro. 21:20).

- *People with self-control know how to turn down temptation.* Someone has explained resisting temptation like so: "Temptation is to see Satan standing outside the back door of your heart. Sin is to unlock the door so that he may have his way. Victory is to open wide the front door of your heart, inviting the Savior to enter and give you strength to bar tight the back door." James 4:7 advises, "Submit yourselves therefore to God. Resist the devil, and he will flee from you."

This list is not exhaustive, but you get the idea. The exercise of this discipline called self-control prevents desire from becoming a dictator. For the person without Christ, the desires dictate and he or she obeys. Those in Christ, living under the authority of His Spirit and ruled by Him, are able to defy this once-powerful dictator. As a result, we experience a transforming change that others notice.[9]

---

9. Swindoll, *The Strength of Character*, 34–35.

CHAPTER 17

No Man Left Behind (6:1–6)

EVERY BRANCH OF THE U.S. military lives by the Soldier's Creed. One part of that pledge declares, "I will never leave a fallen comrade." Perhaps this commitment to the man in the adjacent foxhole was best illustrated in October of 1993 during the Battle of Mogadishu. In the midst of a secret operation, Army pilot Michael Durant and his Black Hawk helicopter were shot down. Durant soon became the world's most famous POW as his story was broadcast on national news. Durant ended up spending eleven grueling days incarcerated by a Somali warlord.

In his book, *In the Company of Heroes,* Durant retells what it was like when he awoke in the wreckage of the Black Hawk helicopter as the enemy was closing in on his position:

> I woke up in the silence of my own grave. At least that's what I believed in that first moment, because in my last flash of consciousness I had already seen the clawing hand of the Grim Reaper . . . The chopper's windshield was completely gone, pierced and disintegrated by a slab of corrugated metal that had stopped only inches from my face . . . I reached up to shove the thing from my cockpit and then the pain swept over me like a wave of molten lava. My back was broken. *Super-Six Four* had come down like Dorothy's house in *The Wizard of Oz,* spinning fast, falling even faster, and finally slamming its nine tons of steel into the hard-packed ground. Two of my vertebrae had smacked together on impact displacing the disk between them and pulverizing each other. Every muscle in my back must have tried to prevent that catastrophe and been ripped apart in the effort, and it felt like some evil giant had me on his worktable squeezing my spine in an iron vise . . . I was dead for sure if I couldn't get myself out of the cockpit. A Blackhawk's hard enough to get out of when your healthy . . . And just then, Randy Shughart and Gary Gordon appeared on the right side of

our chopper . . . More than once I had befriended them and other members of their teams prior to the assault on the city . . . They were the kind of professionals that could pick off a rabbit from a roller coaster with a BB gun. To me they were Batman and Robin, only much better. They had just walked up to my aircraft like they were out for a stroll in the park. "Rescue Force!" was the first thing that leapt to my mind . . . here were the best of the best setting up to get us all out of here."[1]

In many respects, the Christian life is a battlefield. We have an Enemy who has come to steal, kill, and destroy (John 10:10). We are told that the world is hostile territory (1 John 2:15–17, 5:19). We are constantly engaged in spiritual warfare (Eph. 6:12) in which we are pulling down Satan's strongholds (2 Cor. 10:3–6). One thing is for sure—as long as bullets are flying, there are going to be casualties. Sooner or later, on the battlefield of life, you will find yourself wounded, trapped by unforeseen circumstances, and in desperate need of rescue.

In Galatians 6:1–6, Paul introduces an often overlooked area of the Christian life—the ministry of restoration. As believers we are to care for the spiritually wounded and bare the burdens of those who have fallen by the wayside. However, what often happens in the Christian life is quite the opposite of a valiant rescue. Rather than living by a "no man left behind" mentality, the church can become a place where we shoot the wounded. This is especially true in smug, self-righteous, legalistic circles where instead of helping hands, you get pointing fingers and wagging tongues.

You want a good indicator for where people's hearts are with God? Then just wait until someone in the church falls in sin and see how people react—some will descend on them like a pack of hungry wolves and others will stand by arrogantly saying, "What a pity." Very few will actually roll up their sleeves, get involved, and lend a helping hand in trying to get the wounded back on their feet again. But one thing I have learned is that a little encouragement can make the difference between giving up or going on. When a Christian returns after falling into sin, we must avoid a "well, you've really done it this time" attitude. Instead, we should convey love, acceptance, and a desire to see him fully restored. That's not to say we're to take his disobedience lightly, but when a person sincerely repents and comes back to the Lord, the best way to help him is to give him a warm, "Welcome home!" In the passage before us, Paul lays out for us a simple and

---

1. Durant, *In the Company of Heroes*, 25–28.

No Man Left Behind (6:1–6)

practical guide for how to care and bear with our Christian brothers and sisters who have gotten caught in sin.

How to Restore a Fallen Believer (6:1)

Paul begins by contrasting two kinds of Christian—the stumbling believer and the spiritual believer. "Brothers, if anyone is caught in any transgression, you who are spiritual should restore him in a spirit of gentleness. Keep watch on yourself, lest you too be tempted" (6:1). From this single verse we can mine-out several important truths that relate to the ministry of restoration.

First, if we are going to be a restorer, we must *be qualified*. The main prerequisite for this ministry is that rescuers be "spiritual." What exactly does he mean by this? In the immediate context, Paul is talking about the person who exhibits the fruit of the Spirit listed in 5:22–23. The spiritual person is the one who is controlled by the Holy Spirit and they exercise wisdom when it comes to applying biblical principles in life.

In other words, not every Christian is qualified to be a restorer. Why? Because not every believer is spiritually mature enough to handle their own life, much less help someone else. Moreover, there are some people you don't want helping you up because you know they can't be trusted. Some people talk out of both sides of their mouth and use "prayer requests" as a chance to gossip.

There is the old story of a young Catholic priest who was serving in the confessional booth for the first time and was being watched over by an older priest. Throughout his shift, several people came by and confessed their darkest, most secret sins to the young priest. At the end of the day the older priest took the young man aside and said, "When a person finishes confession, you have to say something other than, "WOW!"

Before we can help a fallen brother or sister in Christ, we must be trustworthy and capable or else it will be a case of the blind leading the blind. If you are living in sin and are half-backslidden, then you are not a good candidate for being a restorer. That would be like sending a man who never graduated swimming class out with a team of Coast Guard divers to rescue drowning sailors from a sinking ship.

It's also important for every potential restorer to know the Word of God well enough to be able to give solid biblical counsel and not just personal opinion or the latest in pop-psychology from Dr. Phil. You wouldn't ask a guy who flunked ninth grade algebra to tutor your kid in math, and this also applies with Christians who are shallow when it comes to God's Word. In order to be a restorer, you must be a mature, Spirit-filled, fruit-bearing disciple of Christ—not just any ole' Joe Christian.

Second, in order to be a restorer you must *be willing.* This seems obvious, but the reason why many of us do not get involved in the lives of others is because we are not willing to get our hands dirty. It's much easier to stand on the shore and shout swimming directions to a drowning victim than it is to put ourselves in harm's way and go after them.

Remember the parable that Jesus told of the Good Samaritan in Luke 10:25-37? The priest and the Levite (the religious folk) passed right by the dying man and were not willing to get involved because it was going to be inconvenient and messy. They might get blood on their hands and what if others from their peer group saw them dealing with an undesirable? For the same reason, there are many Christians who don't want to get involved in binding the wounds of the fallen because they don't want to be inconvenienced with the investment it's going to take to restore them. Howard Hendricks once wrote:

> Drowning victims often fight their rescuers in the hysteria of that terrifying moment. The same is true for those who are floundering spiritually because their faith has suffered a shipwreck. I had a dear brother who went down the tubes morally. It was a bad case of spiritual defection. By the grace of God he was brought back into the fellowship and he was ultimately restored to the ministry. After it was all over, we were talking and I asked him, "Where are we failing as a church when it comes to helping those who went through what you went through?" He said, "When I fell into sin it was like going down in the surf. I was looking over at the shore that was filled with believers that I knew and some of whom were crying, 'Isn't that tragic?' Others were cursing, 'You're supposed to know the Word of God, why did you allow that to happen to you?' But there was only one who risked the surf to pull me out while I was drowning. I fought him, but he pushed me, grasped me, put a life jacket around me and took me to shore. By the grace of God, he was the reason I was restored. He would not let me go."[2]

If we know that a brother or sister is drowning in sin and we don't go after them, do we really love them? If you don't have compassion and love for others, then you can't be a restorer.

---

2. Swindoll, *Swindoll's Ultimate Book of Illustrations and Quotes,* 487

No Man Left Behind (6:1–6)

Third, a restorer must *be gentle*. Paul reminds us of the attitude we are supposed to have when restoring a brother, "restore such a one in a spirit of gentleness." Paul uses an interesting Greek word in the text to refer to the act of restoration—it's the word *katartizo*. This is a medical word that was used to describe the setting of a broken bone. It is also used in the Gospels to refer to the disciples "mending their nets" (Mark 1:19). *Katartizo* means to restore something back to its original condition.

The emphasis here is focused on a methodology that seeks restoration and not condemnation. This is especially important in the context of legalism because nothing reveals the wicked heart of a legalistic Christian than the way they treat those who have fallen in trespass. The legalist will use someone else's stumbling block as their podium on which to exhort themselves and their superior morality. John MacArthur has written in a tongue-and-cheek way, "I have often thought that if I ever fall into a trespass, I pray that I will not fall into the hands of those censorious, critical judges in the church. Let me fall into the hands of barkeepers, street walkers, or dope peddlers, because such church people would tear me apart with their long, wagging, gossipy tongues, cutting me to shreds."[3]

The last thing a fallen brother or sister needs is more guilt heaped upon them. Perhaps the reason why many believers will never darken the door of a church again is because they know that when they walk in, they are going to be impaled by the knives coming out of two or three sets of eyes. This doesn't mean that we simply ignore the sin issue, but it does mean that we try to do everything in our power to cover the messy situation in love.

When I worked in my dad's woodshop, often times one of my jobs was to refurbish old creaky chairs. This meant that I would totally dismantle it, number and label each part, clean the parts, and put it back together again with fresh glue in every joint. I learned the hard way that taking apart an old chair requires tender, loving care. If you jump into the project without doing a full survey, you can really mess up the piece even more. Some of the antique pieces were put together with tiny finish nails and if I didn't take the time to remove every nail with a set of pliers, then when I started taking it apart, the nails would rip out large chunks of wood. Then I was in real trouble because you can't put that back together.

We need the hands of a surgeon when we go to restore a broken brother or sister. The fallen don't just need Bible verses quoted at them. What they need is grace and truth. They don't need a stern face of rebuke.

3. MacArthur, *Galatians*, 178.

They need a loving Christian to come along and be willing to help remove the things that prevent them from being put back together.

Jesus did this with Peter after he denied Him three times. Jesus didn't take Peter aside and beat him over the head and pour salt into an open wound. Instead, in John 21 the Lord asked him three times, "Do you love me?" and lovingly brought him back. Love looks past the sin and goes after the soul of the person. Moreover, James 5:19–20 says, "My brothers, if anyone among you wanders from the truth and someone brings him back, let him know that whoever brings back a sinner from his wandering will save his soul from death and will cover a multitude of sins." Tony Evans adds:

> When people need to be cut out of cars after a bad accident there is often a tool used called the "jaws of life." These big cutters can remove doors and metal to give access to people who are trapped. Even when drivers have had wrecks through no one's fault but their own, rescue crews still employ the "jaws of life" to get them out of trouble. Christians are supposed to be the "jaws of life" to each other. When a person is trapped, whether through their own fault or through the fault of another, we should be ready to rescue one another. We should be willing to offer a life line to our brothers and sisters when they are stuck."[4]

Fourth, when restoring a fallen believer we must *be cautious*. Tagged on to the end of this verse Paul adds a warning, ". . . considering yourself, lest you also be tempted." In other words, he says, "Don't rush into this situation somehow thinking you are immune to the trap that caught the fallen brother." Just as a doctor can contract a disease from the patient he is treating, so too a spiritual Christian can become entangled in the same sin if they are not careful. We should never be so prideful to think that we can't fall in the same way. Paul reminds us to approach every opportunity of restoration with a heart of humility and meekness because the day may come along when we will need to be restored by someone else.

How to Relieve a Heavy Burden (6:2–6)

The second aspect of restoration is not just picking a fallen brother up, but also holding them up. It's not enough just to help someone up and then wave good-bye. Paul explains that part of caring is bearing. There are at least three ways we should help in burden-bearing.

4. Evans, *Tony Evans' Book of Illustrations*, 252–253.

No Man Left Behind (6:1–6)

We should *carry the load with humility*. I heard about a storm that flooded a major city in the Midwest. People were gathering their goods to save what they could. One of the policemen saw a sight that touched his heart. He saw a little boy carrying another little boy on his shoulders, all while trying to carry goods and luggage and everything else. The policemen went over to help the boy out and said, "Son, you're trying to do too much. You've got all these bags and then you've got that boy on your shoulders. It's too much weight for you. It's too heavy." The little boy looked at the policemen and said, "He ain't heavy. He's my brother." That attitude of servanthood is at the heart of becoming a burden-bearer.

"Bear one another's burdens, and so fulfill the law of Christ. For if anyone thinks he is something, when he is nothing, he deceives himself." (6:2–3). God does some of His best work through people and one of those works is to shoulder the weight of a cumbersome load that is burying a friend. A burden can be lots of different things depending on the situation—it could be a financial strain, a physical disability, an unbreakable addiction, or a prayer request for a prodigal family member. A burden refers to some weight that is too heavy to carry alone.

John Abruzzo is alive today because his friends took Galatians 6:2 literally. At 8:45 AM on Tuesday, September 11, he was working on the 69th floor of the south tower of the World Trade Center in New York City. That's when the first hijacked plane hit the north tower. Seeing the flames and debris filling the sky, everyone scrambled to evacuate the building. Everyone, that is, except John Abruzzo. A quadriplegic since a diving accident years ago, there was no way he could make it down sixty-nine flights of stairs by himself. Eight men and one woman stayed behind to help him. Easing his 6' 4", 250-pound frame into a special sleigh-like device that itself weighed 150 pounds, they began to take him to safety. It wasn't an easy trip. After they had descended a few stories, the south tower shuddered when the second hijacked plane hit it. Soon the stairwell was filled with hot smoke and panicked workers racing to escape the doomed building. When they got to the 20th floor after an hour, they heard a roar outside. It was the sound of the north tower collapsing. The lights in the stairwell went out. When they reached the lobby, it looked like a deserted war zone: broken windows, smoke, debris, doors on their hinges, furniture overturned. There was no one in sight. As they exited the building, a fireman urged them to run for their lives. They followed the crowds to a high school three blocks away. Ten minutes after they left the south tower, it too collapsed.[5]

Next, we should *carry a burden with responsibility*. "But let each one test his own work, and then his reason to boast will be in himself alone and not in his neighbor. For each will have to bear his own load." (6:4–5). If we consider our context, we know that Paul has already addressed the need for helping other believers who have been caught in sin. Yet it would be very easy to examine and evaluate ourselves by comparing our walk with theirs. We could see the pattern of sin which has trapped that person and quickly pat ourselves on the back for not having fallen prey to the same sin. But the standard for examination is not a fallen comrade, nor is it the world about us. Instead, it's the objective, unchanging Word of God and Christ.

You might be thinking that there seems to be an apparent contradiction between verse 6:2 which says, "Bear one another's burdens," and verse 6:5 which says, "For each one shall bear his own load." However, Paul uses two different Greek words to differentiate what each is supposed to carry. In 6:2, it's "burden." In 6:5, it's "load."

Keep in mind that a burden is something too heavy to carry by oneself, while a load is the normal amount everyone has to carry in their day-to-day routine. In fact, the Greek word in 6:5 translated as "load" literally refers to the backpack a soldier would carry into battle. This verse speaks of being personally responsible for the stewardship of our time, talents, and treasure—those things only we can carry.

Each one of us will have to give an account at the Judgment Seat of Christ for the things God has entrusted to us individually (Rom. 14:10–12, 2 Cor. 5:10). On that day, the Lord will not compare our load with that of the Apostle Paul's, Charles Spurgeon's, or Billy Graham's. We will all be responsible for managing the load we were tasked with carrying. Just as someone else cannot eat and drink for you, neither can anyone else read the Word and pray as you need for your spiritual life. No one else can worship for you. No one else can witness to the people in your social circle except you. No one else can give and tithe for you. No one else can do the confession and repentance that you need for your daily walk with Christ. Each one has the responsibility to shoulder their backpack.

Finally, *we can carry a burden financially*. "Let the one who is taught the word share all good things with the one who teaches" (6:6). Upon a first read, this verse doesn't seem to fit with the context. However, when Paul

---

5. 9/11 Memorial Story Corps.

No Man Left Behind (6:1–6)

speaks of sharing "all good things" with teachers of the Word, he is actually referring to another kind of burden-bearing. One important way to offset the cost of the ministry is to give regularly to the local church. Every person in the body of Christ has the responsibility of helping to carry the financial load of the church. This spreads out the expenses of the church over the whole body and doesn't expect twenty percent of the people to do eighty percent of the giving as it is in most congregations. You can't run a church on spare time and pocket change. The minister should not have to work in the secular world and at the same time also be expected to devote himself to the study and ministry of God's Word. The great reformer Martin Luther understood this, "It is impossible for one man both to labor day and night to get a living, and at the same time to give himself to the study of sacred learning as the preaching office requires."[6]

I was watching a documentary a while back about the U.S. Navy Seals. A large portion of their training revolves on learning how to work together as a team. One of the training exercises these teams of cadets had to do in their boot camp was carry a Zodiac raft, which weighs several hundred pounds, on their shoulders up and down the beach for several miles. As they carried this raft, the man in front would get tired and he would yell for relief. Then the man behind him would step up and move into his position and the man in the front would move to the back and everybody would shift up one spot. What impressed me was that for a few grueling moments the cadets under the boat carried more than their load long enough for one man to get relief until he could jump back in. They had to find a way to keep going because they succeeded or failed as a team—not as individuals.

The church is no different. We are one body that succeeds or fails as a unit. We ought to be willing to step in and shoulder the burden for another believer so they can catch their wind and then get back in the fight. God help us not to add to the burdens of anyone but to make them lighter.

---

6. Luther, *Commentary on the Epistle to the Galatians*, 552.

CHAPTER 18

Spiritual Laws of the Harvest (6:7–10)

One afternoon in the late summer, I was visiting my papaw at his home in the country. As we sat on the front porch, chatting and waiting for the next cool breeze to blow our way, I noticed something peculiar. Growing up close to the foundation of his house, in the midst of shrubs and a flower bed, was an apple tree. It was not an ideal place for a tree to be sprouting, but there it was bearing perfectly shaped green apples. I picked one from the tender boughs and proceeded to slice it with a pocket knife. One bite proved to be crisp, sour, and juicy. These were perfect candidates for fritters or a pie.

Still I wondered why there was an apple tree growing in such a strange place? I asked my papaw the story behind the tree and best he could remember, it was a happy accident. He told me that a few years ago he was walking around the yard eating an apple. When he gnawed it down to the core, he simply tossed it to the side without really paying attention to where it landed. Apparently, it fell among the flowers and, by and by, the seeds germinated and a new tree took root. He decided to let it keep growing and now it was bearing healthy apples.

As I thought about that story, I was reminded of sowing and reaping. My papaw wasn't trying to grow an apple tree, but he inadvertently laid the seeds in fertile soil and nature did the rest. How true this principle is in our lives as well. Often times we don't realize how our words or actions can be planted and later take root. For good or ill, the "law of the harvest" is in action whether we realize it or not. If there is one universal principle that runs through the Bible, it's the "law of the harvest," otherwise known as "sowing and reaping." This cause and effect relationship can be applied to almost every area of life, not just agriculture.

In the area of technology it's true because the data you put into a software program affects what you get out of it. Perhaps you remember the little

Spiritual Laws of the Harvest (6:7–10)

phrase from the early days of computers—"Garbage in, Garbage out." Often abbreviated as GIGO, this is famous computer axiom means that if invalid data is entered into a system, the resulting output will also be invalid. Anyone who has ever entered an invalid email address or misspelled a website's URL knows how this works.

Anybody who knows anything about finance can tell you that it takes money to make money. In other words, if you are not willing to invest in a business or a stock on the front-end, then don't expect a payday on the back-end. In athletics, the common phrase is "no pain, no gain." Sowing and reaping is critical in sports because you play like you practice. If a quarterback doesn't put in the effort to practice, workout, and learn the playbook, then he's going to reap a loss on game day.

In the passage before us, the apostle Paul lays out what is perhaps the most basic principle to spiritual living. In fact, its simplicity is deceiving because we might have the tendency to overlook the profound implications it can have on every area of life. For not only does the law of harvest pertain to this life, but it also extends into eternity. The decisions we make in this life determine our gain or loss of reward in eternity. If we truly understood the powerful implications of this teaching, then our everyday decisions would be seen in light of their eternal significance.

The Permanence of Sowing and Reaping (6:7)

"Do not be deceived: God is not mocked, for whatever one sows, that will he also reap" (6:7). The law of the harvest is as fundamental to life as the law of gravity or the certainty of death and taxes. Even though we may not like the laws of physics, there is nothing we can do to change them. One time I saw a t-shirt with the phrase, "Gravity—it's not just a good idea, it's the law." After that I always thought they should make a shirt that says, "Sowing and Reaping—it's not just a good idea, it's the law," with the verse, Galatians 6:7, underneath. In the same way that gravity or the speed of light are fixed constants of our universe, so too are sowing and reaping immutable standards.

Notice that the law of the harvest is enforced by the sovereignty and unchanging character of God. The word "mock" in the text literally means, "to turn your nose up." In other words, Paul is warning us, "Don't be so foolish to think that this doesn't apply to you." The law of the harvest has been woven into the very fabric of the universe and the consequences of our choices cannot be avoided. Some people think that if they disbelieve in God, it somehow magically exempts them from truth of the Bible. However, the Bible and the principles it teaches are true despite what man thinks or feels. Therefore, the principles of sowing and reaping apply to everyone irrespective if they accept or reject the reality of God and His Word.

Evangelist D. L. Moody had just started preaching a sermon on Galatians 6:7 when a man in the audience stood up and shouted, "I don't believe it." Moody replied, "My friend, that doesn't change the fact. Truth is truth whether you believe it or not, and a lie is a lie whether you believe it or not." When the meeting ended, a police officer was at the door to arrest the man. Earlier that day the man had shoplifted. In order to escape the pursuit of the police, he ducked into Moody's evangelistic meeting thinking that the cops would never find him there. He was convicted of theft and sent to prison. Moody observed, "I really believe that when he got to his cell, he believed that he had to reap what he sowed."

The permanence of this law is both convicting and comforting. On one hand, it's convicting if you are living a life of sin because it promises that there will be a payday someday. On the other hand, it's comforting because it promises that no one gets away with anything. If you have been wronged, mistreated, or gotten the short end of the stick because someone else deceived you, then don't worry because either in this life or the next God's justice will be carried out.

The Principles of Sowing and Reaping (6:7–10)

The law of the harvest operates by a predicable set of rules. Understanding them is key to benefitting the most in our spiritual life. First, we must note *the principle of investment: you only reap if you sow*. There is no such thing as reaping without an investment. Every gardener knows that if you want to enjoy good vegetables in August, you have to invest the time and labor into planting, watering, and weeding from April through July. It's a full-time job keeping the critters from eating away at all your hard work. But it all pays off on Sunday afternoon when you slice open a hot biscuit and lay some cream-style corn over the top of it.

The principle of investment is especially true in the area of giving and tithing. You can't expect to harvest the blessings of God in your life if you refuse to invest in His kingdom. How many times have you heard the excuse or used it yourself, "Well, I will give when I am more financially stable"? The truth is that if we all lived by that logic, then no one would

Spiritual Laws of the Harvest (6:7–10)

ever give to God. That's the point of giving anyway—it's based on faith and it is predicated on the belief that God can stretch your ninety percent after tithing farther than what you could do with all of it. Sadly, there are many Christians who never experience the harvest God wants to give them because they believe it's possible to out-give God.

The investment principle also applies to Christian growth. If you want a vibrant relationship with God, you have to invest time in spiritual things. When you are born again, you receive the Holy Spirit. But the Spirit won't read your Bible for you, nor will He pray for you or get you out of bed on Sunday morning. One of the reasons why people stay baby Christians for decades is because they never decide they want to grow up. The extent of their desire for the things of God never moves beyond the church pew. I have often wondered how many preachers or missionaries or worship leaders the church is missing because they have never been motivated enough to develop their own potential and invest in God's kingdom.

A man came up to a preacher one day who was renowned for his understanding of Scripture and he said, "What can I do to get the knowledge of the Bible you have?" The preacher looked at him and replied, "You can't. You're fifty years too late." The man was not satisfied with that answer, "What do you mean?" The preacher explained, "I started studying the Bible diligently fifty years ago and that's how I know what I know today. You can't have the knowledge of the Bible that I have because you are fifty years too late. You should have sown that seed back then if you wanted the harvest." Never expect to reap a harvest from a field that you didn't sow into.

Second, there is *the principle of identity: you only reap what you sow*. ". . . for whatever one sows, that will he also reap. For the one who sows to his own flesh will from the flesh reap corruption, but the one who sows to the Spirit will from the Spirit reap eternal life" (6:7–8). The kind of harvest that we receive is determined in advance by the kind of seed that we sow. If a farmer puts corn in the ground, he's going to get corn. If he plants potatoes, he's going to get potatoes and not beans or squash.

When it comes to the area of spiritual living, the same principle applies. If you sow into the flesh—that is the old sinful nature—then you can expect a bitter harvest. On the flipside, if you invest into the Spirit and starve out the flesh, you can expect the blessings of God in your life. This is why Christians need to be careful what they are putting into their lives—whether it's the books we read, the movies we watch, the music we listen to, the people we hang around—it is all contributing to either the flesh or the Spirit.

Free at Last

The profound truth that is imbedded in this principle is that even the things we view as small and insignificant can end up coming back to destroy us or bless us in the end. An acorn isn't very big, but contained within it is the potential for a towering oak tree. As the old saying goes, "sow a thought, reap an action. Sow an action, reap a habit. Sow a habit, reap a character. Sow a character, reap a destiny."

A dear friend of mine has told me several times about his conversion to Christ and the person he was before he came to know the Lord. As a fatherless young man, he tried to fill the existential void in his heart with everything from drugs, to sex, to achievement. I asked him when his journey down the broad path of destruction began and what got him experimenting with drugs and alcohol. Not surprisingly, his descent started when was about ten years old. He told me that he started smoking cigarettes by walking up and down the streets in his neighborhood picking up the half-used butts. He would collect the used cigarette butts and either smoke what was left of them or cut them up and combine the left overs into a hand-rolled cigarette. He sowed that seed of addiction early in his life and reaped the damage of it through his teens and twenties. Only Christ was able to break the chains.

On the flipside of this coin, if we sow into the Spirit, we can expect to reap a good harvest. There is an illustration of this from a famous duo in American history. Lewis and Clark's expedition to the Pacific Northwest in 1804 almost came to an untimely and deadly end. Half-starved and almost frozen, the men staggered out of Idaho's snowy Bitterroot Mountains and into the camp of the Nez Perce Indians. Dayton Duncan and Ken Burns tell the story in *Lewis and Clark: The Journey of the Corps of Discovery*:

> Lewis and Clark were the first white men ever to reach their homeland. In the absence of more prominent leaders, who were out on a war party, a chief named Twisted Hair had to decide what to do with the weak but wealthy strangers suddenly in their midst. According to the tribe's oral tradition, some of the Nez Perce proposed killing the white men and confiscating their boxes of manufactured goods and weapons. The expedition's rifles and ammunition, in particular, would have instantly made the Nez Perce the region's richest and most powerful tribe. But an Indian woman came to the Corps of Discovery's aid. As a young girl, she had been captured by an enemy tribe on the plains, who in turn sold her to another tribe farther to the east. Eventually, she had been befriended and treated kindly by white people in Canada before

Spiritual Laws of the Harvest (6:7–10)

escaping and making her way back to her own people. They called her Watkuweis—"Returned from a Faraway Country"—and for years she had told them stories about the fair-skinned people who lived toward the rising sun. She was aged and dying by the time the explorers arrived. When she learned about possible plans to destroy the expedition, tribal tradition says she intervened. "These are the people who helped me," she said. "Do them no hurt."

A stranger's simple act of kindness—years before—saved the lives of an entire expedition. A little kindness can have amazing and unexpected results.

The end result of sowing in the flesh and sowing in the Spirit could not be more opposite. Sowing in the flesh reaps corruption, but sowing in the Spirit reaps everlasting life. In other words, everything that you put into the flesh is temporary and will fade away. However, everything that is sown in the Spirit will pass the test of time and last throughout all eternity. John describes the same principle in 1 John 2:16–17, "For all that is in the world—the desires of the flesh and the desires of the eyes and pride of life—is not from the Father but is from the world. And the world is passing away along with its desires, but whoever does the will of God abides forever."

So the question each one of us needs to ask ourselves is this—"Is what I'm sowing going to have any eternal value? Or is everything I'm working for going to go up in a puff of smoke at the judgment Seat of Christ?" C.S. Lewis has written:

> Every time that you make a choice, you are turning the central part of you, the part that chooses, into something a little different than what it was before. And taking your life as a whole, with all your innumerable choices, all your life long you are slowly turning into this central thing, either into a heavenly creature or a hellish creature: either a creature than is in harmony with God and with other creatures and with itself, or else into one that is in a state of war and hatred with God and with its fellow creatures and itself.[1]

Third, there is *the principle of increase: you always reap more than you sow*. If this principle were not true, then sowing and reaping would be a futile endeavor. Think about it, if you took one seed and placed it in the ground only to later receive the same seed in return, you would have been better off to keep your original seed. The principle of increase means that even if you sow a little bit, you will get a whole lot in return.

---

1. Lewis, *Mere Christianity*, 92.

Free at Last

This is why it behooves us to give and invest in the things of God as much as we can. In God's economy, the original investment snowballs and the dividends are multiplied exponentially. Paul says in 2 Cor. 9:6, "He who sows sparingly will reap sparingly, and he who sows bountifully will also reap bountifully." However, this principle is just like all the others. It's a two-way street. Sowing into the flesh means that your investment in sin will bring back to you a whole lot more heartache, pain, guilt, and suffering than what you bargained for. The Devil doesn't tell those he's tempting that they are getting a raw deal. Instead, he presents a life of the flesh as being consequence-free.

Consider how this double-edged sword of sowing and reaping worked in the lives of some of the Old Testament saints. When Abraham sowed into the flesh, he got Ishmael. But when he sowed into the Spirit, he got Isaac. When Jacob sowed into the flesh, he stole the blessing from his brother Esau. Years later, he didn't realize that was going to come back and haunt him when Laban deceived him and he got Leah instead of Rachel. Samson sowed into the Spirit and he killed 1,000 Philistines with the jawbone of a donkey, but when he got sidetracked and sowed into the flesh, he ended bald and blind at the hands of the little seductress Delilah. When David sowed into the Spirit, he slew the giant Goliath, but when he sowed into the flesh, he got into a costly affair with Bathsheba.

It is said that the Emperor Charlemagne (742–814 AD) wanted to have a magnificent bell cast for the church he had built. An artist named Tancho was employed by the church to make it. The famous metalworker was furnished, at his own request, with a great quantity of copper and a hundred pounds of silver for the smelting of the bell. However, he kept the silver for his own personal use and substituted in its place a quantity of highly purified tin. When the work was completed, he presented the bell to the Emperor who had it suspended in the church tower. At the inaugurating ceremony of the church, Tancho was given the privilege of ringing the bell for the first time. As fate would have it, when Tancho pulled the rope to ring the bell, the harness that held it in place in the belfry snapped and the bell fell on top the artist and killed him instantly.[2]

That bell-maker's death reminds me of the words of Num. 32:23, "be sure your sin will find you out." He certainly got more than what he bargained for. Life is full of trade-offs. Today's poor choices are a down payment on tomorrow's problems. Sooner or later we will reap what we

---

2. DeHann, "We Reap What We Sow."

Spiritual Laws of the Harvest (6:7-10)

sow and more than we sow, but we have nothing to fear if we sow into the Spirit and not the flesh.

Fourth, there is *the principle of interval: you always reap later than you sow*. "And let us not grow weary of doing good, for in due season we will reap, if we do not give up." (6:9). No farmer plants a crop in the morning and reaps a harvest in the evening. There is always a time gap that allows for the seed to germinate and grow into full maturity. In the area of spiritual living, we probably won't see the effects of our choices immediately or perhaps even in this life, but there will come a day when what we've planted is ready to be picked. The toughest part of this principle to learn is that the interval is based on God's timing and not our own. Paul remarks, "*. . . for in due season* we shall reap if we do not lose heart." If you are impatient, you should be reminded that God is not in a hurry. God's purposes start in eternity, but they are slowly worked out in time.

Since there is an unknown period of time between sowing and reaping, the tendency is either for the saint to become discouraged or for the sinner to think he has gotten away with sin. There are times when we wonder if the good we are doing really matters because even though we are sowing, it appears that nothing is happening. But there is an ironclad guarantee that one day we will see the fruit of our labor. 1 Cor. 15:58 is a good reminder, "Therefore, my beloved brothers, be steadfast, immovable, always abounding in the work of the Lord, *knowing that in the Lord your labor is not in vain*." If you allow a short-range view of things to discourage you, it can sabotage God's plan for blessing your life.

If God has called us to a task, quitting is never fitting. Yet who hasn't trudged through the lowlands of discouragement, looking to every side road for an opportunity to leave a difficult and frustrating work? Satan is quick to suggest that we might as well give up, go elsewhere, or let someone who is more talented do the job. But we are where we are by God's appointment. If we're in this kind of beleaguered situation, the noblest expression of faith is a dogged determination to go on with the task.

There once was a small, rural church in Scotland. The pastor had been forced out by his elders who claimed they saw no fruit from his ministry. The village in which the pastor served was a difficult place. People's hearts were cold and hostile to the truth. During the time the pastor served, there had been no conversions and no baptisms. But he did recall one positive response to his preaching. When the offering plate was passed during a service, a young boy placed the plate on the floor, stood up, and stepped into it. When asked to explain, he replied that he had been deeply touched by the minister's life and while he had no money to give, he wanted to give himself wholly to God.

The boy who stepped into the plate was Bobby Moffat, who in 1817 became a pioneer missionary to South Africa. He was greatly used of God to touch many lives. And it all started with that small church and the faithful work of that unappreciated pastor. Years later, when he was a seasoned missionary, Bobby Moffat returned to his hometown church to see if he could find any willing bodies who would return with him to the mission field in Africa. When he arrived at the church one cold wintry night, he was dismayed that only a small group had come out to hear him. What bothered him even more was that the only people in attendance were old ladies (no offence to you gals out there reading, but Moffat was looking for a male pupil).

Despite the dismal outcome, Moffat preached his message and when he stood up behind the pulpit he nearly overlooked one small boy sitting in the back of the church. Little did Moffat realize that his sermon would have a profound impact on that boy. Moffat's stories of adventuring through the African wilderness inspired and challenged this young man and planted the seed of missions in his heart. When he grew up, he went and ministered to the unreached tribes of Africa. His name? David Livingstone.

Even though you may not see how your small, little life can matter, we must remember that the law of the harvest says that big harvests begin as tiny seeds that we plant and patiently wait to see sprout up. "See how the farmer waits for the precious fruit of the earth, being patient about it, until it receives the early and the late rains. You also, be patient" (James 5:7–8).

Finally, we are admonished with this simple command, "So then, as we have opportunity, let us do good to everyone, and especially to those who are of the household of faith" (6:10). The word "opportunity" comes from the Greek word *kairos*, which is sometimes translated "time." However, it's not a word that means the passing of the hours one by one. It refers to those moments in life when a door of opportunity opens before us and we have a choice to make. Will we go through that door or will we hesitate until it closes?

No door stays open forever. Opportunities come and then they go. A sculptor once showed his studio to a friend who spotted a very strange statue. It was the figure of a man with hair completely covering his face and wings on each foot. "What is the name of that statue?" he asked. The sculptor replied, "His name is Opportunity." "Why is his face hidden?" "Because men seldom know when he comes to them." "Why are there wings on his feet?" "Because he is soon gone and when he departs, he cannot be overtaken."

There are so many opportunities to serve the Lord. Many times, all it takes is for us to ask God to open our eyes to needs around us. Several years ago, an article appeared in *Time* magazine about a doctor who lived through the terrible bombing of Hiroshima. When the blast occurred, Dr. Fumio Shigeto was waiting for a streetcar only a mile away, but he was sheltered by the corner of a concrete building. Within seconds after the explosion, his ears were filled with the screams of victims all around him. Not knowing what had happened, he stood there for a moment, bewildered—one doctor wondering how he could ever handle this "mountain" of patients. Then, still somewhat stunned, Dr. Shigeto knelt, opened his black bag, and began treating the person lying at his feet.[3]

The needs of a broken world are overwhelming, but you can start in a small way. Dr. Shigeto's experience is our own. Having survived alcoholism, divorce, debt, toxic church life, or childhood abuse, what is your ministry? Serve someone near you. Maybe it will begin by teaching a children's Sunday school class. Maybe you can visit the sick, dying, and imprisoned. Perhaps you can give meals to the hungry or pay a single mother's light bill. All that God asks is that you do what you can when the opportunity presents itself.

---

3. "The Atomic Doctor," *Time*.

CHAPTER 19

Boasting Only in the Cross (6:11–18)

Perhaps the most recognizable signature in our nation's history is that of John Hancock. In case you forgot your U.S. history, he was the president over the 2nd Continental Congress. In 1776, he along with 55 other men signed their names to one of the most important documents in history—The Declaration of Independence. If you take a trip to the national archives in Washington D.C., you can see the famous parchment under thick glass and maximum security. Even though it is badly faded because of time, you can still make out the signatures of the patriots who became guilty of treason on that hot July day in Philadelphia when they signed their names to it.

A few years ago, I went to the National Archives and sure enough, under Jefferson's grand words, there is the name of John Hancock in bold, flamboyant calligraphy dwarfing all the other signatures. There is a story which says that Hancock signed his name so emphatically because he wanted King George to be able to read it without his spectacles. Another tradition says that upon writing his name, Hancock said to the Congress, "We must now all hang together," to which Benjamin Franklin replied, "Yes, we must indeed all hang together, or most assuredly we shall all hang separately."

Declaring their independence was a costly move for many of the Founding Fathers. Despite the dangers, they laid their livelihood on the line because they believed that freedom and liberty were the God-given right of every human being. They had the courage to sign their names and become the enemies of Great Britain, the most-powerful nation in the world at that time.

Here at the end of Galatians we have the apostle Paul putting his "John Hancock," if you will, on the Christian's Declaration of Independence. Paul was the original freedom fighter. He was not ashamed of the Gospel

Boasting Only in the Cross (6:11-18)

nor was he afraid to stand toe-to-toe with those who desired to dilute the Gospel of grace.

By signing his name to the letter of Galatians, Paul understood the cost involved. For the rest of this life, he would be doggedly persecuted by the Jewish legalists that wanted the message of grace to die without a memory. Fortunately for you and me, Paul was man of grit and determination. His clarion call to freedom was preserved through the centuries. In this last paragraph, Paul sums up his message and in doing so he reveals how we can boldly share the Gospel as he did.

We Must Share the Gospel without Reservation (6:11)

Paul writes an attention-grabbing line in bold, large font, "See with what large letters I am writing to you with my own hand" (6:11). In the first century, it was customary for letters of correspondence to be dictated to a professional scribe or a secretary called an "amanuensis." This meant that Paul probably didn't actually write most of the body of his epistles. However, in order to prove the genuineness of the letter, Paul usually added his own short salutation and signature at the end.

In this case, we can imagine Paul getting to the end of the letter, pushing the scribe to the side, and saying, "Give me that quill. I've got a thing or two to write on my own." Imagine yourself 2,000 years ago, sitting in the First Baptist Church of Galatia. The pastor gets up one Sunday morning to share this letter he received from Paul. After the service, you examine the letter and you notice that most of it is written in neat, professional cursive. But the last paragraph is scrawled out in all caps and underlined.

Some have speculated that perhaps Paul had bad eyesight and that is why he decided to write in such large print, but I think he just wanted to emphasize and underscore his message. You can imagine that Paul pressed hard against the papyrus as he wrote to convince his readers of the serious matters at hand. He has been dealing with issues relating to the very core of the Gospel. These weren't just box scores on the back of the sports page or even the philosophical doodling of a wise man. No, the most important message ever conveyed—salvation and the Savior—were at stake.

Herein is an important application. When sharing the Gospel, we should not be ashamed of our message or the outcome. Paul pulled no punches in dissecting and condemning the legalism that had infiltrated this church. He attacked the heresies of the Judaizers like a bulldog going after a pork chop. He held nothing back and employed all manner of argumentation to convince the Galatians of their waywardness. In this letter, we saw him employ several tools out of his toolbox—everything from high and lofty theology, to allegory, to name-calling, and now breaking the first-century protocol of letter etiquette. Paul shared the truth without any reservations because eternity and the Gospel hung in the balance.

Unlike Paul, one of the primary deterrents that prevent us from sharing the Gospel is fear. Satan has made a living off of scaring many Christians into silence. We are afraid to open our mouths and speak the truth of Christ for any number of reasons: we are afraid we won't know what to say, we are afraid we will mess up, we are afraid someone will ask us a question we can't answer. Perhaps one of the most tense moments in a Christian's life comes in between the few seconds when you feel the inner prompting of the Holy Spirit to speak up and when you finally get the guts to open your mouth.

That wasn't a problem for Paul or for a young lady whose story was publicized in the national news. An online article explained:

> When a man tried to rob a MetroPCS cell phone store at gunpoint in Pompano Beach, Florida, store manager Nayara Goncalves, 20, calmly talked to the man about Jesus and her faith until he left without taking any money. Goncalves said she doesn't know why she began to talk to him about Jesus. "I believe it was the Holy Spirit of God that really made me want to tell him about Jesus," Goncalves said, "I would never be able to do that myself. I would never think that God could use me the way that he did," she said. A store surveillance camera captured the whole exchange between Goncalves and the would-be robber. The man entered the store and made small talk about the rainy weather. He asked to see a phone, and then showed Goncalves a gun and nervously asked for the money in the register. "I really hate to do this," the gunman told Goncalves. She slowly walked towards the register and started to speak to the man, who told her not to be afraid. "I'm not," she said. "I'm just going to talk to you about the Jesus I have . . ." "Jesus has something way better for you," Goncalves told him. Though the man clearly felt guilty about robbing the store, he hadn't given up on his original goal. When Goncalves showed him the money in the register, he told her he had to take all of it. Once she told him that it would come out of her paycheck, however, he backed down. Before the man left, Goncalves pleaded with him to think about what he had done and to get back in touch with his faith. "Jesus can

help you. He can change your life..." Completely defeated, the man revealed that his weapon was only a BB gun and left the store.[1]

Often, as Christians, we forget that the Gospel is backed by the power of the Holy Spirit. If we have the courage to be the Lord's witnesses, there is no telling whose heart might be touched. Yet if we stay silent, we'll never know the life-changing power of the Gospel. We are not responsible for the outcome of sharing the Gospel, only being obedient to the command to share it and defend it.

We Must Share the Gospel without Religion (6:12–13)

We live in an age where truth is questioned and assaulted on every side. The tendency is to water-down the exclusive claims of Christ and to make His message more palatable. If the culture cannot shut us up, it will try and get us to compromise the Gospel with man's thinking. For nearly six chapters, Paul has labored to make the point that grace and religion are diametrically opposed. If you are not relying on the Cross of Christ, then you are relying on religion to make you presentable to God. Paul draws a contrast between the motives of the Judaizers and his message of grace. He clearly outlines three reasons why his enemies adamantly attacked him and promoted a salvation relying on human works.

First, he says, was to garner *the approval of peers*. "It is those who want to make a good showing in the flesh who would force you to be circumcised ..." (6:12). One motivation for legalism is the desire to impress others. The Judaizers wanted to convert the Galatians so their numbers would make them look high and mighty in the eyes of other men. When the Judaizers returned to Jerusalem, they wanted to be able to stand up with all the people in the missionary meeting and declare that they had traveled far and wide and had a good many scalps to show for their effort. The Galatians cowed down to their back-breaking demands.

Second, they diluted the Gospel *to avoid persecution*. "... and only in order that they may not be persecuted for the cross of Christ" (6:12). Preaching the Gospel of grace will not get you fan mail or a pat on the back. Instead, it will make you a candidate for persecution. The Gospel is an offense which declares that man is utterly broken and incapable of saving himself. The Judaizers added works to their message so as to not hurt

---

1 Wetenhall, "Christian Woman Stops Robbery with Faith."

people's egos with the truth of man's depravity and spiritual bankruptcy. In essence, Paul called them out as shallow cowards because they didn't believe in the Cross enough to endure harassment.

George Whitfield was one of the great preachers of the American frontier during the mid-1700s. Historians estimate that he preached anywhere from forty to sixty hours a week. In fact, he crossed the Atlantic thirteen times between Britain and America, preaching on both continents. His adage was, "We are all immortal until our work for God is done." Believe it or not, Whitfield was hated, especially in America, because when he would come to town the people would flock to hear him at his outdoor meeting rather than listen to the local ministers. Whitfield emphasized a simple message of grace and the clergy in the American colonies would get jealous when people would be converted to Christ. So to get back at Whitfield, they would provoke rabble rousers to disrupt him while he preached. According to Whitfield's journals, it was not unusual for him and his companion, John Wesley, to be pelted with stones, rotten eggs, dirt, and on occasion a dead cat hurled at their heads.[2]

If you preach the Gospel, you might as well never run for public office. The Gospel isn't just an inspirational story that's supposed to makes us feel warm and fuzzy. In fact, the bloody cross and the dying Savior are there to show the incredible lengths to which God went to reconcile the world to Himself. Our sinfulness was the reason Jesus gave His life as a ransom. That is certainly not as appealing to the pride of man as something like, "God helps those who help themselves."

Third, they added works to grace in order *to appear perfect*. "For even those who are circumcised do not themselves keep the law, but they desire to have you circumcised that they may boast in your flesh" (6:13). The legalists wanted everyone to think their nose was clean, when in reality they were just as dirty as everyone else. The Judaizers demanded that the Galatians keep the law, when they themselves lived in contradiction and fell short of their own standards. Paul could not understand why the Galatian believers wanted to follow such hypocrisy.

Years ago, I remember Johnny Cash came out with an album called *American Recordings* and on the front cover of the CD jacket were two dogs. One dog was black with a white stripe and the other dog was white with a black stripe. In an interview, someone asked Mr. Cash what the dogs meant and he said, "Their names are sin and redemption. Sin is the black

---

2. Wiersbe, *50 People Every Christian Should Know*, 42.

dog with the white stripe and redemption is the white dog with the black stripe. Those two dogs tell my life story. When I was in sin, I was bad but not all bad. Then when I got saved, I could try my best to be good, but I wasn't all good. There was that black streak of sin always in me."

Cash was no ivory tower theologian, but he did pretty well with that explanation. The simple fact is that we are like that white dog. Even though we are forgiven and cleansed of our sins, we will never be perfect and we will be trapped in this fallen flesh. It's foolish for any of us to pretend like we've got things "all-together" or that we have arrived. Yet this is the pretense of many legalists. David Jeremiah commented on this passage, "The legalists only wanted to exploit the Galatians for their own bragging rights. This is one of the most notorious signs of legalism—bragging about what we do or don't do instead of bragging about Jesus Christ and what He has done for us."[3]

We Must Share the Gospel without Retreat (6:14–15)

Os Guinness tells of a Jewish man, imprisoned fifteen years by Soviet authorities for political dissidence, who became a Christian while in the terrible Gulag. He was sustained throughout that long ordeal by his faith in the Savior and by the memory of his four-year-old son who he hoped to see again one day. When he was finally released, the man anticipated the reunion with heart-pounding excitement. How thrilled he was to notice as they hugged each other that his son was wearing a cross! After they had talked about many things, he asked his son, now nineteen years old, just what the cross meant to him. His heart was crushed by the answer: "Father, for my generation the cross is just a fashion statement."[4]

As sad as that story is, that is actually more true to life than we might realize. For many, the cross has become nothing more than a piece of jewelry. Many who wear the cross never think of the Christ of the cross. The apostle Paul saw the cross as a symbol of the very core of his faith. It bore witness to his radically transformed life. Paul preached only one message—the Cross of Christ. In fact, you might argue that the guy had a one track mind.

---

3. Jeremiah, *Claiming Faith, Finding Freedom*, vol. 2, 113.
4. Grounds, "Fashion or Faith?"

> For I am not ashamed of the gospel for it is the power of God for salvation to everyone who believes, to the Jew first and also to the Greek" (Rom. 1:16).
>
> "For I decided to know nothing among you except Jesus Christ and him crucified" (1 Cor. 2:2).
>
> "Brothers, I do not consider that I have made it my own: forgetting what lies behind and straining for what lies ahead, I press on towards to the goal for the for the prize of the upward call of God in Christ Jesus" (Phil 3:13–14).

Paul took every opportunity to make sure that people knew that his life was indebted to Christ who gloriously saved him from a rebel's heart. I don't think that redeeming grace ever became a cold and boring doctrine to Paul because when grace snatched him up, he was about as lost as someone could be. While the legalists boasted in their flesh, Paul gloried in the foolishness of the cross. The New Testament gives us three commands of the Cross. One of them is recorded here. We are to carry the cross (Luke 9:23), preach the cross (1 Cor. 1:18–21), and boast in the cross (Gal. 6:14).

Paul noted the *priority of the Cross*. "But far be it from me to boast except in the cross of our Lord Jesus Christ, by which the world has been crucified to me, and I to the world" (6:14). Could there anything more radical and disturbing than this statement? To glory in the cross meant to embrace an instrument of torture, humiliation, and death. Today, we might say, "I revel in the thought of the electric chair. I delight in the sight of a gallows. Lethal injection puts me on cloud nine."

In reality, there was no reason to get sentimental about crucifixion. In the ancient world, thousands of people were executed in this most debasing manner. In 519 BC, for example, King Darius I of Persia crucified 3,000 political enemies in Babylon. After the slave revolt led by Spartacus in 71 BC, the Roman general Crassus captured and crucified 6,000 insurrectionists and hung their bodies on crosses along the Appian Way from Rome to Capua. The cross was a symbol of the swift, brutal, and unforgiving justice of the Roman Empire. There was no uglier sight. That's why I think Dorothy Sayers was right when she said, "It is curious that people who are filled with horrified indignation whenever a cat kills a sparrow can hear the story of the killing of God told Sunday after Sunday and not experience any shock at all." But Paul's boasting was in "the cross of our Lord Jesus Christ." This cross was different because the One who hung upon it was uniquely different than any other crucifixion victim. It is safe to say that up until that

Boasting Only in the Cross (6:11–18)

point in history, no man ever chose the cross as his preferred method of death. Yet with Jesus, the cross was His mission, destination, and goal. To the world it was death, but to Christ's followers it was eternal life.

Paul understood that the cross was the intersection of God's love and justice. Calvary was the place where God reconciled His unbending holiness which had to punish sin and His infinite love which desired to offer mercy to the guilty. The cross was the place where a great Divine transaction took place where the Son of God, who knew only righteousness, and humanity, who knew only sinfulness, traded places (2 Cor. 5:21). With two pieces of timber and a few nails, Jesus bridged the infinite gap between God and man. Moreover, the cross reminds us that evil cannot and will not win. God has ordained that through the brutality of a Roman cross, salvation would come to the world.

People have often wondered what made Billy Graham's evangelistic crusades so successful. How was it that a simple man from a dairy farm in North Carolina could literally change the world with such a simple message? Dr. Graham touched on that when he recalled a lesson he learned early in his ministry after a 1953 crusade held in Dallas. Billy wrote:

> One night my preaching did not seem to have spiritual depth or power, although a number of people did come forward at the Invitation. After the meeting, John [Bolten, who was a close and trusted friend of Graham's] and I took a walk together, and he confronted me. "Billy," he said, "you didn't speak about the Cross. How can anyone be converted without having at least one single view of the Cross where the Lord died for us? You must preach about the Cross, Billy. You must preach about the blood that was shed for us there. There is no other place in the Bible where there is greater power than when we talk or preach about the Cross." At first I resisted his rebuke. The Cross and its meaning were more often than not, a part of my sermons. But that night I could not sleep, and before morning came I knew he was right. I made a commitment never to preach again without being sure that the Gospel was as complete and clear as possible, centering on Christ's sacrificial death for our sins on the Cross and His resurrection from the dead for our salvation."[5]

After 2,000 years of preaching it should be clear that Gospel message is the only message worth preaching. There is no need for entertainment or new programs. Just stay with the simple Gospel. Paul's only boast was in the

---

5. Graham, *Just As I Am*, 284–285.

cross of Christ. What is your boast? Is it your money? Your education? Your family pedigree? Your good connections? Your good grades? Your personal achievements? Your good looks? Paul regarded his family background, his religious heritage, his education, and even his good morality as "dung" compared to the glory of knowing Christ personally (Phil. 3:1–9).

Paul also boasted in Christ because of *the power of the Cross*. "... by which the world has been crucified to me, and I to the world. For neither circumcision counts for anything, nor uncircumcision, but a new creation" (6:14–15). The cross is the believer's rallying cry of victory. It represents having the chains of sin loosed and the bondage of the world broken. Because of the cross of Christ, we are saved from the penalty of sin in a single moment, from the power of sin gradually through our Christian walk, and from the presence of sin when one day we'll receive our glorified bodies. John Piper says, "If we desire that there be no boasting except in the cross, then we must live near the cross. For the believer, the cross of Christ is not merely a past place of substitution, but it is also a present place of daily execution."

The enticements and things of the world lose their luster in the sight of the cross. Why? Because nothing this world has to offer can offer what the cross can. We may place our hope in politics, but even if we get a new man in the White House it won't change the hearts of people. We may place our hope in science, but no matter how sophisticated our technology becomes the utopia we seek always eludes us. Money, pleasure, and the trendy diversions of this life are never large enough to fill the existential void in man's soul. Religion may offer us behavior modification, but it can never bring assurance of where we'll go after death.

However, the cross is not about reformation, but transformation. According to verse 6:15, only Christ has the power to make us a "new creation." This is why circumcision or church membership or mode of baptism are ultimately irrelevant. We must be born from above (John 3:3). In 2 Cor. 5:17, Paul wrote, "Therefore if any man be in Christ, he is a new creature: old things are passed away; behold, all things are become new." The message of the cross is that it doesn't promise to make bad people good but to make dead people alive to God.

The Vietnam Veterans Memorial is striking for its simplicity. Etched in a black granite wall are the names of 58,156 Americans who died in that war. Since its opening in 1982, the stark monument has stirred deep emotions. Some visitors walk its length slowly, reverently, and without pause.

Boasting Only in the Cross (6:11–18)

Others stop before certain names, remembering their son or sweetheart or fellow soldier, wiping away tears, tracing the names with their fingers.

For three Vietnam veterans—Robert Bedker, Willard Craig, and Darrall Lausch—a visit to the memorial must be especially poignant, for they can walk up to the long ebony wall and find their own names carved in the stone. Because of data-coding errors, each of them was incorrectly listed as killed in action. Dead, but alive—a perfect description of the Christian.[6]

We Must Share the Gospel without Regret (6:16–18)

"And as for all who walk by this rule, peace and mercy be upon them, and upon the Israel of God. From now on let no one cause me trouble, for I bear on my body the marks of Jesus. The grace of our Lord Jesus Christ be with your spirit, brothers. Amen" (6:16–18). Paul believed the massage of grace so much that he was willing to suffer intense persecution and suffering. In the face of bumps and bruises, cuts and scrapes, he did not quit. His scars only made the gospel that much more genuine and relevant. 2 Cor. 11:24–25 is a short list of just some of the sufferings Paul endured, "From the Jews five times I received forty stripes minus one. Three times I was beaten with rods; once I was stoned; three times I was shipwrecked; a night and a day I have been in the deep . . ."

In the ancient days, it was customary for slave masters to brand their slaves with a particular tattoo to show whose property they were. Paul was branded for Christ and he wore the scars on his body like a badge of honor. Paul ends by telling his enemies that he has no regrets. In summary, he says, "You Judaizers can take your little circumcision club and go somewhere else. Don't bother me anymore. You like to make marks on the body and call yourself holy. Here are my marks. See the scars. Here is where I was beaten. Here is where I was scourged. And I got these marks when I was stoned and left for dead." Paul laid it all on the line for Christ and the scars were the marks of divine ownership that proved he truly belonged to Jesus Christ. Wiersbe adds, "Paul was not an armchair general; he was out in the front lines, waging war against sin and taking his share of suffering."[7]

With that, Paul has said all he could say. What will the Galatians do? As he writes his final words, not even Paul knows the answer, and the Scriptures never inform us as to what happened to the church in Galatia.

6. Larson, *750 Engaging Illustrations for Preachers, Teachers & Writers*, 98.

7 Wiersbe, *The Wiersbe Bible Commentary: New Testament*, 582.

Having made his argument, the issue now rests with his readers. Will they choose slavery or freedom? It is fitting that the book ends this way, with an unanswered question, because in every generation the church of Jesus Christ faces the same issues in one form or another. Will we choose liberty in Christ or will we succumb to the temptation to return to the slavery of self-effort and law-keeping as a means of pleasing God? Will we decide that God's grace is not enough and that we need to add something else to what God has already done for us? Today, our argument isn't about circumcision, but we quickly substitute other equally good things in place of the simple Gospel of grace. That is why in order to keep our focus on Christ and live in freedom, we must boast only in the cross.

In 1967, a young man named Charles Murray was training at the University of Cincinnati for the Summer Olympics of 1968 as a high diver. A Christian friend spent hours sharing the gospel with him. Charles was not raised in a Christian home, so the story of Jesus fascinated him. He even began to ask questions about forgiveness of sin. One day his Christian friend asked if he was ready to trust Christ as his own Savior. His reply was a definite "No."

Because he was training for the Olympic Games, Charles had special privileges at the university pool facilities. Sometime between 10:30 and 11:00 that evening he decided to go swim and practice a few dives. It was a clear night in October and the moon was big and bright. The university pool was housed under a ceiling of glass panes so the moon shone bright across the top of the wall in the pool area. Charles climbed to the highest platform to take his first dive.

At that moment the Spirit of God began to convict him of his sin. All the Scripture he had read flooded his mind. He stood on the platform backwards to make his dive, spread his arms to gather his balance, looked up to the wall, and saw his own shadow caused by the light of the moon. It was the shape of a cross. He could bear the burden of his sin no longer. His heart broke and he sat down on the platform and asked God to forgive him and save him. He trusted Jesus Christ twenty feet in the air.

Suddenly, the lights came on. The attendant had come in to check the pool. As Charles looked down from his platform, he saw an empty pool that had been drained for repairs. He had almost plummeted to his death, but the cross had stopped him from disaster.[8] No wonder Paul gloried in the cross. It is God's plan to save us from ultimate disaster.

---

8. Ray Pritchard, "Our Crucified God: What the Cross Means to the Church – Galatians 6:14."

Bibliography

"Adopted Minnesota Man Learns He Is a Prince." *ABC NEWS*, 2 June 2005 <http://abcnews.go.com/GMA/story?id=812514> accessed 14 May 2014.
Alcorn, Randy: *The Grace and Truth Paradox*. Colorado Springs, CO: Multnomah, 2009.
Alcorn, Randy. *The Purity Principle*. Colorado Springs, CO: Multnomah, 2003.
"The Atomic Doctor." *Time*, 28 April 1975 <http://content.time.com/time/magazine/article/0,9171,917392,00.html> accessed 11 September 2014.
Baaker, Jim. *I Was Wrong*. Nashville, TN: Thomas Nelson, 1996.
Barnes, Craig M. "How We Act in God's Family," cited by Larson, Craig Brian and Ten Elshof, Phyllis. *1001 Illustrations That Connect*. Grand Rapids, MI: Zondervan, 2008.
Brother Andrew. *The Calling*. Grand Rapids, MI: Revell, 2002.
Bubeck, Mark. *The Adversary*. Chicago: Moody Press, 1975.
Clifford, Ross. *The Case for the Empty Tomb*. Claremont, CA: Albatross, 1991.
Colson, Charles. "Making the World Safe for Religion." *Christianity Today*, 8 November 1993, 33.
Cordeiro, Wayne. *Jesus: Pure and Simple*. Minneapolis, MN: Bethany House, 2012.
DeHann, Dennis J. "Level Ground." *Our Daily Bread*. 15 January 1996, <http://odb.org/1996/01/15/level-ground/> accessed 20 May 2014.
DeHann, Richard. "We Reap What We Sow." *Our Daily Bread*. 16 August 1998 <http://odb.org/1998/08/16/we-reap-what-we-sow/> accessed 15 April 2012.
Dickson, John. *Humilitas*. Grand Rapids, MI: Zondervan, 2011.
Dunn, Holly. "Daddy's Hands," MTM Music, 1986.
Durant, Michael. *In the Company of Heroes*. New York: Puntam, 2003.
Evans, Tony. *Tony Evans Book of Illustrations*. Chicago: Moody Press, 2009.
Federer, William J. *What Every American Needs to Know about the Qur'an*. St. Louis, MO: AmeriSearch, 2011.
Galli, Mark and Olsen, Ted, eds. *131 Christians Everyone Should Know*. Nashville, TN: B&H Publishing, 2000.
George, Timothy. *The New American Commentary—New Testament*. Nashville, TN: B & H Publishing, 1994.
Graham, Billy. *Just As I Am*. New York: Harper Collins, 1997.
Green, Michael P. *1,500 Illustrations for Preaching*. Grand Rapids, MI: Baker, 1982.
Greer, J.D. *Gospel: Recovering the Power That Made Christianity Revolutiona*ry. Nashville, TN: B & H Publishing, 2011.
Grounds, Vernon C. "Fashion or Faith?" *Our Daily Bread*, 20 February 1996 <http://odb.org/1996/02/20/fashion-or-faith/> accessed 16 July 2014.

Bibliography

"Homeless Man, Max Melitzer Learns He's Rich," *Huffington Post*, 18 June 2011 <http://www.huffingtonpost.com/2011/06/18/homeless-man-max-melitzer_n_879860.html> accessed 6 June 2014.

Hordern, William E. *A Layman's Guide to Protestant Theology*. New York: Macmillan, 1955.

Howerton, Mike. *Glorious Mess*. Grand Rapids, MI: Baker, 2012.

Idleman, Kyle. *Not a Fan*. Grand Rapids, MI: Zondervan, 2011.

Janes, Nick. "Former Inmate Arrested after Jumping Fence onto Folsom Prison Property," *CBS Sacramento*, 11 August 2011 <http://sacramento.cbslocal.com/2011/08/11/officers-searching-for-man-who-jumped-fence-into-folsom-prison/> accessed 13 March 2012.

Jeremiah, David. *Claiming Faith, Finding Freedom, vols. 1 & 2*. San Diego, CA: Turning Point, 2011.

Keller, Phillip. *A Shepherd's Look at Psalm 23*. Grand Rapids, MI: Zondervan, 1970.

Lanchin, Mike. "Shoichi Yokoi, the Japanese Soldier Who Held out in Guam." *BBC News*, 23 January 2012 <http://www.bbc.co.uk/news/magazine-16681636> accessed 20 February 2014.

Larson, Craig Brian. *750 Engaging Illustrations for Preachers, Teachers & Writers*. Grand Rapids, MI : Baker Books, 2002.

Lewis, C.S. *Mere Christianity*. San Francisco: Harper Collins, 1952.

Lucado, Max. *A Love Worth Giving*. Nashville, TN: Thomas Nelson, 2002.

Lucado, Max. *God Came Near*. Portland, OR: Multnomah, 1987.

Lucado, Max. *He Still Moves Stones*. Nashville, TN: Thomas Nelson, 1999.

Lucado, Max. *In the Grip of Grace*. Dallas, TX: Word, 1996.

Luther, Martin. *Commentary on the Epistle to the Galatians*. London: James Clarke & Co. Ltd., 1955.

Luther, Martin quoted by Mullett, Michael A. *Martin Luther*. New York: Taylor & Francis, 2004.

Luther, Martin. *Table Talk*.

MacArthur, John. *The MacArthur New Testament Commentary: Galatians*. Chicago, Moody Press, 1987.

McDowell, Josh. *Evidence for Christianity*. Nashville, TN: Thomas Nelson, 2006.

McGee, J. Vernon. *Thru the Bible Commentary Series: The Epistles, Galatians*. Nashville: Thomas Nelson, 1991.

McGlynn, Katla. "17 Ridiculous Laws Still on the Books in the U.S." *Huffington Post*, 2 May 2010 <http://www.huffingtonpost.com/2010/03/02/17-ridiculous-laws-still_n_481379.html> accessed 11 September 2014.

Maxwell, John. *Becoming A Person of Influence*. Nashville, TN: Thomas Nelson. 1997.

Michael, Larry J. *Spurgeon on Leadership*. Grand Rapids, MI: Kregel, 2010.

Miller, Calvin. *Into the Depths of God*. Minneapolis, MN: Bethany House, 2000.

Morrison, Frank. *Who Moved the Stone?* Grand Rapids, MI: Zondervan, 1958.

"Muslim Extremists Throw Acid on Church Leader," *Voice of the Martyrs*, 5 January 2013 <http://www.persecution.net/ug-2012-01-05.htm> accessed 14 December 2013.

Niebuhr, H. Richard. *The Kingdom of God in America*. Middletown, CT: Wesleyan University Press, 1988.

Peterson, Eugene. *The Message: The Bible in Contemporary Language*. Colorado Springs, CO: Nav Press, 1998.

Bibliography

Phillips, Donald T. *Lincoln on Leadership: Executive Strategies for Tough Times.* New York, NY: Warner Books, 1993.

Phillips, John. *Exploring Galatians.* Grand Rapids, MI: Kregel, 2004.

Piper, John. *Let the Nations Be Glad: The Supremacy of God in Missions.* Grand Rapids, MI: Baker, 2010.

Pritchard, Ray "Born Free: Seven Promises You Can Count On." *Keep Believing Ministries,* July 2001 <http://www.keepbelieving.com/sermon/2001-07-01-Born-Free-Seven-Promises-You-Can-Count-On/> accessed 14 May 2014.

Pritchard, Ray. "Our Crucified God: What the Cross Means to the Church–Galatians 6:14," *Keep Believing Ministries* < http://www.keepbelieving.com/sermon/1999-03-28-Our-Crucified-God-What-the-Cross-Means-to-the-Church/> accessed 20 July 2014.

Ryken, Philip Graham. *Galatians: Reformed Expository Commentary.* Phillipsburg, NJ: P & R Publishing, 2005.

Schroeder, Andreas. *Scams: Ten Stories That Explore Some of the Most Outrageous Swindlers and Tricksters of All Time.* New York: Annick Press, 2004.

Sides, Hampton. *Ghost Soldiers: The Epic Account of World War II's Greatest Rescue.* New York: First Anchor Books, 2001.

Spurgeon, Charles. *Spurgeon at His Best.* Grand Rapids, MI: Baker, 1988.

Stott, John R.W. *The Message of Galatians.* Downers Grove, IL: InterVarsity, 1968.

Swindoll, Charles R. *Elijah: A Man of Heroism and Humility.* Nashville, TN: Thomas Nelson, 2000.

Swindoll, Charles R. *The Grace Awakening.* Nashville: Thomas Nelson, 2010.

Swindoll, Charles R. *The Strength of Character: 7 Essential Traits of a Remarkable Life.* Nashville, TN: J. Countryman, 2007.

Swindoll, Charles R. "Peace That Exceeds Understanding." *Insights.* April 2001, 1-2.

Swindoll, Charles R. *Swindoll's Ultimate Book of Illustrations and Quotes.* Nashville, TN: Thomas Nelson, 1998.

Tenney, Merrill C. *Galatians: The Charter of Christian Liberty.* Grand Rapids, MI: Eerdmans, 1957.

Vairin, Donald. "His Mysterious Ways." *Guideposts,* September 1999, 39.

Wetenhall, John. "Christian Woman Stops Robbery with Faith." *ABC News.* 30 June 2010. <http://abcnews.go.com/US/faith-stops-florida robbery/story?id=11288067#.T3xq7PDOUko> accessed 11 September 2014.

Wiersbe, Warren. *50 People Every Christian Should Know.* Grand Rapids, MI: Baker, 2009.

Wiersbe, Warren. *Be Free.* Colorado Springs: David C. Cook, 1975.

Wiersbe, Warren. The Wiersbe Bible Commentary—New Testament. Colorado Springs, CO: David C. Cook, 2007.

Wilkins, J. Steven. *Call of Duty: The Sterling Nobility of Robert E. Lee.* Nashville, TN: Cumberland House, 1997.

Willard, Dallas. *The Divine Conspiracy.* San Francisco: Harper One, 1998.

Worden, Amy. "Pennsylvania Man Lived the Drama that Inspired 'Unstoppable.'" *The Philadelphia Inquirer,* 12 November 2010 < http://articles.philly.com/2010-11-12/news/24955089_1_rail-crossings-rail-yard-runaway-train> accessed 10 August 2014.

Wurmbrand, Richard. "Love Pardons the Enemy," *The Voice of the Martyrs.* April, 2002.

Yancey, Philip. *What's so Amazing about Grace?* Grand Rapids, MI: Zondervan, 1997.

Zacharias, Ravi. *Recapture the Wonder.* Nashville, TN: Integrity, 2003

"9/11 Memorial Story Corps." <https://www.911memorial.org/storycorps> accessed 11 September 2014.

www.ingramcontent.com/pod-product-compliance
Lightning Source LLC
Chambersburg PA
CBHW071444150426
43191CB00008B/1229